Luxury Philosophy

Luxury Philosophy

John Armitage

BLOOMSBURY ACADEMIC
LONDON · NEW YORK · OXFORD · NEW DELHI · SYDNEY

BLOOMSBURY ACADEMIC
Bloomsbury Publishing Plc
50 Bedford Square, London, WC1B 3DP, UK
1385 Broadway, New York, NY 10018, USA
29 Earlsfort Terrace, Dublin 2, Ireland

BLOOMSBURY, BLOOMSBURY ACADEMIC and the Diana logo
are trademarks of Bloomsbury Publishing Plc

First published in Great Britain 2025

Cover image: *The Swing*, Jean-Honore Fragonard, c. 1767,
Wallace Collection, London, England, UK.
Contributor: photosublime / Alamy Stock Photo

Bloomsbury Publishing Plc does not have any control over, or responsibility for,
any third-party websites referred to or in this book. All internet addresses given
in this book were correct at the time of going to press. The author and publisher
regret any inconvenience caused if addresses have changed or sites have ceased
to exist, but can accept no responsibility for any such changes.

A catalogue record for this book is available from the British Library.

A catalog record for this book is available from the Library of Congress.

ISBN: HB: 978-1-3504-1483-9
          PB: 978-1-3504-1484-6
          ePDF: 978-1-3504-1485-3
          eBook: 978-1-3504-1487-7

Typeset by Integra Software Services Pvt. Ltd.
Printed and bound in Great Britain

To find out more about our authors and books visit www.bloomsbury.com
and sign up for our newsletters.

Contents

1

Luxury Philosophy: An Introduction

Luxury Philosophy offers a comprehensive guide to the foremost philosophers in luxury philosophy from the eighteenth century to the twenty-first century. The book includes critical discussion of seven philosophers who have dominated the moral and political, economic, social, and cultural debate over luxury since 1750 and a concluding commentary on luxury philosophy today. In disciplinary extent, these figures include moral philosophers and political economists, phenomenologists, and literary, critical, and cultural theorists. The contributions of these separate figures to luxury philosophy constantly clarify the benefits to knowledge of studying sumptuousness and the autonomy of very well-off living or environs, while focusing their reflections on luxury and the luxurious across numerous subjects. The important figures in the historical and contemporary philosophical life of luxury—Jean-Jacques Rousseau and Jean François de Saint-Lambert, Karl Marx, Emmanuel Levinas, Georges Bataille, Theodor W. Adorno, and Roland Barthes—suggest interdisciplinary analyses of subjects and objects that are often seen as inessential but which offer gratification and ease, and historical and contemporary services that are attractive, costly, or difficult to acquire or do.

The reason leading me to author this book has been a rising awareness of fundamental conceptual and moral transformations taking place in the past 270 years. Throughout the twentieth century especially, many prevailing negative viewpoints in luxury philosophy from the eighteenth and nineteenth centuries were exposed to continued critique, undoing, and rebuilding. Enlightenment and counter-Enlightenment luxury philosophy has been actively analyzed and assessed, with new constellations of knowledge about luxury, comprising phenomenology and cultural theory, critical theory, structuralism, and poststructuralism, developing. Traditions of philosophy regarding luxury that hitherto had been powerful, such as Enlightenment and counter-Enlightenment philosophies, have come under scrutiny across luxury philosophy. There has also been an explosion of new discourses and luxury philosophies, including post-phenomenology, postmodern cultural and critical theory, in addition to evocative research programs such as the luxury philosophy connected particularly with Roland Barthes's (1993) structuralist and poststructuralist approach (see, also, Armitage 2020).

Certainly, these events in luxury philosophy have been for many people simultaneously intimidating and exciting: intimidating because the main traditions of eighteenth- and nineteenth-century luxury philosophy look deeply strained in the face of the fundamental moral transitions now sweeping the world; exciting because their connotations and results are not only philosophically significant but indicate new possibilities for change in the cultural, political, and social meaning of luxury. Of vital importance here are spectacular changes to the twentieth-century and contemporary development of luxury philosophy. Among these changes are to be considered the reassessment of the eighteenth- and nineteenth-century luxury philosophers and their influence; twentieth-century and contemporary continental philosophers furthering the study of luxury by moving beyond Rousseau, Saint-Lambert, and Marx; the immediate and the long-term impact of the seven important luxury philosophers discussed in this book; the growth of luxury philosophy within the history of philosophy; the spread of contemporary philosophies of luxury, their utilization, and development; and the increase in topics regarding the globalization of luxury, of its artistic, visual, and cultural politics.

In view of these philosophical and moral changes, there is an urgent need for continued critical discussion of the consistency and diffusion of eighteenth-century, nineteenth-century, twentieth-century, and contemporary luxury philosophy in the hands of its principal experts. *Luxury Philosophy* represents an effort to meet this need. The original contribution of this volume is that it critically introduces and discusses seven illustrious international luxury philosophers and presents chapters on their work, accompanied by a closing review of luxury philosophy today, that are published here for the first time. To facilitate the reader-friendly intention of the book, each of the main chapters, 2–8, presents a biographical outline and positions the work of luxury philosophers concerning numerous schools of thought; and each chapter presents a thorough explanation and critique of the individual figures. Each of the central chapters (2–8) ends with a comprehensive bibliography of the luxury philosopher's chief works on luxury in English translation, together with the particulars of secondary references. Chapter 9, by contrast, considers the influence of luxury philosophy today and concludes the book. The chapter raises the question of whether the work of the seven important luxury philosophers examined in this volume has imparted material for subsequent contemporary luxury philosophers to utilize and develop through a commentary on the influences of luxury philosophy that have been published since the millennium, such as Mehita Iqani and Simidele Dosekun's (2019) *African Luxury: Aesthetics and Politics*. Consequently, *Luxury Philosophy* is an up-to-date explanation of the subject.

In this introduction, I shall outline a background for the critical discussion of individual luxury philosophers and the influence of luxury philosophy today that follow. My goal is limited. In reviewing some of the most important developments in eighteenth-century, nineteenth-century, twentieth-century, and contemporary luxury philosophy, I shall outline key topics and traditions that stimulate the work of prominent luxury philosophers, of philosophical movements, and of explanatory methods. I shall divide my commentary around five subjects, or sets of debates, in eighteenth-century, nineteenth-century, twentieth-century, and contemporary luxury philosophy: luxury; luxury philosophy; virtue, the luxury of appearances, and Marxist philosophy; voluptuosity, expenditure, and the dual character of luxury; and luxury mythology, luxury philosophy today, and its influence.

Luxury

Among the multiplying themes that have always concerned philosophers from time immemorial, one question in the present context is notable as of essential significance: that is, the question of the composition of the concept of luxury. The issues in the balance in the historical and contemporary creation, deconstruction, and reconstruction of luxury are deep and intense. Some of the essential concerns that have matured over the centuries comprise the following: the psychological, cultural, political, and social forms through which people are constructed as luxurious; the multifaceted, inconsistent ways in which people describe themselves as ostentatious, tremendously well-to-do, and living in luxurious settings; the emotional investments that people come to have in their identification with objects that are not vital but which supply indulgence and well-being and to which they feel entitled; and the impact that luxuries carry for comprehending the production and reproduction, disturbance, and transformation of culture, politics, and society.

It was not until the eighteenth century, among philosophers of different affiliations, that the concept of luxury fell within a space of more careful consideration and critical practice. Although the project of understanding luxurious objects that are pleasing but high-priced or problematic to attain or do had been at the center of Western philosophy, such as that of Plato (2007), for 2,000 years, the appearance of new discursive orientations concerned with questioning the nature of luxury began with the appearance of distinctive currents of thought in response to the main direction taken by modern European philosophy and, in particular, the Enlightenment: the intellectual and philosophical movement that occurred in Europe in the seventeenth and eighteenth centuries, with ongoing global influences and effects (Hyland 2003). The Enlightenment included a range of ideas centered on the value of human happiness, the pursuit of knowledge obtained by means of reason and the evidence of the senses, and ideals such as natural law and liberty, progress, toleration, fraternity, constitutional government, and separation of church and state (Robertson 2022). Following the Enlightenment and, in particular, the philosophical upheavals of Denis Diderot, Montesquieu, and Voltaire, among many others, numerous important figures in eighteenth-century intellectual life reassessed anew the claims of traditional metaphysics, religion, and morality, combining it with admiration for the methods of the natural sciences. These Enlightenment philosophers, in various ways, fostered interest in comparing natural science with other claims to knowledge that seemed insecure to their rational philosophy, which sought to place artistic, moral, and even religious truths on more logically defensible, more scientific, and thus more secure, foundations. However, they also, perhaps inadvertently, encouraged attentiveness to the nature of the concept of luxury, in the nature of yearning, in the interpersonal nature of conceptions of excess, the experience of extravagance, and in how luxury combines and connects with people's identification with objects that are sought-after, but which are often understood to be unnecessary. Nineteenth- and twentieth-century critics of the philosophy of the Enlightenment, such as Georg Wilhelm Friedrich Hegel and Søren Kierkegaard, Friedrich Nietzsche, Edmund Husserl, Martin Heidegger, Jean-Paul Sartre, Hans-Georg Gadamer, Jürgen Habermas, Jacques Derrida, Michel Foucault, and Jean-François Lyotard, and particularly those who argued that the efforts of Enlightenment thinkers were doomed from the start, have been fundamental to the post-Enlightenment undertaking of decentering and analyzing numerous concepts, inclusive of luxury, as such critical thought deeply rearranges the relation of the self, including the luxurious self, and Other. Critics of the philosophy of the Enlightenment have also been used by post-Enlightenment philosophers to interrogate the positioning of the Enlightenment philosophers, predominantly the failures and difficulties that they met with in their attempts to provide secure, rational foundations for the moral, religious, and artistic dimensions of human knowledge, failures and difficulties that were, in fact, signs of the inevitable consequences of a distorted, one-sided, philosophical approach; to expose the connection between scientific method and enlightenment; and to warn of the philosophical idealizations and fantasies governing Enlightenment visions of rational, objective, and definitive answers to philosophical questions.

If critics of the philosophy of the Enlightenment have appeared large in the language of the post-Enlightenment, they have played a similarly significant role in the understanding of topics from cultural profligacy to the politics of necessity to issues of social indulgence. Why this influence? What can critics of the philosophy of the Enlightenment offer luxury philosophy? In the understanding of enjoyment, riches, comfort, and plush living, to identify only a few themes, the critique of the philosophy of the Enlightenment is engaged with critically to examine afresh the objects through which people represent the cultural, political, and social worlds of objects that are thought an immoderation instead of a necessity internally and externally. Through the critique of the philosophy of the Enlightenment, luxury philosophers are able to investigate, interrogate, and critique the pleasant objects, the sometimes-imaginary satisfactions of luxurious reality and, perhaps, eventually, of luxurious independent selfhood (see, e.g., Rousseau 1968: 58). Of import here is the conflict or chasm between awareness of luxury, the irrationality of, for example, lechery, and extreme agency on the one hand, and unconscious desire for wastefulness, dreams of luxurious material and immaterial objects, and feelings concerning luxurious goods and services that are beneficial to bodily relaxation on the other. The idea that conscious awareness of resplendent living is occasionally incorporated within, or overwhelmed by, the unconscious forces of a mind fixed on unrestricted excess has been integral to the study of the luxurious self and its philosophical satisfactions alike. Here the debate over the necessities of life and the contentments and amusements offered by luxurious objects is especially significant, as is historical and present-day concern with the ways in which other ways of attending to prodigality through increasingly endless choice may be adding another, possibly unnecessary, layer to people's experience of luxury in the contemporary world (Armitage and Roberts 2014).

Conceivably more than anywhere else, critics of the philosophy of the Enlightenment have made their largest impact in the philosophy of pleasure as something that is out of the ordinary that is permitted to the self (see, e.g., Saint-Lambert 1965). In general terms, critics of the philosophy of the Enlightenment have been adopted by philosophers of pleasure not as an addition to, or dislocation of, the history of unusual objects that are consented to by the self, but as reexamining them, as containing the possibility of another way of appreciating forms of self-indulgence that might be perceived by some to be foolish or worthless. In this area of debate as in others, the critique of the philosophy of the Enlightenment means different things to different people.

In European philosophy, and particularly in the work of philosophers concerned with pleasure, the philosophy of pleasure engages with Enlightenment and post-Enlightenment thought concerning, for instance, desire, to trace the objects that are exceptional, that are sanctioned by the self, and that are framed by wishes and wants—with specific stress on longing, craving, and yearning. Critics of the philosophy of the Enlightenment who style themselves as philosophers of pleasure take their prompt more from critical Enlightenment thinking concerning disproportionate interest in the procuring, indulging in, and the providing of sexual activity. More exactly in this critical Enlightenment setting, luxury and luxuriance are considered as voluptuous, sensual pleasures; the power of the order of luxury is to bring attention to those objects that are extraordinary and that are facilitated by the self as pleasure so joyfully that it becomes almost impossible to see the emotional investment that people have in eadness, the happiness that is derived from luxury and wealth. What might be called the philosophy of pleasure plays with new methods of figuring eadness and with alternative possibilities for reimagining those objects that are remarkable that are approved of by the self. The innovative contributions to these debates in the philosophy of pleasure and critical Enlightenment thought are deliberated and debated in numerous chapters of this book.

Luxury Philosophy

Captivated by the discourse of the debate between supporters and critics of the philosophy of the Enlightenment, what I am naming luxury philosophy in this book from the eighteenth century to the twenty-first became engaged with the difficulties and controversies of "continental philosophy," which includes the variety of thinkers and philosophical methods discussed in *Luxury Philosophy* and which can be contrasted with "analytical philosophy." Analytical philosophy is typified by its stress on language, clarity, and thoroughness in argumentation and it makes use of formal logic, mathematics, and the natural sciences in an effort to concentrate philosophical consideration on smaller problems that lead to answers to bigger questions. Moreover, analytical philosophy has dominated academic philosophy in the English-speaking world for most of the twentieth and twenty-first centuries (Dummett 1993). This debate emerged from the thought of alternative and distinct modes of continental philosophy from that of supporters of the philosophy of the Enlightenment which incorporates not only thinkers such as Hegel and Kierkegaard, Nietzsche, Husserl, Heidegger, Sartre, Gadamer, Habermas, Derrida, Foucault, and Lyotard but also those luxury philosophers included in this book, namely, Rousseau and Saint-Lambert, Marx, Levinas, Bataille, Adorno, and Barthes. The one thing that arose from this debate over currents of thought—throughout a series of disagreements wherein Hegelian idealism and Marxism, the critical theory of the Frankfurt School, existentialism, hermeneutics, phenomenology, structuralism, poststructuralism, and postmodernism reigned supreme—is that there is no single, homogeneous, continental philosophical tradition. Instead, there is a diversity of connected currents of thought operating from within the languages of the supporters and the critics of the philosophy of the Enlightenment. Continental critics of the philosophy of the Enlightenment are differentiated from supporters of the philosophy of the Enlightenment, especially, by their focus on thinking in a recognizable continental style, which is an approach to philosophy, inclusive of luxury philosophy, centered on the history of thought and its lines of intellectual descent—mainly in the contrasting philosophical substance and critical mode, but in the sometimes sympathetic, sometimes hostile, critique of early modern and modern European philosophy and, particularly, the Enlightenment as well. In this interpretation, the critique of the philosophy of the Enlightenment denotes an intellectual deliberation upon the work of supporters of the philosophy of the Enlightenment, its upheavals, and skepticism about the assertions of traditional metaphysics, religion, and morality, not to mention its veneration of the methods of the natural sciences.

The critique of the philosophy of the Enlightenment, by contrast, describes a change of emphasis at the level of science, skepticism or doubt, and human knowledge (see West 2010). Various critiques of natural science—of knowledge, enlightenment, art, morality, religion, truth, and rationality—have been used to signify a break with the supporters of the philosophy of the Enlightenment, to proclaim that the endeavors of these thinkers to discover scientific and secure philosophical foundations were hopeless from the beginning, and to point out that the disappointments and problems that they met with in their efforts to provide secure, rational foundations for the moral, religious, and artistic elements of human knowledge were indications of the unavoidable consequences of a distorted, biased philosophical approach. Numerous chapters in this book outline the compound, incongruous ways in which the instinct to critique the philosophy of the Enlightenment has been differentiated from Enlightenment and scientific forms typical of the work of supporters of the philosophy of the Enlightenment. The outcome was numerous original intellectual approaches to continental philosophy and critique drawn from, for instance, the writings of Johann Gottfried von Herder, the German Enlightenment philosopher, theologian, poet, and literary critic, but, especially, from the philosophy of Hegel: whether developing it or countering it, few ignore the thought of Hegel and the Hegelian system, with its tripartite emphasis on the science of logic, the philosophy of nature, and the philosophy of spirit (Taylor 1975). However, for some, the isolation of a distinct tradition of continental philosophy has dogged the utilization of these critiques because the term "continental philosophy" is controversial, even aberrant, and ethnocentric, as, obviously, only the European continent is meant. Such a perspective thus makes continental philosophy a variant of Western philosophy, which, as is well known, draws on a shared history from the pre-Socratics and Plato to Aristotle, Christianity, Judaism, and Islam as well as on the work of modern European philosophers such as René Descartes and John Locke, David Hume, Gottfried Wilhelm Leibniz, Benedict de Spinoza, and Immanuel Kant. Yet, for others, the discourse of the supporters of the philosophy of the Enlightenment and the critique of the philosophy of the Enlightenment has highlighted the fact that continental philosophy started life as a category of exclusion, given that the analytical philosophy dominant within the English-speaking countries of the West (the United States, the UK, Australia, Canada, and New Zealand) has routinely disregarded philosophical work produced on the continent of Europe since Kant. But, whereas Kant's importance is recognized within analytical and continental philosophical traditions, especially since his transitional philosophy was partially a reply to radical skeptics such as Hume, the work of Hegel, whose ideas result from his criticism of Kant, has been mainly discounted, as has the post-Hegelian philosophy of many other eighteenth-, nineteenth-, twentieth-, and twenty-first-century continental thinkers. What is of importance in the current context are the lines of ideational connection between the supporters of the philosophy of the Enlightenment and the critique of the philosophy of the Enlightenment in light of luxury philosophy; there are, I argue, high levels of enclosure, containment, translation, and amalgamation in the interrelating forms of the supporters of the philosophy of the Enlightenment and the critics of the philosophy of the Enlightenment. The organizing framework for this argument is, I suggest, the critique of the philosophy of the Enlightenment as the philosophy of the Enlightenment without exclusions. The critique of the philosophy of the Enlightenment acknowledges that it has often been ignored by analytical philosophers, and welcomes, for example, literary philosophers such as the novelists Sartre and Albert Camus. Yet the critique of the philosophy of the Enlightenment does not eclipse the philosophy of the Enlightenment. The philosophy of the Enlightenment and the critique of the philosophy of the Enlightenment crisscross and interweave—occasionally across different continents, forms of philosophy, and frequently around their Hegelian and associated responses to Kant.

However, as a category of exclusion, the critique of the philosophy of the Enlightenment as continental philosophy was first recognized less as a literary philosophical tradition and more as a separate philosophical tradition from the perspective of an emergent analytical philosophy. A wide variety of twentieth-century analytical philosophers from Gottlob Frege to Bertrand Russell to G. E. Moore came to be labeled as "analytical," as having broken with idealism and Hegelianism, as having created new philosophical concepts intended to revive the skeptical, scientific spirit of the Enlightenment with the assistance of technical developments in logic and mathematics. The subsequent principles and techniques were used against the assertions of continental metaphysical idealism, traditional religion, and morality. Analytical philosophy also often employs "Hume's fork" (see, e.g., Fogelin 1993). Here Hume (2007: 28–9; original emphases) maintains that "All the objects of human reason or enquiry may naturally be divided into two kinds, to wit, *relations of ideas* and *matters of fact*." The former comprise the truths of mathematics and logic, which are "discoverable by the mere operation of thought, without dependence on what is anywhere existent in the universe" (Hume 2007: 28). The latter are contingent truths about the world which, according to Hume (2007: 29; original emphases), "seem to be founded on the relation of *cause* and *effect*." Anything that belongs to neither category, including metaphysics and religion, is exposed as valueless from the standpoint of truth and the natural sciences, reason, or genuine knowledge. Contemporary analytical philosophers continue to work in the spirit if not always in the letter of Hume's principles because, for these philosophers, philosophy is neither a branch of logic or mathematics nor a natural science but the examination of concepts. As stated by analytical philosophers, such a philosophy is interpreted as encompassing the investigation of the structure of thought, which in turn consists in the investigation of language (Dummett 1993). In contrast, numerous continental philosophers have, in defiance of Hume's dismissals, come to regard the critique of the philosophy of the Enlightenment as pertinent to their own conceptions of metaphysics, morality, and modes of experience. *Luxury Philosophy* provides new sources of insight into the uniqueness of, and interconnectedness between, those critics of the philosophy of the Enlightenment concerned with luxury philosophy. Although it is certainly clear that there is no one approach to the critique of the philosophy of the Enlightenment, there are nonetheless many fundamental themes that run through the writings of luxury philosophers. These themes involve existential and moral, ethical, and aesthetic questions that arise from an engagement with the critique of the philosophy of the Enlightenment and with those cultural, political, and social conditions entailing philosophical issues about luxury and the meaning of life, with luxury and questions of right and wrong or with luxury and the meaning of art and beauty. The questioning of traditional ideas of luxury philosophy, metaphysics, and methodology; the continuing decentering and deconstruction of the conceptual examination of luxury; the reflexive study of sensation; the questioning of "scientific" tools and approaches to the "facts" or "truths" of luxury; the raising of human necessity and human needs as locations for philosophical critique: these themes are integral to the cultural, political, and social project that is the critique of the philosophy of the Enlightenment concerned with luxury philosophy. The distinctive modulations of these themes are given in the philosophy of authors focused on luxury, including Rousseau and Saint-Lambert, Marx, Levinas, Bataille, Adorno, and Barthes, are discussed in the chapters that follow.

The conditions of this broadening of the critique of the philosophy of the Enlightenment to include luxury are chiefly historical and relate predominantly to the antagonism between the philosophical camps of continental and analytical philosophy. It has frequently been argued that this antagonism does not indicate a critical break between the supporters and the critics of the philosophy of the Enlightenment; this line of commentary is inclined to underline that this antagonism and their interconnectedness across continents and modes of philosophizing had their geneses over a century ago in the sometimes-abusive, sometimes-reconciliatory opposition between continental and analytical philosophy and the rise of nationalistic, even fascistic, political ideologies in geographical terms and interpretations (see West 2010). However, there are strong signs that there are numerous incongruities that surround any geographical understanding of the difference between analytical and continental philosophy, involving analytical philosophers who were German and Austrian (Gottlob Frege, Ludwig Wittgenstein); whose British analytical philosophy was, in part, influenced by the German phenomenology of Husserl (Gilbert Ryle); and those contemporary English-speaking and North American analytical philosophers who have drawn on and developed continental ideas (Richard Rorty, Alasdair MacIntyre, Charles Taylor), in addition to the rise of analytical philosophy in France, Germany, and Eastern Europe, especially in Poland. One cannot detect such a stress upon the geographical basis for the identification of two equally isolated traditions in many current approaches within Western philosophy. It might, for example, be emphasized that while there is evidence that the difference between analytical and continental philosophy is more a result of rivalries between philosophical groups, it is not easy to classify doctrinal differences or to describe the two approaches in terms of themes, methods, or even dispositions. It might also be proposed that attempts to demarcate differences between analytical and continental philosophy have not only functioned to inhibit intellectual engagement as much as to identify dissimilarities but also to misconstrue cultural and historical, political, social, and intellectual traditions and loyalties. In this framework, the antagonism between the two distinct philosophical camps of continental and analytical philosophy is a double-edged phenomenon, producing fruitful debate on the one side, and philosophical and intellectual antagonism between thinkers on the other.

Virtue, the Luxury of Appearances, and Marxist Philosophy

One topic that concerned luxury philosophers in the eighteenth century was the topic of human virtue. The questions at issue in the eighteenth-century creation, analysis, and restoration of virtue were multifaceted. A few of the important concerns that manifested in the 1750s comprise: the mental, social, and cultural forms through which civilized people were raised and understood as virtuous; the composite, paradoxical ways in which people expressed themselves as free from vice; the public investments that people came to have in their identities as theatergoers and civil members of communities; and the implications for virtue when attempting to comprehend the staging of plays and their claimed harmful social and cultural effects on citizens.

During the 1750s, among luxury philosophers of various affiliations, human virtue became an arena of careful consideration and critical practice. Whereas the project of the defense of virtue had been integral to Western philosophy since ancient Rome and Greece, the advent of novel discursive emphases focused on the deterioration of virtue started where the philosophy of ancient Greece and Rome left off. After the ancient Roman Ovid's (43 BCE–17/18 CE) erotic poetry (1982), for example, several prominent figures in eighteenth-century scholarly life reevaluated once more the junctions of luxury and obscenity, of luxury and debasement, of luxury and immodesty, of luxury and corruption, of luxury and appearances, and of luxury and shame. At this juncture, the philosophical perspectives of Rousseau (Chapter 2) and Saint-Lambert (Chapter 3) are crucial. These luxury philosophers, in many different ways, stimulated awareness of the nature of human virtue, in the questioning of the benefits of the sciences and the arts, in the vice-ridden nature of the human experience of enervation, and in the critique of the sciences and the arts as producers of luxury objects. What Saint-Lambert (1716–1803) calls "the luxury of appearances" (1965: 217), and specifically his revisiting of class analysis, was fundamental to the philosophical undertaking of producing, decentering, and dismantling the idea of virtue, because his thought about class greatly repositioned the relation between individual virtue and money. The luxury of appearances has also been employed by luxury philosophers such as Saint-Lambert to probe the positioning of people within the class structure, above all when people within the class structure begin spending more money than they can afford; to demystify—through ideas of intra- and interclass spending—the relation between luxury and one particular class; and to forewarn of the romanticism of appearances and the chimeras of excess that dominated early modernist desires concerning the love and seeking of wealth.

The luxury of appearances was central to the language of eighteenth-century luxury philosophers such as Saint-Lambert. Yet it has also played a correspondingly important part in fields from political economy to social psychology to cultural and media studies in the nineteenth and twentieth centuries. But what can the notion of the luxury of appearances contribute to luxury philosophy? Not only in the works of Rousseau and Saint-Lambert but also in the works of Bataille (Chapter 6) and Barthes (Chapter 8), to mention only two, the luxury of appearances is engaged with analytically to examine anew the real and symbolic forms through which people signify to themselves and to others the social and cultural domain of luxury. By means of the concept of the luxury of appearances, luxury philosophers are equipped to survey, look into, and evaluate the rich, often-fantasy configuration of luxurious reality and perhaps in due course the nature of human virtue itself (Saint-Lambert 1965: 217). Of crucial significance here is the collision between the nobles on the one hand, and ordinary people on the other. The view that the old social hierarchy might collapse was at the core of Saint-Lambert's study of the noble self and ideas of social superiority. Here the debate over how the luxury of appearances became a burden for everyone was especially noteworthy, as was eighteenth-century anxiety with the ways in which the luxury of appearances formed a danger to social morality in the early modern world of Europe (Saint-Lambert 1965: 217).

The idea of the luxury of appearances also made an important impact in nineteenth-century Marxist philosophy and luxury studies. Generally, the luxury of appearances was taken up by Marx not as an appendage to, or supplanting of, the history of capitalism and luxury studies, but as quizzing them, as encompassing the prospect of a distinctive method of appreciating luxury objects as commodities. In this space of deliberation, as in others, the luxury of appearances denotes different ideas and issues to different luxury philosophers. In Marx's *Capital Volume I* (1976), and specifically in his work on the commodity (1976: 125–77), Marx engages with the commodity to map the luxurious framing of this most basic form—with precise stress on the wealth of capitalist society and its appearances. As a German luxury philosopher, Marx does not take his lead from Saint-Lambert's luxury of appearances but from the truth that, for him, capitalism is a world of appearances. More explicitly in this setting of the luxury of appearances, capitalism is regarded dialectically in terms of method; the power of the luxury of appearances is to establish luxury commodities so firmly that it becomes virtually impossible to see the inner essence of capitalism or its laws of motion. Marxist philosophy introduces original methods of envisioning capitalism and with alternate options for imagining luxury. The radical contributions to these debates concerning the luxury of appearances and Marxist philosophy are examined and discussed in Chapters 3 and 4 of this book.

Voluptuosity, Expenditure, and the Dual Character of Luxury

Launching a discourse concerned with the problem of people being powerless to hide from themselves, luxury philosophy in the mid-twentieth century became increasingly intrigued with the notion that people sense that their selves are fastened to their being, by ideas of an unusual and separate form of experience Emmanuel Levinas called "voluptuosity" (1969) or the experience of human beings in search of the exceeding of their own being through sensual pleasure. What developed from this deliberation of the problem—throughout Levinas's succession of often controversial statements in which issues of male and female sexuality, being, luxury, and the world dominated—is that various primary differences function from within the luxurious beyond or the voluptuous. Voluptuosity is distinguished from luxury, most of all, as a return to the self or to the world—largely as an engaged participant in a space of meaning, but in terms of an objectless space of human satisfaction also. In this evaluation, elucidated in Chapter 5, voluptuosity exemplifies an exhilarating process of self-reflection by luxurious beings upon their cerebral aspirations and corporeal boundaries.

Expenditure, on the other hand, describes a shift of perspective at the level of luxury as a principle of loss and as the justification of luxurious human activity in the modern world (see Bataille 1985). A key critical expression—"the notion of expenditure" was utilized by Bataille (1985) to designate a disagreement with modern economic thought, to declare the beginning of an alternative form of modern consciousness, and to embrace the pursuit of being luxurious as the pursuit of the impossible (Bataille 1991). Several luxury philosophers in this volume delineate how the urge toward expenditure can be differentiated from social and cultural forms of thought characteristic of analytical rationalist thought concerning luxury. For some luxury philosophers, such as Bataille, an unsatisfactory level of attention to the continental philosophy of Nietzsche and Hegel has inhibited the development and use of the term "expenditure," whereas for other luxury philosophers, such as Barthes (see Chapter 8), the discourse of luxurious expenditure has generated useful knowledge. Also of importance in the present context are the connections between analytical and continental luxury philosophy, such as the connections between Hume's (1987) and Saint-Lambert's discussed in Chapter 3. Yet the continental luxury philosophy of expenditure moves beyond analytical luxury philosophy through its recognition of the principle of loss. The continental luxury philosophy of expenditure appreciates the unproductive and sometimes perverse character of modern luxurious living, and openly welcomes the study of seemingly wasteful and aberrant issues of mourning and war, cults, and the construction of sumptuary monuments. However, as Saint-Lambert's largely positive discussion of the work of Hume demonstrates, the continental does not necessarily hide or overshadow the analytical. Analytical and continental orders intersect—on occasion amid discussions of diverse forms of luxurious life, and frequently within debates over language and other games (see, e.g., the use of the work of the analytic philosopher Wittgenstein [1967] by the continental philosopher Lyotard [1984]).

A comparable ambiguity is evident at the level of continental luxury philosophy itself. For one thing, a variety of luxury philosophers, from Levinas to Bataille, can be described as "continental," as having broken with the problems of language and logic as identified by analytical philosophy, and as having unveiled new philosophical hypotheses calculated to question extant eroticism and economic culture. In spite of that, many of these same luxury philosophers did not so much come to refuse the label "continental" as applicable to their own philosophical and political efforts as associate themselves with other labels that are, in fact, subdisciplines of continental philosophy, such as phenomenology (Levinas) and cultural theory (Bataille). *Luxury Philosophy* presents new understandings of the distinctiveness of, and interconnections between, continental luxury philosophers. Even though it is undeniably true that there is no one approach to continental luxury philosophy, there are nevertheless various underlying topics that pervade the work of continental analysts of the luxurious philosophical condition. The questioning of traditional beliefs about luxurious phenomena, luxurious art, and luxurious sexuality as voluptuosity; the constant decentering and deconstruction of unproductive economic and political forms; the reflexive undermining of modes of luxury consumption; those forms of expenditure characterized by loss; the raising of unconditional expenditure contrary to the economic principles of balanced accounting, acquisition, and rationality as a site for criticism—these topics are at the center of the project of continental luxury philosophy. The characteristic nuances these topics are given in the writings of Levinas and Bataille are discussed in Chapters 5 and 6.

The conditions of this enlarging of continental luxury philosophy are predominantly cultural and political and connect in part to what Adorno (1981: 86) calls the "dual character of luxury." In Chapter 7, it is demonstrated that Adorno argues that the duality of luxury does not indicate a critical break from the social powers of efficiency, exchange, and profit; his explanations accentuate that the duality of luxury has its beginnings in the production of human resistance to expectations of people's submission to capitalism.

Still, for Adorno, there are strong indications that the duality of luxury also encompasses: a singular experience; an understanding of luxury that does not only focus on one side of its dual character; an appreciation that not all of the social product benefits human needs; the development of human happiness through squander, and the questioning of an obsolete capitalist system. One can perceive such an accent upon what might be called "the other side of luxury" and its dual character across the use of parts of the social product in Adorno's modern methodology that takes place within the realms of sociology and politics, luxury philosophy, and critical theory. Adorno, for instance, does not highlight the reproduction of expended labor either directly or indirectly. However, he does advocate that much more consideration should be given by luxury philosophers to the social and cultural, economic, and political experiences of people who, for whatever reason, and for however long, are not completely under the influence of the utility principle. In this framework, the duality of luxury is an ambiguous experience, producing power, efficiency, exchange, and profit in one way, and human resistance, the pursuit of liberation, and a critique of capitalism in another.

Luxury Mythology, Luxury Philosophy Today, and Its Influence

Luxury philosophy was, and remains, responsive to the exterior cultural, social, and political milieu within which it functions. It would be extraordinary if this were not the case, in the sense that luxury philosophy must be a consideration of the era wherein it is situated, revealing the main cultural and economic, political, and social transformations of luxury of the period. Luxury mythology has been, and continues to be, an insightful and continuing influence on twentieth-century and contemporary luxury philosophy. In composing *Luxury Philosophy*, I have tried to demonstrate and investigate some of these influences through the writings of Barthes (1993) in Chapter 8 and, for instance, Paula von Wachenfeldt and Magdalena Petersson McIntyre in Chapter 9. In fact, possibly every luxury philosopher in this volume has been, at some time, influenced by luxury mythology.

The twentieth century saw important shifts in the nature of luxury mythology. The literary and cultural critics of structuralism and poststructuralism (exemplified here especially by Barthes) endeavored to further a critique of luxury mythology as a specific aspect of a critical philosophy of modern society through an investigation of the associations between literature (particularly Sartre and Jean Racine in the case of Barthes) and semiotic theory—the study of signs and symbols, chiefly as components of language or other systems of communication, and encompassing semantics, syntactics, and pragmatics; the fluctuating nature of fashion in capitalism (for example through Barthes's studies of clothing and women's magazines); and the social origins of signs. Barthes also expounded a more complex interpretation of the mystifications of luxury culture and communication. These critical evaluations of luxury mythology amounted to the production of a multifarious and extensive corpus of luxury philosophy.

Barthes's critique of luxury mythology was also influenced by his discovery of, for instance, washing powder advertisements, which led him to contemplate the human world of luxury mythology in everything from novels to striptease to plastic, its philosophical culture, and its comprehension of popular culture. Barthes's interest in luxury mythology was also enthused in 1950s France by the then emergence of consumer culture that drew his awareness to the significance of philosophy for luxury, and to the importance of developing his own understanding of myth with regard to cultural studies. Barthes's interest in the themes of popular culture, mythical thought, and rituals was also partly derived from, but not dependent upon, the writings of the French anthropologist Claude Lévi-Strauss whose *The Savage Mind* (1966) came to have a lasting relevance to the analysis of rituals and modes of symbolic representation, diverse cultures, and political systems and societies. Barthes's discovery of advertising as a form of luxury mythology provides some of the philosophical framework for the growth of luxury philosophy today in Europe and North America. The structuralism and poststructuralism of Barthes who was influential in the development, for example, of the luxury fashion, cultural, and media studies of von Wachenfeldt and Petersson McIntyre, are currently joined by the advance of poststructuralist luxury philosophy which, in the case of luxury philosophy today, is being developed by Verena Andermatt Conley, whose work is examined in Chapter 9.

These developments in the critique of luxury mythology are especially significant in Italy where Patrizia Calefato, whose writings are examined in Chapter 9, is developing her perspective on contemporary luxury in society through the framework of Barthes's and Bataille's critique of fashion and capitalism. The emergence of lifestyle studies (Chaney 1996) is a crucial watershed in luxury philosophy, and numerous scholars such as Calefato have become fascinated with the relationship between luxury, lifestyle, and expenditure. This fascination has come to influence Calefato's interpretations of luxury mythology as a philosophy, and her investigation of consumerist extravagance has come to critique contemporary luxury mythology. The unleashing of unbridled luxury consumer desire in the present period highlights the sense of competition for status (a topic that is also discussed in Chapter 3) that begins with luxury consumption but ends with the confusions of the nature of contemporary economic value. As the pursuit of luxury does not seem to offer any solutions to the dilemmas of contemporary capitalism, the legitimacy of luxury mythology as a luxury philosophy becomes an important issue. With the death of Levinas in 1995, there was a general sense of the need to refresh the critique of luxury mythology, and the sense of that need has brought numerous luxury philosophers to reassess the ideas and influences of luxury philosophy. There is a broad sense among African feminist luxury philosophers such as Mehita Iqani and Simidele Dosekun, for instance, discussed in Chapter 9, that the contemporary period has produced an environment of widespread reassessment and revisiting of the legacy of eighteenth-, nineteenth-, and twentieth-century luxury philosophy.

This refreshment of the critique of luxury mythology will certainly develop into a redirection of previous work. The critique of luxury mythology still provides a crucial focus for an emerging luxury philosophy that incorporates cultural studies, political economy, and social thought, and offers a critical consideration of the fundamental aspects of luxury within society—aesthetics, the visual, and material culture being clear examples. As *Luxury Philosophy* shows, it is impossible to comprehend eighteenth-, nineteenth-, twentieth-, and twenty-first-century luxury philosophy without an in-depth grounding in the critique of luxury mythology. The critique of luxury mythology has also had a vital contribution to make to the understanding of luxury consumption and to the development of Marxism, critical theory, structuralism, and poststructuralism. The critique of luxury mythology will continue to be essential since it provides at least one possibility of incorporating moral philosophical examination with cultural and political, economic, and social thought, and because it profoundly interrogates the division between the facts of luxury and the values of luxury. It has consequently made a substantial contribution to the dismantling of taken-for-granted ideas about luxury and, today especially, to the critique of West-centric notions of the luxurious. As it becomes apparent that the market-driven culture of luxury consumption is not a solution to many of the difficulties of the twenty-first century, one can feel sure that there will be a continued interest in, along with the supplementary development of, the critique of luxury mythology.

A Finite Choice

In endeavoring to choose luxury philosophers for inclusion in *Luxury Philosophy* I have been faced with a finite choice. My chief goal has been to obtain some equilibrium in my representation of luxury philosophy. In my explanation of luxury philosophy from the eighteenth century to the twenty-first century, for instance, it is apparent that, on the whole, luxury philosophy has been more influential in France than in Germany—a difference that reflects the different history of luxury philosophy in France and Germany. I have tried to give some representation of German and French luxury philosophers, accepting that the Marxian and critical theoretical traditions of German continental philosophy have not preferred luxury philosophy per se.

I have also endeavored to attain some equilibrium in my choice from numerous subdisciplines of continental philosophy, particularly Enlightenment and counter-Enlightenment thought (Rousseau and Saint-Lambert), Marxism (Marx), phenomenology (Levinas), cultural theory (Bataille), critical theory (Adorno), structuralism, and poststructuralism (Barthes). I have also sought to acknowledge that, historically and contemporaneously, luxury philosophy as such is fundamentally interdisciplinary, especially today, and the continental philosophers whom I have included have made wide-ranging contributions across several fields, inclusive of moral philosophy and political economy, existentialism, cultural and critical fashion, media, and cultural studies.

My primary criterion of choice has, though, been that the luxury philosopher must be *a continental philosopher*, which explains the absence within this book of, for instance, chapters on well-known British analytical philosophers of luxury such as Hume (1987) and German and French sociologists of luxury such as Werner Sombart (1967) and Pierre Bourdieu (1984). I have tried to investigate those luxury philosophies that have made, and are currently making, a major impact on the study of early modern, modern, and contemporary cultural values, social forms, and the politics of eroticism, consumption, and ideology. I have been unable to avoid being primarily focused on male luxury philosophers because, in the history of continental philosophy, no female philosophers have yet produced a comprehensive luxury philosophy. However, I have attempted to represent a number of feminist critiques of Levinas's luxury philosophy in Chapter 5 while making it apparent in Chapter 9 that by far the majority of luxury philosophers contributing to contemporary debates in the field are female. The luxury philosophers included in *Luxury Philosophy* are generally people who have been active and important from the eighteenth to the twenty-first century, and whom I foresee will continue to be important in the decades to come.

Conclusion

The chapters that follow underline that a flexible divergence of research agendas is creative and useful for historical and contemporary luxury philosophy. Such divergence, developing from traditions of thought extending from the Enlightenment and the critique of Enlightenment philosophy to Marxism, phenomenology, cultural theory, critical theory, structuralism, and poststructuralism, produces new methods for conceptualizing a sometimes-confusing collection of luxurious phenomena, cultural, political, and social subjects and objects, and philosophical discourses in historical and contemporary eras. Therefore, a critical luxury philosophy receptive to these interdisciplinary standpoints and themes should consider the demand for different kinds of indulgence and self-indulgence (physical, mental, cultural, historical, political, and social) as a promising basis for remapping the landscape of eighteenth-, nineteenth-, and twentieth-century luxury philosophy, and for mapping the landscape of contemporary luxury culture, of the politics of luxury, and of the role of luxury in society. In my estimation, the primacy of concern for diverse cultures of gratification and social divergence in much present-day luxury philosophy arises not just from epistemological breaks, such as those between Enlightenment thought and the critique of Enlightenment thought. Instead, today, as deliberated in Chapter 9, it also arises from a new sociocultural context of the globalization of objects that are essentially whims and desires, the transnationalization of luxury conglomerates such as LVMH Moët Hennessy Louis Vuitton, the virtualization of communication and interaction with "objects" in the metaverse (Armitage 2023) that exude qualities which are possessed by real objects that are excessively expensive, the individualization or personalization and customization of luxury, luxury's supposed "democratization" (Berry 2022), and so on. Yet, a critical luxury philosophy attentive to the shifting character of the self and luxury must be founded as much on the identity or identification with luxurious subjects and objects as on different kinds of lavishness and the otherworldliness of sumptuosity, and this unavoidably necessitates an engagement in cultural and economic, moral, political, and social debates concerning everything from splendor and wealth to opulence and the state of being rich and affluent. It is my hope that the reader will find *Luxury Philosophy* a helpful and informative guide to the parameters of luxury-related philosophical tendencies and of the character of luxury critique.

References

Adorno, T. W. (1981), "Veblen's Attack on Culture," in S. Weber and S. Weber (trans. and eds.), *Prisms*, 73–94, Cambridge, MA: MIT Press.

Armitage, J. (2020), *Luxury and Visual Culture*, London: Bloomsbury.

Armitage, J. (2023), "Rethinking Haute Couture: Julien Fournié in the Virtual Worlds of the Metaverse," *French Cultural Studies*, 34 (2): 129–46.

Armitage, J. and J. Roberts (2014), "Luxury New Media: Euphoria in Unhappiness," *Luxury: History, Culture, Consumption*, 1 (1): 113–32.

Barthes, R. (1993), *Mythologies*, trans. A. Lavers, London: Vintage.

Bataille, G. (1985), "The Notion of Expenditure," in A. Stoekl (ed.), *Visions of Excess: Selected Writings 1927–1939*, trans. A. Stoekl, et al., 116–29, Minneapolis: University of Minnesota Press.

Bataille, G. (1991), *The Impossible*, San Francisco: City Lights Books.

Berry, C. J. (2022), "Democratic Luxury: An Oxymoron?," *Luxury Studies: The In Pursuit of Luxury Journal*, 1 (1): 11–24.

Bourdieu, P. (1984), *Distinction*, trans. R. Nice, London: Routledge Kegan & Paul.

Chaney, D. (1996), *Lifestyles*, London: Routledge.

Dummett, M. (1993), *Origins of Analytical Philosophy*, Cambridge, MA: Harvard University Press.

Fogelin, R. J. (1993), "Hume's Skepticism," in D. F. Norton (ed.), *The Cambridge Companion to Hume*, 90–116, Cambridge: Cambridge University Press.

Hume, D. (1987), "Of Refinement in the Arts," in E. F. Miller (ed.), *Essays: Moral, Political, and Literary*, 268–80, Indianapolis, IN: Liberty Fund.

Hume, D. (2007), "Skeptical Doubts Concerning the Operations of the Understanding," in S. Buckle (ed.), *An Enquiry Concerning Human Understanding and Other Writings*, 28–40, Cambridge: Cambridge University Press.

Hyland, P., ed., with O. Gomez and F. Greensides (2003), *The Enlightenment: A Sourcebook and Reader*, Abingdon: Routledge.

Iqani, M. and S. Dosekun, eds. (2019), *African Luxury: Aesthetics and Politics*, Bristol: Intellect.

Levinas, E. (1969), *Totality and Infinity: An Essay on Exteriority*, trans. A. Lingis, Pittsburgh, PA: Duquesne University Press.

Lévi-Strauss, C. (1966), *The Savage Mind*, London: Weidenfeld & Nicolson.

Lyotard, J.-F. (1984), *The Postmodern Condition: A Report on Knowledge*, trans. G. Bennington and B. Massumi, Manchester: Manchester University Press.

Marx, K. (1976), *Capital Volume I*, trans. B. Fowkes, Harmondsworth: Penguin.

Ovid (1982), *The Erotic Poems*, trans. P. Green, London: Penguin.

Plato (2007), *The Republic*, trans. D. Lee, London: Penguin.

Robertson, R. (2022), *The Enlightenment: The Pursuit of Happiness 1680–1790*, London: Penguin.

Rousseau, J.-J. (1968), *Politics and the Arts: Letter to M. d'Alembert on the Theater*, trans. A. Bloom, Ithaca, NY: Cornell University Press.

Saint-Lambert, J. F. (1965), "Luxury," in N. S. Hoyt and T. Cassirer (trans.), *Encyclopedia: Selections—Diderot, d'Alembert and a Society of Men of Letters*, 203–32, Indianapolis, IN: Bobbs-Merrill.

Sombart, W. (1967), *Luxury and Capitalism*, trans. W. R. Dittmar, Ann Arbor: University of Michigan Press.

Taylor, C. (1975), *Hegel*, Cambridge: Cambridge University Press.

West, D. (2010), *Continental Philosophy: An Introduction*, 2nd edn, Cambridge: Polity.

Wittgenstein, L. (1967), *Philosophical Investigations*, 3rd edn, trans. G. E. M. Anscombe, Oxford: Blackwell.

2

Jean-Jacques Rousseau: Luxury as the Enervation of Virtue

Biographical Details and Philosophical Context

Jean-Jacques Rousseau was born in Geneva, Switzerland, in 1712, but his father, Isaac, fled Geneva in 1722 to avoid arrest, leaving Rousseau boarding with siblings Jean-Jacques and Gabrielle Lamberrier. Rousseau's early years are recorded in his 1782–9 autobiography *The Confessions* (1973). Rousseau grew up in Geneva (where he was apprenticed to an engraver, Abel Ducommun) but also lived in Italy, France, and England. The theme of the arts remained a significant motif of his philosophy, including the philosophy of music, theater, and literature. Broadly speaking, anybody who takes the calling of a philosophical life seriously cannot ignore the arts. Rousseau received a prize from the Académie de Dijon and condemnation from the authorities in Switzerland and France. He fled to England in 1766.

Rousseau's first appearance in print was in 1750 when he published his "Discourse on the Sciences and the Arts" (1987), a discourse which argued that the sciences and the arts corrupt human morality. In France, Rousseau came under the influence of the *philosophes*, the intellectuals of the eighteenth-century European Enlightenment who applied reason to the study of philosophy and history, science, politics, economics, and society (Robertson 2022). From the 1750s, Rousseau became increasingly connected with and involved in the French philosopher, art critic, and writer Denis Diderot's (1713–84) and Jean le Rond d'Alembert's (1717–83) *Encyclopédie, or a Systematic Dictionary of the Sciences, Arts, and Crafts*, better known as the *Encyclopédie*, which was published in France between 1751 and 1772, with later supplements, revised editions, and translations (d'Alembert 1995). In 1754, Rousseau visited Geneva and converted back to Protestantism, having converted to Catholicism in 1728. In 1755, Rousseau published *A Discourse on Inequality* (1984) and *Discourse on Political Economy* (2008), during the writing of which much of his philosophical research became critical of the leading figures of the French Enlightenment such as Diderot and d'Alembert. In 1758, Rousseau's *Politics and the Arts: Letter to M. d'Alembert on the Theater* (1968; hereafter *Letter to M. d'Alembert on the Theater*) was published, which is a refutation of d'Alembert's suggestion that Geneva establish a public theater (1968).

Following the official suppression of the *Encyclopédie* in 1759, Rousseau published his 1761 novel *Julie, or the New Heloise: Letters of Two Lovers Who Live in a Small Town at the Foot of the Alps* (1997; hereafter *Julie, or the New Heloise*). In 1762, Rousseau published, first, *Of the Social Contract* (2012a), which theorizes how to establish legitimate authority in a political community that is compatible with individual freedom and, second, *Emile, or On Education* (1991), Rousseau's treatise on education and the nature of humanity, both of which were condemned by the authorities in Paris and Geneva. Throughout the 1760s and 1770s, Rousseau remained a critic of Swiss politics and education policy, the constitution of human knowledge, truth, reality, and society, writing, in 1764, for example, *Letter to Beaumont, Letters Written from the Mountain, and Related Writings* (2013). Rousseau died at Ermenonville, outside Paris, in July 1778, prior to the publication in 1780 of his *Rousseau: Judge of Jean-Jacques* (2012b), his 1782 *Reveries of the Solitary Walker* (1979) and, in 1782 and 1789, the first and second halves of his *The Confessions* (1973).

Rousseau made two important contributions to luxury philosophy. Arguably, his apparently separate contributions (to the sciences, the arts, and to the theater) converge around a sustained critique of European philosophical assumptions about corruption, manners, and morals, namely, around the philosophical critique of the theater. This chapter therefore largely concentrates on Rousseau's *Letter to M. d'Alembert on the Theater*, the study by which his historical and global philosophical reputation was not so much launched as sustained and enhanced. A conclusion suggests that a major component of Rousseau's discussion of the arts and the theater has been neglected, namely his tentative moves toward what might be called "a morality of inner feelings," which, by a series of examples, attempts to chart a way out of the problems Rousseau associated with the theater.

Luxury Philosophy and Contributions

Rousseau's luxury philosophy has broadly two principal components. First, in 1750, he developed a view of the sciences and the arts in "Discourse on the Sciences and the Arts" (1987) through the writing of an essay for a prize competition sponsored by the Académie de Dijon, contending with the question of whether human morality had been worsened or enhanced by the renaissance of the arts and sciences. "The moment I read this," wrote Rousseau in *The Confessions*, "I beheld another universe and became another man … What I remember quite distinctly about this occasion is that … I was in a state of agitation bordering on delirium" (1973: 327–8). Rousseau won the prize with "Discourse on the Sciences and the Arts," wherein he defended ancient Roman civil virtues against what he considered Athenian vice-ridden literary poets and orators. "The Discourse on the Sciences and the Arts" made Rousseau's European reputation, even attracting criticism from as far afield as the King of Poland (Riley 2001: 8). Consequently, from 1750 onward, Rousseau was a leading citizen of the eighteenth-century *République de lettres* or the scholarly world of early modern Europe. Second, Rousseau made a major contribution to the debate over the theater in his 1758 *Letter to M. d'Alembert on the Theater* (1968), a contribution that marked the beginning of the loosening of his links to the *philosophes*, largely because Rousseau opposed d'Alembert's (1968) scheme to found a public theater in Geneva. Rousseau advised that such a public theater would be contrary to civil virtues and that, for example, staging a production of Molière's 1666 comedy of manners in verse, *The Misanthrope* (2000), would have harmful effects on the citizenry of Geneva. Rousseau's work as a whole has given rise to much praise and to much controversy, but the debate around his views on the theater has not, to date, been particularly robust. Within the 453 pages of Patrick Riley's (2001) otherwise excellent edited collection, *The Cambridge Companion to Rousseau*, for instance, the concept of the theater features only in one chapter (Dugan and Strong 2001). Rousseau's work presupposes a particular engagement between the arts, the sciences, and philosophy. I shall discuss Rousseau's analysis of the arts before developing a full exposition of his views on the theater.

Discourse on the Sciences and the Arts

Eighteenth-century European societies could not assume that the restoration and development of the sciences and the arts either cleansed or debased behaviors and morals. Philosophers of the arts such as Rousseau no longer necessarily had, nor necessarily needed, the authority of traditional culture and critique behind them when they came to pronounce on questions concerning, among other topics, luxury. Many had as a result stopped being cultural arbiters of honesty and dishonesty and became, instead, sociocultural interpreters of philosophy and politics, religion, rationality, and progress. With the growth of the age of the Enlightenment, philosophers of the arts became increasingly uncoupled from traditional culture and critique (Robertson 2022).

In the eighteenth century, with the permitted rise of alternative cultural views to those of, for instance, the Catholic Church, philosophers of the arts, such as Voltaire (1694–1778), the French Enlightenment writer, philosopher, historian, and author in 1790 of *Candide, or Optimism* (2006), his satiric novel of the pitfalls of hopefulness in a world of hardships, were important in defining alternative cultural beliefs. Hence, for example, the significance of philosophical publications in redefining and reshaping core political values, religious, and sociocultural standards. Rousseau's memorable commentaries on, arguments about, and questioning of luxury in the early modern period (approximately 1350–1800), together with his transformation of academic thought about luxury in France and elsewhere, undermined the then-contemporary role and statements of many other philosophers of the arts (Bayly 2004). Indeed,

Rousseau's study of luxury in the "Discourse on the Sciences and the Arts," coupled with his natural disposition toward the extremes, was indicative of the changes in Europe in the early modern period. As a philosopher of the arts, Rousseau no more automatically had, nor automatically wanted, the authority of traditional culture and critique that had characterized the philosophers of the arts in, for instance, the ancient Roman Empire, such as Petronius (27–66 CE), the Roman courtier, "Arbiter of Good Taste," lazy and dissolute lover of luxury, and author of *The Satyricon* (2011), his satirical novel, believed to have been written during the era of Emperor Nero (r. 54–68 CE).

Rousseau acknowledges these changes in the philosophy of the arts in his analysis of luxury in the "Discourse on the Sciences and the Arts." Writing of luxury as enervation, as debilitation or enfeeblement in ancient Athens and Rome, Rousseau (1987: 6) discusses their earlier absence of the excesses of corruption, the role of the progress of the arts, and the subsequent dissolution of customs that, according to him, follow directly upon one another. Rousseau also deliberates on his alternative cultural judgment that a traditional culture can never be revitalized once its body politic has been affected by luxury through the arts and their enervating impact. The deterioration by luxury of ancient cities such as Athens and Rome, the obscenities produced by their increasingly debased writers, such as the Roman Ovid's (43 BCE–17/18 CE) erotic poetry (1982), in common with their views that offend against modesty, reinforced the feeling among philosophers of the arts such as Rousseau that not only were there no longer any virtues, but that such corruption imposes a certain shame on one's own culture. The philosophical and artistic context of eighteenth-century cities such as Geneva and Paris had thus changed radically since the heydays of ancient Athens and Rome.

However, these changes in luxury and in the authority of philosophers of the arts in the eighteenth-century Europe did not have the same impact on Rousseau, given his close interest in cultural and political dissolution. The issue of his involvement in attempting to reshape human conceit from a standpoint founded on "happy ignorance" and "eternal wisdom" probably explains many of the tensions and ambiguities in the "Discourse on the Sciences and the Arts" (1987: 10). The "Discourse on the Sciences and the Arts" is concerned partly to chart the distance between the then contemporary philosophers of the arts such as Rousseau and the world of "vain inquiries," a cultural distance reinforced by nature's "heavy veil" and the challenges to its processes (Rousseau 1987: 10). The tension for Rousseau is that on the one hand he recognizes that historically philosophers of the arts have been central to understanding nature's lessons (through, for example, the production of human knowledge) and on the other that to be critical they have to be, like Rousseau, to some extent critical of what people have learned or gained from nature's lessons. As a result, neglect of nature's lessons and its protection is the main vice of philosophers of the arts.

The role of philosophers of the arts is therefore bound up inevitably with the creation and the critique of the sciences, the arts, and the fact that they owe their origin to humanity's vices. A philosopher of the arts like Rousseau is an influential figure because he disbelieves that the benefits of the sciences and the arts have anything to do with human virtues; indeed, for him, critics of the sciences and the arts must highlight that the flaw of their derivation is evident in the luxury objects that they produce. The critical philosopher of the arts must go beyond the arts in particular to assert and to explore the luxury that nourishes them, that is, to question the reason for the arts, to consider what the development of luxury might become, and to speculate on how the arts nourished by luxury impacts upon people and nature (Rousseau 1987: 10). Often this critical stance will look like questioning received truths, but it means ultimately that the radical philosopher of the arts is always a philosopher alive to truth and, equally importantly, to truth in retreat.

Rousseau could be criticized because his view of the philosopher of the arts as a critic of the evil of the arts in particular tends to preclude the possibility that philosophers of the arts could themselves be either lazy persons or conceited ones or both. Rousseau rejects the possibility of the philosopher of the arts as a combination of vain luxury and necessity. Because it rules out the possibility that philosophers of the arts could ever indulge in vain luxury and influence from within the development of the sciences and the arts, it could be regarded as a romantic view of the activities of philosophers of the arts whose roots, for Rousseau, lie inside the ancient view of the Greek philosopher Plutarch (46–119 CE), one of Rousseau's favorites, whose *Greek Lives* (2008) emphasizes that philosophers of the arts should concentrate on virtues to be imitated and vices to be shunned. Rousseau (1987: 12) supports this emphasis by recognizing that luxury produces the splendor of states while simultaneously claiming that luxury is completely opposed to the extension of empires and to decent morals. For Rousseau, philosophers of the arts of the early modern period must bring a critical sociocultural perspective to the ambiguities of lives lived in luxury and wealth and to the merits and demerits of virtue, trade, and money.

This view of the philosopher of the arts as the arbiter of what is at stake in the question of luxury is, as Rousseau recognizes, a somewhat romantic political and moral image. In eighteenth-century philosophy, the European philosopher of the arts was quite likely to be driven by questions concerning the luster of luxury and "the taste for ostentation" with, according to Rousseau (1987: 13), little concern for critical public debate over "the taste for honesty" (on the question of luxury and taste in early modern Europe, see also: Hont 2006; Ilmakunnas and Stobart 2017). Rousseau takes note of the pressures on the intellects of the then contemporary philosophers of the arts to resist humiliation by a multiplicity of useless needs; to resist falling from prominence and, by implication, to resist their own depletion of strength and subsequent dearth of courage. Rousseau's (1987: 14) somewhat modest solution to these difficulties is to criticize the slide toward the dissolution of customs wherein luxury must be regarded as equally important and to resist "the corruption of taste." Although certainty about talented people in the arts who have "firmness of soul" is problematic in the degraded climate of the world of the early modern philosopher of the arts, talented people must equally not give themselves over to "childish productions," to the decoration of "carriage panels," and to the further dissolution of customs (Rousseau 1987: 14). The tension for philosophers of the arts is to remain loyal and effective within their own alternative cultural opinions, especially where those alternative cultural opinions are under threat from, for instance, "lascivious pictures," and to remain loyal to ancient Greek philosophers such as Plutarch on customs and "the simplicity of the earliest times" (Rousseau 1987: 14).

Rousseau's defense of the simplicity of the earliest times was, for many eighteenth-century philosophers of the arts, such as Voltaire, running contrary to their experience of the increasing number of enjoyable amenities of life. As early as 1737, for example, Voltaire had written his "Defense of the Worldling or an Apology for Luxury," which is a critique of the claimed link between poverty, virtue, and national importance, with his crucial argument being that "luxury, which destroys a state that's poor, enriches one that's great" (quoted in Hont 2006: 413). For Voltaire, and for others, Rousseau's defense of simplicity looked problematic, given Rousseau's apparent commitment to the earliest times rather than to contemporary times in the "Discourse on the Sciences and the Arts." More specifically, Rousseau (1987: 15) overtly adopted the critique of the arts and luxury on the basis of their enervation of virtue; furthermore, he did so from the perspective of the earliest times with a view to characterizing the notions of the sciences and the arts as distractions from military exercise through the production of "idle and sedentary occupations." Rousseau (1987: 15) thus challenged kings and their courtiers, their princes, and their nobility by arguing that the study of the sciences and the arts is "much more apt to soften and enervate courage than to strengthen and enliven it." In this chapter on Rousseau, I argue that his critique of the arts and luxury on the basis of their enervation of virtue is a crucial theme of his *Letter to M. d'Alembert on the Theater* and that it is consistent across his work. Consequently, the critique of the arts and luxury on the basis of their enervation of virtue is fundamental in Rousseau's writing sooner than decorative. As a result, Rousseau (1987: 15) embraces a critical standpoint on the demise of virtue not only in ancient Rome but also in the then contemporary cities of early modern Europe, such as Geneva, on account of their inhabitants becoming "connoisseurs of paintings," engravers of gold vessels, and promoters of the fine arts.

Letter to M. d'Alembert on the Theater

Rousseau's eighteenth-century philosophical preoccupation with the theater is a testimony to the then contemporary assumption that any adequate cultural knowledge of the reality of luxury must consider the effects of the theater which constitutes the stage and the players who perform, and makes possible such cultural knowledge. What I shall call "the taste for luxury" within the theater can only be understood as an interplay of the effects of the theater, and thus interpretations of this culture of adornment are also an effect of the frequenting of the theater. This principle of the effects of the theater and cultural knowledge of the reality of luxury, which is central to the philosophy of Rousseau, is clearly illustrated by the history of European understanding of the theater. While the early modern debate about European views of the theater was reestablished by Rousseau's 1758 *Letter to M. d'Alembert on the Theater* (1968), the philosophical controversies about the character and culture of the theater can be traced back through the European encounter with the ancient Greek and Roman theater of, for instance, Aeschylus (525/524–456/455 BCE), the father of tragedy (2003), and Seneca (4 BCE–65 CE), the Stoic philosopher, statesman, dramatist, and satirist (2011). Rousseau's controversial paradigm had the effect of establishing the notion of "theater" as a distinctive and pervasive ideology about the taste for luxury. His critique laid the eighteenth-century foundation for an extensive inquiry into the problematic relationships between theatrical effects, costumes, the jewelry the players wear, and the theater's interruption of the course of civil and domestic affairs at particular hours. For Rousseau (1968: 58), the theater is a "resource to idleness," a "place to forget oneself," and to become concerned with "foreign objects." But he asks, is the theater beneficial or damaging to the habits of citizens, their formation and development of new morals? This is an issue that, for Rousseau, hinges on the contemplation of the spectators of the theater and on the transformations that the theater brings them. "It is, then," Rousseau writes, "from the situation of each at the beginning that the differences must be estimated" (1968: 58).

In the philosophical literature, Rousseau's criticisms of the traditions of the theater are typically associated with the article on "Geneva" written by d'Alembert (1968) in his and Diderot's *Encyclopédie*. D'Alembert's representation of the prospect of a theater in "Geneva" is seen to be a manifestation of enduring and novel discursive paradigms that constantly reproduce the theater as an object of cultural knowledge for the citizens of the city of Geneva and elsewhere. This emphasis on the work of d'Alembert is not so much mistaken as perhaps misdirected, because it fails to recognize the obvious fact that Rousseau was more an important philosopher of luxury than he was a philosopher of the theater. For Rousseau (1968: 96), for example, the theater was not only in contradiction of ancient truisms but, for the citizens of Geneva, a "monument of luxury and softness" that deserves anger because it will be built on the wreck of their "antique simplicity" and endanger their public liberty. Yet d'Alembert was a significant influence on Rousseau's approach given the former's argument in "Geneva" that the city would be enhanced by permitting theatrical performances, which were not at that time allowed. As d'Alembert wrote in "Geneva," provided that the behavior of the actors themselves was accordingly controlled by law:

> Geneva would have theater and morals [manners], and would enjoy the advantages of both; the theatrical performances would form the taste of the citizens and would give them a fineness of tact, a delicacy of sentiment, which is very difficult to acquire without the help of theatrical performances … Geneva would join to the prudence of Lacedaemon the urbanity of Athens.
>
> (quoted in Rousseau 1968: 4)

D'Alembert's "Geneva" is thus a study that incorporates commentaries on the behavior of the theater players, their legal regulations, and the possible transformation of Geneva's morals whereby the citizens of the city would enjoy the benefits of theatrical performances as well as the creation and growth of their own cultural tastes. The importance of d'Alembert on citizenship and as an authority on refinement and tact is recognized explicitly in *Letter to M. d'Alembert on the Theater* (Rousseau 1968: 3). In this perspective, Rousseau's *Letter to M. d'Alembert on the Theater* does for French philosophical representations of the theater what "Geneva" attempted in terms of the promotion of the refinement of feeling for European theatrical tradition from Molière's *The Misanthrope* to Voltaire's 1753 *L'Orphelin de la Chine* (*The Orphan of China*; 2018), his play based on *The Orphan of Zhao*, a thirteenth-century Chinese play attributed to Ji Junxiang. Furthermore, if d'Alembert provided the philosophical tools for the analysis of Geneva it was Rousseau's assertion that the theater could only succeed if it delivered pleasurable yet distracting and diversionary "amusement" for the spectators that provided the reconceptualization of the theater. To show these dependencies in philosophical and aesthetic genealogies on d'Alembert, Molière, and Voltaire is not to present a criticism of Rousseau by showing his work to be derivative. It is in the nature of philosophical work to derive ideas, and in any case where would one start the story? From whom did d'Alembert derive the brilliant idea of theatrical representation as a "toy for sick children" (Grimsley 1963: 137)?

Rousseau's thesis and its criticisms are well known and I shall merely summarize its major components (Grimsley 1963: 136–7, 1983: 154; Fermon 1997: 102). The theater is constructed in European ideology as a permanent and enduring if "amusing" and distracting object of cultural knowledge in opposition to what I shall call "people discovering their pleasure in performing their public duties" as a positive and alternative pole. The reality and the discourse of the theater enervate traditions and feelings that divert people from the good persons they truly are through the deterioration of their divergent and complex morality; the theater gratifies and strengthens existing sociocultural tastes and produces incoherent and fake passions for the gaze of European spectators and their own discourse founded on artificial sensations. The theater is the location where the dreamlike is represented and people disengage from their involvement with important matters. In a lengthy critical treatment of these ideological forces, the theater is called up and called to account by Rousseau through his discussion of Molière's *The Misanthrope*. While people discovering their pleasure in performing their public duties are seen by Rousseau to develop historically in terms of the various stages of good, honest, people, in Molière's theater of *The Misanthrope*, such people are depicted as ludicrous and disgraceful. For Rousseau, Molière's *The Misanthrope* contends that charming men of the world are far superior to good, honest folk, and can easily defeat them. Yet Rousseau emphasizes that *The Misanthrope* is a play of brilliance which shows the power of the theater; however, because it also shows human virtuousness being ridiculed it cannot be said to show the role of the theater as a power for good.

Another of Rousseau's arguments in *Letter to M. d'Alembert on the Theater* is that many plays are constructed around the "love interest" (1968: 47). This love interest animates the obsessions of women in intolerable ways; for instance, Rousseau understands women through their perceived desires and pleasures. What will happen to women if a theater is founded in Geneva? As a result, the theater produces "theatergoers" for whom the theater is defined by the demand for fine clothes: women in particular will want to go out to "see" and "be seen" in their luxurious attire; the pleasure will be removed from the necessary and useful duties of the family and community; expenditure and sloth will take their place; legislation will be ineffective to control these harmful results; such legislation would only be effective if people shared the anxieties that it aimed to nurture; and the founding of a theater, the attendance at performances, and the subject matter of plays all counteract a sense of collective life and faithfulness that the law needs to employ to obtain compliance. In the philosophy of Rousseau, such theatergoers find their ultimate expression in his image of them sitting confined in the darkness as isolated individuals, an image he hopes to dispute by pointing out the need for people to live and labor together to maintain a fair and wealthy community. However, it does not follow that in Rousseau's world there should be no entertainments. Rousseau (1968: 125) sought numerous entertainments yet to be born, and encouraged those already in existence to "flourish with a truly festive air" in his *Letter to M. d'Alembert on the Theater*. The difference between the theater and the festival, however, is that while theatergoers are confined in the darkness as isolated individuals, "festivalgoers" assemble together, and "form among themselves sweet bonds of pleasure and joy" in "the open air, under the sky" (Rousseau 1968: 125).

In the geography of the cultural imagination, the theater is that part of the philosophical and aesthetic map by which Europe has historically gathered and oriented itself toward people's pleasant emotions and their satisfaction. The theater is a satisfied arena; that is, the theater and its luxuries offer the players' heads crowned with gold and garlands of flowers, a positioning that constitutes a sociocultural gathering in a condition of togetherness and spectacle. The theater and its luxuries as mental practices divide the world into players and spectators, with the theater's endless entertainments redefining the players and the spectators alike. The theater is a playhouse wherein the taste for luxury is enacted, an auditorium which defines the individual edges and boundaries of the love of the self and the world, and thus regulates the transgressive possibilities not only of one's own culture but also that of others. Against the theater and the taste for luxury, the model that people should abide by, suggests Rousseau, is that of Sparta, the prominent city-state in Laconia in ancient Greece, whose citizens indulged in "modest festivals and games without pomp": even in ancient Athens, Rousseau argues, amid the fine arts and "in the lap of luxury and softness, the bored Spartan longed for his coarse feats and his fatiguing exercises" (1968: 133). Rousseau's contention is that the people who discover their pleasure in the performance of their public duties are part of the festival, of the cultural customs of Europe that celebrated the festival as a type of local entertainment and active participation rather than passive consumption.

It is this satisfied taste for the luxury of passive consumption that increasingly defines people's reluctance to actively participate in modern games in the city; people amuse themselves in arenas other than those of public prizes or sailing, which are active and, according to Rousseau, "useful and so agreeable" (1968: 126). In *Letter to M. d'Alembert on the Theater*, Rousseau claims that the early modern identity of people in Europe is not defined by bread and their life as it is lived in their appropriate sociocultural station, but by living in that station "pleasantly, in order that they fulfil duties better, that they torment themselves less over changing their stations, that public order be better established" (1968: 126). Within the paradigm of Rousseau's *Letter to M. d'Alembert on the Theater*, good morals are defined as contingent more than is often supposed on people being content in their station. Dishonesty and conspiracy originate from restlessness and anger. For example, in the evolution of the theater and its luxuries, all goes badly when the characters of a play aspire to the station of another. *Letter to M. d'Alembert on the Theater* emphasizes that people must enjoy their occupation to perform within it properly. For Rousseau, "the disposition of the state is only good and solid when, each feeling in his place, the private forces are united and co-operate for the public good instead of wasting themselves one against the other as they do in every badly constituted state" (1968: 126). From Rousseau's viewpoint, people require festivals and pleasures, amusements, and distractions from their work. But this last is because they not only need the time to earn their bread but also the time in which to consume it with delight. Bustle and recreation, training and rest, are all crucially important. For people to be active and to be working hard, Rousseau (1968: 126) argues, festivals and amusements are vital to the maintenance of social order and to the deterrence of revolution as well as to increases in labor productivity.

Appraisal of Key Advances in Luxury Philosophy and Controversies

Having briefly described the principal features of Rousseau's argument in *Letter to M. d'Alembert on the Theater*, I can now indicate some of the major criticisms of Rousseau's perspective. He presents ingenious paradoxes about the European philosophical and aesthetic discourse on the taste for luxury and he also offers a philosophical and moral rhapsody that characterizes the theater from the standpoint of moral and aesthetic issues. In the eighteenth century, and even today, it was and is difficult to classify neatly and unambiguously such figures as d'Alembert, the aloof intellectual and careful scientist, in Rousseau's paradigm as occupying the same location within the field of the theater. In any case, Rousseau concentrates primarily on heartfelt matters (his beloved Geneva and its citizens) and not on an argument directed against d'Alembert individually. Employing the theater as a mirror of people discovering their pleasure in performing their public duties, Rousseau the radical writer used the taste for luxury as a device to attack or to question eighteenth-century European culture.

If the theater expresses a particular combination of the power of effects on those who frequent it seeking cultural knowledge, then it and its spectators must vary and change over time and between different urban, regional, and national configurations and traditions. Because Rousseau's attack on the theater concentrated primarily on the prospect of a theater in Geneva, he offered a philosophical and moral rhapsody only on the refusal of Genevans to allow a theater in their city and the negative feelings he attributed to Geneva's religious authorities concerning the question of a theater being built in the city. Also, while there is good reason to believe that the theater contributed to the taste for luxury, for instance as d'Alembert's "toy given to sick children," the theater and its ever-changing discourse were for d'Alembert at the time nothing more than "a regrettable but necessary antidote to the insidious malady of boredom" (Grimsley 1963: 137). In the mid-eighteenth century, the theater was, however, also understood by d'Alembert to have "the simultaneous advantage of inculcating useful lessons disguised under the appearance of pleasure" (Grimsley 1963: 137). These somewhat contradictory attitudes reflected the changes brought about by, and the growth of, the European Enlightenment philosophy of reason on the one hand, and the steady decline of matters of religious faith on the other, throughout the eighteenth century; one can see these contradictory attitudes and changes at work in the theater in, for example, Voltaire's 1759 play, *Socrates: A Play in Three Acts* (2009), which is set in ancient Greece during the events just before the trial and death of Greek philosopher Socrates, yet which is also heavy with satire specifically at government authority and organized religion. It is important to recognize that there were significant changes in the theater in the eighteenth century which themselves reflected changes in religious thinking with the rise of Enlightenment philosophy, the changing status of philosophers of the arts such as Rousseau and d'Alembert in early modern society, and personal changes following the publication of Rousseau's *Letter to M. d'Alembert on the Theater* and d'Alembert's lesser known reply to Rousseau, which has yet to be translated into English, his *Lettre à J-J Rousseau, citoyen de Genève* ("Letter to J-J Rousseau, citizen of Geneva" in Grimsley 1963: 137). In short, the upsurge of Enlightenment thought brought about more of a sense of philosophical argument and of aesthetic reexamination in the world of learned questioning, a sense of allies and adversaries in the then contemporary commentaries and retorts, speeches, and opinions about Rousseau's work in *Letter to M. d'Alembert on the Theater*.

Rousseau's work in *Letter to M. d'Alembert on the Theater* did not consider and perhaps could not countenance the responses to these theatrical and other changes, namely the growth of Enlightenment thought in France as a defensive protest against incorporation and dilution into European government authority and European-organized religion. With the publication of Rousseau's *Letter to M. d'Alembert on the Theater*, a critique of the taste for luxury and Enlightenment thought was one of the few remaining personal and political options in Rousseau's world as a protest against rational moral principles and government authority, if not organized religion. One can also see Rousseau's critical analysis of the taste for luxury in the same light in his 1761 best-selling novel *Julie, or the New Heloise* (1997: 447–9), whose subtitle signposts the letters of Héloïse d'Argenteuil and Peter Abelard (Clancy 2003), which detail a famous medieval tale of desire and Christian renunciation. The plot of *Julie, or the New Heloise* also unfolds through letters, which depends on the impulsive love between Julie d'Étanges, an aristocratic Swiss young woman living in Vevey on Lac Léman, and her teacher, a lower-class person who has no name but is given the pseudo-saint's name of St. Preux by Julie and her main confidante, her cousin Claire. *Julie, or the New Heloise* is consequently one of Rousseau's later attempts to counter the rise of rational moral principles and people's incorporation into a European model of blind social compliance with government authority. Rousseau's critical assessment of the taste for luxury and Enlightenment thought thus sought to challenge what he saw as the vice-ridden claims of European inauthentic selfhood, and he offered an alternative model of understanding premised on the virtues and significance of the authentic self. In the context of the expansion in Enlightenment thought, Rousseau therefore continually questioned the increasing dominance of European rational moral principles, which resulted in his defense of people's inner principles and feelings as key constituents of their core identity.

Because Rousseau associated the theater very closely with the taste for luxury, there is a fundamental cultural and political problem about the relationship between luxury, the enervation of virtue, and the theater. If the fostering of people's desires represents one new form of dominance to those which control them, the repeated luxurious emotions which are sensed in the theater arouse people, enervate them, weaken them, and make them less capable of withstanding their cravings, presents another (Rousseau 1968: 57). Molière's *The Misanthrope* and Voltaire's *Socrates: A Play in Three Acts* express the enervation of virtue of seventeenth- and eighteenth-century France. There is a general enervation of virtue in the European theater of the eighteenth century, wherein antagonism to theories of virtue has often accompanied hostility to practices of virtue. Generally speaking, Rousseau's critique of the theater did not so much not notice but did not develop the connection between these two forms of "sterile interest," namely indifference to practices of virtue and indifference to theories of virtue (1968: 57). In his *Letter to M. d'Alembert on the Theater* Rousseau writes concerning the enervation of virtue and the theater that "those of my compatriots who do not disapprove of the theater in itself are in error" (1968: 57). Rousseau also noted the parallels between the taste for luxury and the enervation of virtue. There are thus two discourses of the theater for the virtuous, one relating to the taste for luxury and the other to the taste for virtue. While the taste for luxury is defined by its lavishness and so forth, the taste for virtue is defined by Rousseau through its origins in the barbarous nature of sexual relations in Sparta where, for instance, Spartan men and women lived together but not in the same way: hence, for Rousseau, Spartan women, while healthy and brave, did not enervate their men according to his analysis in *Letter to M. d'Alembert on the Theater* (1968: 103). For Rousseau, the taste for Spartan virtues that are energetic, strong, and invigorated was undermined by men who compel the entire world, excluding themselves, "to be just, so that everyone will faithfully render unto him what is due him, while he renders to no one what he owes" (1968: 24). The European theater oriented its identity between two poles—practices of virtue and theories of virtue. Rousseau criticized the taste for luxury because it led to the enervation of virtue, to a debilitation of virtue that people love indisputably, but only in other people since they themselves expect to benefit from it; theories of Spartan virtue suffered from the fact that people want no virtue for themselves, as it would be expensive to them (1968: 24). "What then," Rousseau writes, does the theatergoer "go to see at the theater? Precisely what he wants to find everywhere: lessons of virtue for the public, from which he excepts himself, and people sacrificing everything to their duty while nothing is exacted from him" (1968: 24).

Throughout the eighteenth century, Rousseau suggests, theories of virtue disturbed the consciousness of the theatergoers of Europe because the "theater has rules, principles, and a morality apart, just as it has a language and a style of dress that is its own" (1968: 26). The notion of "heroic" theories of virtue pinpoints the idea that people say to themselves that whatever takes place inside the theater is not appropriate for them outside of it: people, Rousseau argues, would believe themselves as preposterous to assume the virtues of the theater's heroes "as it would be to speak in verse or to put on Roman clothing" (1968: 26). People's vaunting of theories of virtue arose from their theatrical experience of witnessing grand opinions and dazzling sayings on the stage. While theories of virtue emphasize the theater's language and style of dress, the theater was also guilty of presenting virtue to its spectators as a diversionary entertainment. Now rejection of these two stereotypes, of the theater's "heroic" theories of virtue, and the viewing of excellent adages, was crucial if theatergoers, as the foundation of European values, were to maintain their difference and distance from mere public amusement. Precisely because for Rousseau the taste for virtue and the taste for luxury shared so much in common (excellence and refinement, sociocultural value, high standards, and taking pleasure in doing what is right) they had to be separated culturally and socially by a discourse of duty. The taste for Spartan virtues, for the separation of theatrical comedies and tragedies from "the duties of man," raised significant questions about the theater and the character of its "passing and sterile emotions that have no consequences," not to mention theatergoers clapping their own bravery in acclaiming that of others, their kindness in sympathizing with evils that they themselves could have eradicated, and their "charity in saying to the poor, God will help you!" (Rousseau 1968: 26).

To summarize this discussion it is important to show that, for Rousseau, the theater can be described in terms of two dimensions. First, there are internal and external dimensions of the theater in which Rousseau's attention is focused inward on the discourse of duty or outward toward the theater's externalized language (its eyepopping axioms on the stage) and style of dress. Second, there is a dimension that is divided into positive and negative evaluations. The theater involves a negative/external framework of public rejection of the theater's language (its alluring aphorisms on the stage) and style of dress as inappropriate and preposterous beyond its walls. The practices and heroic theories of virtue perfectly express this interpretative option. In the opposite direction, that of the positive/internal, people discovering their pleasure in performing their public duties identify with some discourses of duty within the theater as a positive expression of identity and consciousness. For example, Jean Racine's 1670 play *Bérénice* (1988), a five-act tragedy taken from the Roman historian Suetonius (66–122 CE), recounts the story of the Roman emperor Titus and Bérénice of Cilicia, the sister of Agrippa II. When discussing the play, Rousseau notes that the effect of the characters of Titus and Bérénice on the identities and consciousness of spectators is positive and pleasurable because Titus and Bérénice's "sacrifices made to duty and virtue … have a secret charm, even for corrupted hearts; and the proof that this sentiment is not the work of the play," writes Rousseau (1968: 53–4), is that spectators have it before the play starts. This position contrasts with the internal/negative, with people discovering their *dis*pleasure in performing their public duties. In *Bérénice*, for instance, Rousseau remarks, Titus abdicates the throne at the feet of Bérénice who, "affected by such a great sacrifice, … feels it her duty to refuse the hand of her lover, but nevertheless accepts it" (1968: 54). Finally, there is the positive/external, that is, as Rousseau puts it, "when the people is corrupted, theater is good for it" (1968: 65). This typology helps us to understand that the theater not only produces people who discover their pleasure in performing their public duties, but also that Rousseau's "sterile interest" and "sterile emotions" can be positive and negative.

The account of the theater provided by Rousseau in *Letter to M. d'Alembert on the Theater* is in large measure devoted to the culture and politics of his native city, Geneva. Nowhere in Rousseau's writings is his idea of cultural and political association more thoroughly described than in his *Letter to M. d'Alembert on the Theater*, where Rousseau endorses companionable festivities "in the open air, under the sky" (1968: 125). However, by 1758, Rousseau had ended relations with his previous allies, the *philosophes*, and was concerned with critiquing two philosophers' work that attempted to transcend the narrow limitations of the pre-Enlightenment theatrical tradition. In this respect, Rousseau's observations on d'Alembert and Voltaire are instructive, because they provide a model of what Rousseau himself called "a morality apart" (1968: 26).

As stated, following a period of sociable interactions during his *Encyclopédie* days when Rousseau accorded to d'Alembert the esteem owing to a foremost French intellectual, he made the publication of d'Alembert's article "Geneva" (1968) the reason for an attack upon the proposal that a theater should be founded in that city. While the conflict of principle and argument was acute, the publication of *Letter to M. d'Alembert on the Theater* in 1758 did not have a damaging impact upon their affiliation and no personal hostility was stimulated either by Rousseau's *Letter to M. d'Alembert on the Theater* or by d'Alembert's official response, his *Lettre à J-J Rousseau, citoyen de Genève* (Grimsley 1963: 137). Insofar as Rousseau was concerned, the *Letter to M. d'Alembert on the Theater*, while directed to d'Alembert, included only unimportant individual references to d'Alembert and was mostly devoted to his own explanation of morality and art. On d'Alembert's part also there was no animosity. Immediately prior to the publication of his work, Rousseau wrote to alert d'Alembert of the approaching production. D'Alembert responded with a pleasant note wherein he asserted: "Far from being offended by what you may have written against my article 'Geneva,' I am, on the contrary, very flattered by the honor you have done me; I am very anxious to read your work and profit by your observations" (Grimsley 1983: 195). That these statements of interest were not empty utterances is demonstrated by the practical efforts which d'Alembert undertook to further Rousseau's work by securing its admission into France from Switzerland and even offering to function as its official censor.

Voltaire plays an equally important role in Rousseau's struggle over the destiny of Geneva (Wokler 2012: 85–6). Rousseau saw Voltaire's recent residence in Geneva and endorsement of the idea of establishing a theater there as nurturing the cultural and philosophical accoutrements of European moral corruption and the political suppression of its citizens. He devised his *Letter to M. d'Alembert on the Theater* with the constitution of Geneva and his conscious dedication to the restoration of its democratic principles in mind, both so much corroded in practice under the reign of Voltaire's governing patrician associates, according to Rousseau. For his part, Voltaire condemned the austere, transcendent, fanatical, and opinionated variety of patriotism that he saw Rousseau as supporting, and Voltaire believed justice was well performed when the Calvinist pastorate, which he reviled for much the same reasons, joined the patriciate of Geneva in denouncing Rousseau's philosophy. Nonetheless, Voltaire, after questioning Rousseau's ideas, assumed the republican cause that Rousseau supported and sought reforms in Geneva which proved too extreme for patricians and democrats alike. There are many inconsistent characteristics about Voltaire's and Rousseau's Genevan battles, not all of them about the fate of European theater, its language, and dictums: among them are such facts as that the sovereign assembly, whose powers Rousseau wanted to reinstate, had always been the realm of only a small portion of its population; and that when Rousseau became the patron saint of the republican cause in the 1760s he refused to enroll in it, instead renouncing his citizenship and subsequently urging his supporters to ask Voltaire for advice, whom they might otherwise have avoided. In short, the ideological and personal differences between Rousseau and Voltaire emerge most noticeably in their assessments of the culture and politics of Geneva.

My contention is that Voltaire's presence in Geneva and enlightened approach to the theater provided the impetus, if not the model, for Rousseau's own *Letter to M. d'Alembert on the Theater*. Rousseau's critical account of Voltaire's residence in Geneva and promotion of a theater there (see, e.g., Wokler 2012: 80), is, however, tempered, if somewhat caustically, by an appreciation of Voltaire's talents in *Letter to M. d'Alembert on the Theater*. As Rousseau put it: "Let M. de Voltaire deign to compose tragedies for us on the model of *la Mort de César* and the first act of *Brutus*; and, if we must absolutely have a theater, let him engage himself always to fill it with his genius and to live as long as his plays" (1968: 121–2). Rousseau's discussion of Voltaire recognized the importance, if not the scale, of Voltaire's achievements, which were to promote the rise of the theater in Geneva as part of the republican cause and its interconnections with radical reforms. If Rousseau's attempt to restore Geneva's democratic principles recognized and addressed Voltaire's governing patrician friends, then Voltaire taking up the republican cause recognized the existence of a dense and reactionary world to which post-Enlightenment Europe and European theater had to establish an orientation. Voltaire's account implicitly looks at the problem of philosophers such as Rousseau tussling over the fortune of Geneva and the prospect of erecting a theater there through a refutation of Rousseau's alleged rise of cultural and moral decadence. In my view, Voltaire rather than d'Alembert set the agenda for Rousseau, which was first to understand European theater's adoption of the taste for luxury alongside Voltaire taking up the republican cause, and second to begin to probe the philosophical problem of the future of Geneva and the likelihood of instituting a theater there. Certainly, Voltaire was Rousseau's mortal rival and not an ally in the same faction. As Wokler writes, for Rousseau, Voltaire "had destroyed the morals of Genevans by introducing the love of luxury, satire, and theater in their midst, with the loss of their liberty the likely outcome and permanent monument of his stay among them" (2012: 80).

Rousseau's critical analysis of philosophers of the arts like d'Alembert and Voltaire prepared the groundwork for his subsequent reflections on the relationship between philosophers of the arts and the wider public

(Rousseau 1968: 6). In *Letter to M. d'Alembert on the Theater*, d'Alembert and Voltaire are critiqued, often implicitly, because their relationship to their audience was unambiguously endeavoring to bolster "the influence of [the] Enlightenment over the hearts and minds of the people" (Furniss 2004: 604). They were committed to the superiority of European Enlightenment values and their dream of society ruled by reason, but this relationship to moral values and rationality was far more unambiguous in d'Alembert and Voltaire than in Rousseau's *Letter to M. d'Alembert on the Theater*. Rousseau, in his own fictional writing on love and ethics, marriage, imaginary communities, virtuous individuality, and the extended family, steadfastly maintained his moral position to his public. Rousseau's controversial writing on society and the Enlightenment wherein he attempts to reconcile the Enlightenment's initial doctrines with piousness and the energy of virtue, with honesty, and with republican values is clear in the text that followed *Letter to M. d'Alembert on the Theater*, his 1761 novel *Julie, or the New Heloise* (1997). The core of this position is not to reject community and philosophy, the arts, and the sciences, but to build an alternative community that incorporates them into the practical arts (e.g., horticulture), into the ties of affection, the need for clarity between people, and the attainment of virtuousness, or, in simple terms, a morality apart. Rousseau's *Julie, or the New Heloise* expresses it perfectly: a morality apart educates its children not to "make scholars of them," but to "make them ... charitable and just" (1997: 610).

In conclusion, I suggest that Rousseau's ethical vision of the philosopher of the arts can be regarded as a defense of his morality apart, which can be defined as the ethical world view of this philosopher of the arts in a mid-eighteenth-century European context where fiction and nonfiction were beginning to rewrite the traditional agenda of the theater. Rousseau's philosophical analysis of the work of letters and love in *Julie, or the New Heloise* provides a model of a morality apart prepared by a philosopher of the arts and for a conception of the art of living "in a small town at the foot of the alps" which I now wish to sketch in this concluding comment. For a discussion of Rousseau's morality apart, fictional letters of love are important for two reasons. First, Rousseau argues that the proper topic of the novel is the character and influence of the novel itself, and second, that it is not until people realize that the theater is both a foundation of and cure for dishonesty, depravity, and vice in large cities such as Geneva that they can appreciate that novels play a comparable dual role regarding entire peoples such as the Swiss or the French. Perhaps it is not too fanciful therefore to believe that, because of their exposure to eighteenth-century European concerns and issues, the morality apart promoted by Rousseau the philosopher of the arts might, in recognizing the increasing ubiquity of large cities in the 1750s, reject all claims to the escalating cultural superiority and political dominance of the theater. This is the central message of *Letter to M. d'Alembert on the Theater* and *Julie, or the New Heloise*: that in reality the world of people is too immoral and debased to be (mis)represented solely by the theater and must be supplemented by people discovering their pleasure in performing their public duties through novels. Precisely because people were exposed to the eighteenth-century European forces of immorality, any morality apart, any philosopher of the arts living "in a small town at the foot of the alps," should welcome a stance that supports the diverse value of letters and love and celebrates the teeming diversity of human cultural dialogue, imaginary or real. With an awareness for the tensions between a localized philosophy and a European-wide Enlightenment, a morality apart and its renovation of virtue might come to recognize a difference between arguments that pertain to the city and arguments that pertain to the countryside.

A morality apart can be defended ethically, because Rousseau counseled his readers that his letters on love were not written by "French, wits, academicians, philosophers; but provincials, foreigners, solitary youths, almost children, who in their romantic imaginations mistake the honest ravings of their brains for philosophy" (1997: 3). For Rousseau, people did not need an analysis of Enlightenment philosophy but a positive alternative to it that would celebrate the unpretentiousness of "sensible youths," where the only interest is what is in their hearts, which is the "single sentiment" of love (1997: 11). One can suggest that the components of Rousseau's notion of a morality apart and its renovation of virtue are as follows: the art of living "in a small town at the foot of the alps" as a method and as a mentality to achieve some emotional distance from "philosophizing"; and reflexiveness with respect to "everything" (the lovers in *Julie, or the New Heloise*, writes Rousseau, "get everything wrong" [1997: 11]); the revelation of nothing but oneself as an appealing individual; a morality apart founded not on knowledge but on the worth of one's inner feelings, especially the self-detached from the real world arising from an awareness of its precarious condition and hence acceptance of the fiction of another world distinct from the real one; and a creative appreciation of an "authentically new spectacle," especially "in the open air, under the sky" (Rousseau 1968: 125, 1997: 11). These values flow generously from Rousseau's analysis of the pitfalls of the prospect of a theater in Geneva in 1758, his view of the philosopher of the arts, and his sincere engagement, in the second half of *Julie, or the New Heloise*, with a prototype of human society that functions as a genuine alternative to that proposed by the Enlightenment thought of d'Alembert and Voltaire.

References

Aeschylus (2003), *Prometheus Bound and Other Plays*, trans. P. Vellacott, London: Penguin.

Bayly, C. A. (2004), *The Birth of the Modern World 1780–1914: Global Connections and Comparisons*, Oxford: Blackwell.

Clancy, M. T., ed. (2003), *The Letters of Abelard and Heloise*, trans. B. Radice, London: Penguin.

d'Alembert, J.-B. (1968), "Geneva," in A. Bloom (trans. and ed.), *Politics and the Arts: Letter to M. d'Alembert on the Theatre*, 139–48, Ithaca, NY: Cornell University Press.

d'Alembert, J.-B. (1995), *Preliminary Discourse to the Encyclopedia of Diderot*, trans. R. N. Schwab, Chicago: University of Chicago Press.

Dugan, C. N. and T. B. Strong (2001), "Music, Politics, Theater, and Representation in Rousseau," in P. Riley (ed.), *The Cambridge Companion to Rousseau*, 329–64, Cambridge: Cambridge University Press.

Fermon, N. (1997), *Domesticating Passions: Rousseau, Woman, and Nation*, Hanover, NH: Wesleyan University Press.

Furniss, T. (2004), "Rousseau: Enlightenment Critic of the Enlightenment?," in M. Fitzpatrick, et al. (eds.), *The Enlightenment World*, 596–609, Abingdon: Routledge.

Grimsley, R. (1963), "D'Alembert and Rousseau," in R. Grimsley, *Jean d'Alembert (1717–83)*, 132–56, Oxford: Clarendon Press.

Grimsley, R. (1983), *Jean-Jacques Rousseau*, Brighton: Harvester Press.

Hont, I. (2006), "The Early Enlightenment Debate on Commerce and Luxury," in M. Goldie and R. Wokler (eds.), *The Cambridge History of Eighteenth-Century Political Thought*, 377–418, Cambridge: Cambridge University Press.

Ilmakunnas, J. and J. Stobart, eds. (2017), *A Taste for Luxury in Early Modern Europe: Display, Acquisition and Boundaries*, London: Bloomsbury.

Molière (2000), *The Misanthrope and Other Plays*, trans. J. Wood and D. Coward, London: Penguin.

Ovid (1982), *The Erotic Poems*, trans. P. Green, London: Penguin.

Petronius (2011), *The Satyricon*, trans. J. P. Sullivan, London: Penguin.

Plutarch (2008), *Greek Lives*, trans. R. Waterfield, Oxford: Oxford University Press.

Racine, J. (1988), *Bérénice*, Paris: Le Livre de Poche.

Riley, P., ed. (2001), *The Cambridge Companion to Rousseau*, Cambridge: Cambridge University Press.

Robertson, R. (2022), *The Enlightenment: The Pursuit of Happiness 1680–1790*, London: Penguin.

Rousseau, J.-J. (1968), *Politics and the Arts: Letter to M. d'Alembert on the Theater*, trans. A. Bloom, Ithaca, NY: Cornell University Press.

Rousseau, J.-J. (1973), *The Confessions*, trans. J. M. Cohen, London: Penguin.

Rousseau, J.-J. (1979), *Reveries of the Solitary Walker*, trans. P. France, London: Penguin.

Rousseau, J.-J. (1984), *A Discourse on Inequality*, trans. M. Cranston, London: Penguin.

Rousseau, J.-J. (1987), "Discourse on the Sciences and the Arts," in *Basic Political Writings of Jean-Jacques Rousseau*, trans. D. A. Cress, 1–24, Indianapolis, IN: Hackett.

Rousseau, J.-J. (1991), *Emile, or on Education*, trans. B. Foxley, London: Penguin.

Rousseau, J.-J. (1997), *Julie, or the New Heloise*, trans. P. Stewart and J. Vaché, New Haven, CT: Dartmouth College Press.

Rousseau, J.-J. (2008), *Discourse on Political Economy and the Social Contract*, trans. C. Betts, Oxford: Oxford University Press.

Rousseau, J.-J. (2012a), *Of the Social Contract and Other Political Writings*, trans. Q. Hoare, London: Penguin.

Rousseau, J.-J. (2012b), *Rousseau: Judge of Jean-Jacques*, trans. C. Kelly and J. R. Bush, New Haven, CT: Dartmouth College Press.

Rousseau, J.-J. (2013), *Letter to Beaumont, Letters Written from the Mountain, and Related Writings*, trans. C. Kelly and J. R. Bush, New Haven, CT: Dartmouth College Press.

Seneca (2011), *Phaedra and Other Plays*, trans. R. S. Smith, London: Penguin.

Voltaire (2006), *Candide, or Optimism*, trans. T. Cuffe, London: Penguin.

Voltaire (2009), *Socrates: A Play in Three Acts*, trans. F. R. Morlock, San Bernardino, CA: Borgo Press.

Voltaire (2018), *The Orphan of China. A Tragedy. Translated from the French of M. de Voltaire. First Acted at Paris, on the 20th of August, 1755* [translator not named], Farmington Hills, MI: Gale.

Wokler, R. (2012), "The Enlightenment Hostilities of Voltaire and Rousseau," in R. Wokler (ed.), *Rousseau, the Age of Enlightenment, and Their Legacies*, 80–7, Princeton, NJ: Princeton University Press.

3

Jean François de Saint-Lambert: The Luxury of Appearances

Biographical Details and Philosophical Context

Jean François de Saint-Lambert was born in Nancy in northeastern France in 1716 and brought up on his parents' estate at Affracourt, a village in Lorraine. Saint-Lambert studied at the university at Pont-à-Moussan, started writing poetry, and, by 1733, had commenced work on *Les Saisons* (*The Seasons*; 2014), his chief poetical work, which was not published until 1769. In 1739, Saint-Lambert joined the Heudicourt regiment in the Lorraine Guards, spending a good deal of the 1740s fighting in the Italian campaigns of the War of the Austrian Succession (1740–8). Moving to Paris in 1750, Saint-Lambert awarded himself the title of Marquis de Saint-Lambert, to which he had no entitlement. In 1752, Saint-Lambert instigated a love affair with Sophie d'Houdetot. This amorous relationship is notable for scholars of luxury philosophy because, in 1757, while Saint-Lambert was absent on military duty in the Seven Years' War (1756–63), the philosopher Jean-Jacques Rousseau (see Chapter 2) fell in love with Sophie, a love that Rousseau recorded in his autobiography, published between 1782 and 1789, *The Confessions* (1973). Sophie spurned Rousseau and she and Saint-Lambert stayed together until his death. Saint-Lambert left the army in 1758 and devoted himself to literature. Thanks mainly to the success of *The Seasons*, Saint-Lambert was elected to the Académie française in 1770.

Saint-Lambert found the French Revolution of 1787–99 distasteful because he preferred a paternal monarchy with privileges for the nobility and the church, organizations that he considered crucial to such a form of government. Losing much of his wealth in the revolution, and backing those unsympathetic to it, Saint-Lambert sought refuge with Sophie in the country near Paris while continuing to write on philosophy and science, morality, and religion. Drawing a pension from Napoleon's post-revolutionary government in 1800, Saint-Lambert returned to the newly reinstated Académie française and to public life but he was increasingly in poor health. Saint-Lambert died in Paris in February 1803.

Saint-Lambert made one important and influential contribution to eighteenth-century luxury philosophy. He wrote on one of the most controversial questions concerning luxury philosophy in his 1765 essay "Luxury" (Saint-Lambert 1965), a contribution to Denis Diderot and Jean le Rond d'Alembert's co-edited *Encyclopédie* (Saint-Lambert 1765), which was the general encyclopedia published in France between 1751 and 1772, with later supplements, revised editions, and translations (d'Alembert 1995). The notion of luxury as harmful or beneficial was explored in "Luxury" through the dispute regarding its effects; a dispute that dates back to classical times and to classical authors such as Plato's discussion of luxury in his 375 BCE *Republic* (2007). Saint-Lambert made his decisive contribution to luxury philosophy in "Luxury" through his consideration of previous periods and the wide-ranging eighteenth-century accord that luxury was harmful to society. His somewhat controversial contribution to the study of luxury in "Luxury" recognized that a slow transformation in economic and political circumstances was underway in the 1760s under the influence of, among many other publications, Bernard Mandeville's 1714 *The Fable of the Bees* (1989), which defends the paradox that social benefit is the unintended consequence of personal vice. Throughout Saint-Lambert's career he was a close student of other eighteenth-century authors, especially those such as Voltaire (1694–1778), the French Enlightenment writer, philosopher, satirist, and historian, whom Saint-Lambert met in 1747, and David Hume (1711–76), the Scottish Enlightenment analytic philosopher, historian, economist, librarian, and essayist, whom Saint-Lambert considered fellow travelers in questioning the traditional consensus that luxury was damaging to society. Saint-Lambert's work addressed issues relating to luxury and to the question of whether the term "luxury" was any longer sufficient to explain the multifaceted philosophical, social, economic, and political issues involved. Finally, he addressed the extravagant, expensive, and self-indulgent aspects of luxury in terms of wealth or a level of comfort that permits unnecessary spending.

Although Saint-Lambert covered a wide range of questions in his luxury philosophy, his perspective is remarkably consistent and its central focus is not so much that of Hume's well-known essay on luxury of 1752, "Of Refinement in the Arts" (1987), but that of the philosophical, political, and economic aspects of luxury. In this discussion of Saint-Lambert, it should be recognized that his work is historically adjacent to the luxury philosophy of Jean-Jacques Rousseau, with whom he profoundly disagrees, namely Rousseau's 1750 "Discourse on the Sciences and the Arts" (1987a). Although this chapter is exclusively about Saint-Lambert, it is in reality difficult to ignore the related contributions of Saint-Lambert and Rousseau. Both philosophers significantly developed luxury philosophy and the study of the arts, where for instance Rousseau's "Discourse on the Sciences and the Arts" has been highly regarded since its publication.

Luxury Philosophy and Contributions

This discussion of Saint-Lambert's luxury philosophy demonstrates that he had a significant influence over eighteenth-century luxury philosophy in Europe. It is surprising, therefore, that, apart from specific studies that incorporate Saint-Lambert's luxury philosophy (e.g., Lough 1971: 351–4; Kors 1976: 192–3), his impact upon "The early Enlightenment debate on commerce and luxury" (Hont 2006), and his contribution to the political economy of virtue and other debates (see, e.g., Shovlin 2006, 2008; Hont 2008), there have not been more comprehensive and critical evaluations of his work as a whole, even if Saint-Lambert's moral tale "Ziméo" of 1769 has recently been reassessed by scholars of French literature concerning the topic of slave revolution (Bandau 2017).

The Political Economy of Desire: Loving and Seeking Wealth

Saint-Lambert's luxury philosophy is overtly and self-consciously based on the traditions of eighteenth-century luxury philosophy, especially Voltaire, author in 1736 of the poem "Le Mondain" ("The Worldling" or "The Man of the World"; 2011), which defends a way of life focused on worldly pleasure, and Hume's important essay from 1752, "Of Refinement in the Arts" (1987). Hume's essay states that luxury stimulates people to work harder, inspiring "an assiduity in honest industry," which, in turn, gratifies their "natural appetites, and prevents the growth of unnatural ones, which commonly spring up, when nourished by ease and idleness" (1987: 270). Second, writes Hume, luxury helps to make people more intelligent: it puts "the minds of men … into a fermentation," at which point "profound ignorance is totally banished, and men enjoy the privilege of rational creatures, to think as well as to act, to cultivate the pleasures of the mind as well as those of the body" (1987: 271). Finally, Hume argues that luxury helps to bring people together in cities, clubs, and conversation, and that "they must feel an encrease in humanity from the very habit of conversing together and contributing to each other's pleasure and entertainment" (1987: 271). In brief, Hume considers that "*industry, knowledge*, and *humanity*, are linked together by an indissoluble chain, and are found, from experience as well as reason, to be peculiar to the more polished, and, what are commonly denominated, the more luxurious ages" (1987: 271; original emphases). This eighteenth-century tradition is seen initially by Saint-Lambert through the framework of eighteenth-century European notions of desire, a term that he uses frequently throughout his essay on "Luxury." The work of Rousseau (e.g., Rousseau 1973, 1987a) has, for instance, been important in understanding the everyday world of desire, if not for Saint-Lambert. However, the principal interpretative claim of this chapter is that Saint-Lambert's luxury philosophy is dominated by the political economy of desire. To achieve clarity in understanding Saint-Lambert's luxury philosophy, it is important to study his definition of luxury as "the use men make of wealth and industry to assure themselves of a pleasant existence" (1965: 204). Saint-Lambert is completely explicit about "the first cause of luxury," which "lies in that dissatisfaction with our condition, that desire to increase our well-being, which is and must be present in all men" (1965: 204). Consequently, the political economy of people's desires, of their passions, of their virtues, and of their vices is crucial to the development of Saint-Lambert's work. In this interpretation of Saint-Lambert's luxury philosophy his dependence on the concept of desire should not be either ignored or neglected. In particular, human desire with respect to its role of necessarily making people love and seek wealth is carried over into Saint-Lambert's work on government; it is the tension between the human impulse of desire and the then radical agenda of founding government on equality and community of property that makes Saint-Lambert's luxury philosophy interesting and problematic. Saint-Lambert's luxury philosophy has a critical dimension that deconstructs the mainsprings of everyday reality by uncovering its taken-for-granted assumptions about the desire on the part of people to accumulate wealth. This humanistic luxury philosophy promises to expose the disguises that cloak people's cultural and economic, political, and social worlds of desire, but paradoxically Saint-Lambert also demonstrates that people need these disguises to make their world safe for the necessity that is luxury: "hence," Saint-Lambert comments, "luxury exists in all states and in all societies" (1965: 204).

In general terms Saint-Lambert argues that luxury has been the subject of moralists who have censured it and the object of praise by (unnamed) "political thinkers" who have spoken of it "more as befits a man of business or a clerk than a philosopher or a statesman" (1965: 204). By this, Saint-Lambert means that the praise by political thinkers maintains that luxury: encourages population growth; increases the well-being of states; facilitates the circulation of money; refines manners and fosters individual virtue; favors the progress of knowledge and of the fine arts; and increases equally the power of nations and the happiness of citizens (1965: 204–5). Saint-Lambert does not accept such political claims at face value, noting, for example, that there is "much luxury in Japan, and yet in that country manners are still cruel" (1965: 206). Similarly, as with the praise of luxury, Saint-Lambert also addresses the moral censure of luxury, a critique which upholds that luxury causes: inequality of wealth and the useful arts to be surrendered to those that give pleasure; the ruination of the countryside by attracting people to the cities; depopulation;

the weakening of courage; and the stifling of honor and love of country (1965: 206). These positive and negative evaluations of luxury provide the basis for Saint-Lambert's political and economic explanation not for the origins of people's love and seeking of wealth but for his recording of what are "the salient points" in praise of luxury and in its censure and to "showing that history contradicts the one as much as the other" (1965: 207). Saint-Lambert adopts this position to argue that, since the philosophers who have censured luxury fall into moderate and bad-tempered groups, it is especially important to construct an argument against those luxury philosophers, such as Rousseau, who, in an effort to have people evade the evil results of luxury, would put people "back in the woods and into a certain primitive state that never was and cannot be" (1965: 207). This argument is complemented by Saint-Lambert's suggestion that the most extensive positive opinion of luxury in France in 1765 was that it was necessary to elevate a nation from its flaws and anonymity, to give it the strength, the coherence, and the wealth that will lift it above other nations. It is interesting therefore that one of the most important contributions to the eighteenth-century debate about luxury in France was in fact based upon an argument that luxury must continue to grow to promote the arts, industry, and commerce, and to bring nations to that point of maturity that is necessarily followed by their old age and ultimately their obliteration. "This opinion," explains Saint-Lambert, "is quite widely held, and even Mr. [David] Hume shares it" (1965: 208). Such an argument concerning luxury and the arts, industry, commerce, and national ascent and descent may explain why Saint-Lambert's critical reception of Rousseau and rather unenthusiastic reception of Hume is characterized by a profound concern for the first principles of government (Shovlin 2008: 218; Hont 2008: 283). Saint-Lambert's interest in luxury and the arts, industry, commerce, and nationhood points to a rather humanist theory of the love and the seeking of wealth, while his position on luxury in France in philosophical terms implies a thorough criticism of the taken-for-granted nature of wealth.

The core of Saint-Lambert's work is a philosophy of people's love and seeking of wealth. Society is characterized by laws and regulations and therefore people freely constitute legislation so as to have a stable structure within which to operate. People are defined by their personal interest, which is often in conflict with the general interest, and as a result people tend to diverge from the latter, a divergence that, if it is to be prevented, requires the building of a sense of social morality. People's love and seeking of wealth are the bridge between people and their history and it is through this love and seeking of wealth that people's lives become coherent as part of a nation, meaningful concerning industry, and continuous in terms of social progress. In thriving within the context of laws and regulations, people's love and seeking of wealth provide them with, for instance, variety in the arts, a variety generated by, among other things, the very presence of laws and regulations. Over time, people's love and seeking of wealth are taken for granted and become part of the background of social action. The foreground is occupied by reflexive, practical, and conscious activities regarding, in the present context, the pursuit of luxury. However, with the securing of a pleasant existence through the work of others, there is a process of government corruption with the result that the background becomes ever more reliant on personal interest, more open to corruption, constitutionally thinner and increasingly an object of reflection for those preoccupied with the love of wealth, pleasure, and those passions that stimulate luxury. Accordingly, the foreground of personal interests, habits, and prejudices expands, and life is seen to be faulty and defective within the setting of constitutions which, apart from any influence of luxury, entails the corruption of governments. The decadent and corrupt ways of loving and seeking wealth of past empires, such as those of the ancient Persians, the ancient Athenians, and the ancient Romans do recede, and early modern European life in, for example, Italy becomes more luxurious yet not warlike: it is peaceful and humane, charming; indeed, it is a nation where the private virtues are refined under the power of a priesthood and governments whose object is to maintain peace. In fact, according to Saint-Lambert people in Italy live in a world of civil laws, civil administration, and the arts, a world wherein the love and seeking of wealth are anything but frowned upon by governments (1965: 211–12). There are profound economic and political, national, and geographical consequences associated with these changes. Premodern Europeans, such as the Dutch and the Swiss, the Portuguese, and the Spanish had trade and industry, land, exports, and fertile regions, that is, firm and definite economic and political, national, and geographical structures that corresponded with their reliance on the background of their love and seeking of wealth. In early modern societies, such as Saint-Lambert's France, the French had commerce that abounded in prosperity, and the love and seeking of wealth were achieved through France's colonies, its exports, and its fashions (1965: 212). The economic and political, national, and geographical pressures on the people of France were profound and to some extent France's early modern peoples were confronted with the uncertainties of increasingly international forms of production, manufacture, and industry, not to mention the prospective ruination of the ever more porous boundaries of the French colonial nation-state that stretched from the Americas and Asia to the Caribbean and the Middle East (Smith 2023).

Saint-Lambert's luxury philosophy can be interpreted as an application of the concept of desire to the specific field of luxury and to specific domains of early modern society, such as the prosperity of nations. Saint-Lambert's reflections on luxury consumption, luxury production, and the luxury industries have a characteristic line of argumentation. People's love and seeking of wealth that they take for granted and regard as natural are shown not just to be socially but historically constructed and, in the case of luxury, precariously variable with national prosperity. People, observes Saint-Lambert, become aware of "the function of luxury" as being "the same for a nation as for an individual: the number of pleasures must be in proportion to the means for enjoying them" (1965: 212). However, Saint-Lambert then shows that, while people's love and seeking of wealth are constructed, it is socially necessary, and indeed collective life would be poorer and boring without such love and the desire for enjoyment. Indeed, the implications of Saint-Lambert's deconstructive analysis of wealth are to suggest by implication that people would be wise to remember their philosophical awareness that luxurious consumption, luxurious production, and the luxury industries are socially and historically constructed, because their stimulation of the arts and industry depends on their taken-for-granted instinct and passion for luxury.

Having succinctly discussed Saint-Lambert's conception of desire and philosophy concerning people's love and seeking of wealth, it is useful to now turn more directly to his account of the construction of the political and economic aspects of luxury. Saint-Lambert approaches the question of the political and economic aspects of luxury in society through a political-economic methodology that specifies three moments in the construction and production of the political and economic aspects of luxury: industrialization, modern governmentality, and social morality. The first concept is closely related to Saint-Lambert's account of "the new arts" in "Luxury" where the human world of industry is built by people in terms of giving them new means of subsistence (which leads to an increase in population) (1965: 213). Modern governmentality is the process by which the humanly created world of the constitution of the state and civil laws encourages and protects private property: it is a world wherein the state and its wealth come to signify importance and power and that "whoever strives to gain wealth is useful to the state and that whoever, being rich, wants to enjoy his wealth is a reasonable man" (Saint-Lambert 1965: 213). Finally, this increasingly industrialized world must be reappropriated by governments as they transform but also preserve this industrialized and modern world through the fostering of social morality in their citizens. This whole process is parallel to Saint-Lambert's earlier discussion of luxury in the critical philosophy of Hume. The citizens who populate the early modern world are in fact constructs or projections of a human world that requires the furthering of social morality, whereby the love of property is kept alive and stimulated by modern governmentality. The pursuit of luxury is both a form of social morality and a desire to increase one's possessions and one's enjoyment of them. For Hume, that luxury rouses people to work vigorously, to remain truthful and trustworthy, and to be diligent was the first reason to support it. For Saint-Lambert, it is the government that "must concern itself with the manner in which its citizens wish to gain riches and to enjoy them" (1965: 214).

Eighteenth-century luxury philosophies occupy positions on a philosophical continuum between Saint-Lambert's perspective that luxury must grow to nurture the arts and Rousseau's viewpoint that luxury must shrink to stave off corruption and the dissolution of mores in the progress of the arts. For instance, Rousseau's radical standpoint denies that there are given or fixed reasons as to why luxury must promote the arts and asserts that knowledge of the social reality of luxury not only is socially constructed but also has an enervating effect upon people (1987a: 6). By contrast, Saint-Lambert emphasizes the existence of luxury in all states and in all societies, while remaining hostile to the proposition of Rousseau that the reality of luxury is constructed through categories of understanding based on degeneracy and perceptions founded on obscenity. In eighteenth-century luxury philosophy, the most radically held position was that of Rousseau's wherein luxury was charged with encouraging immodesty and crime and with hastening the disgrace of nations and the rise of barbarism. Rousseau's radicalism was significantly influenced by a variety of sources: d'Alembert, the Greek philosophy of Plutarch, and the writings and plays of Voltaire (Rousseau 1968; Plutarch 2008; Wokler 2012). The interesting dimension of Saint-Lambert's writings is that they combine support for the gaining of riches, which must contribute to the wealth of the state, with support for private property contributing to the good of the community: "the well-being of one class of citizens," declares Saint-Lambert, "must not be sacrificed to the well-being of another" (1965: 214). People have to construct the world of luxury, because their desires provide them with that which leads to luxury. Thus, according to Saint-Lambert, people's love and seeking of wealth through luxury must be subordinated to social morality and to the welfare of the community. Saint-Lambert's version of private property contributing to the good of the community and to the well-being of all classes of citizens is, however, problematic because, as he himself recognizes, it is not easily reconciled with the ignorance of those who govern or with their ill will or with their neglect of the governed and even of their own systems of government (Saint-Lambert 1965: 215). In short, Saint-Lambert's version is basically unable to deal with governments that overload their populations with taxes, misuse their legitimate authority, and make vulnerable or demean their own citizens. Yet Saint-Lambert's luxury philosophy is rooted in an epistemology that recognizes support for the gaining of riches, which must contribute to the wealth of the state, and the need to acknowledge that monopolies not only exist but also prevent the distribution of their own products (Shovlin 2006: 121, 2008: 219). Because Saint-Lambert deconstructs government animosity and the abandonment of the governed from an interpretation of the essential social and geographical, economic, political, and moral characteristics of people (namely their laws and regulations) one could imagine that Saint-Lambert could be categorized as a political economist of luxury. The point is not necessarily to criticize

Saint-Lambert's eighteenth-century political economy of luxury, but to note that commending private property contributing to the good of the community and to the well-being of all classes of citizens, together with support for the gaining of riches, provided that it contributes to the wealth of the state, are not typically combined. For example, Saint-Lambert's contemporary, the Chevalier Louis de Jaucourt (1704–79), the French scholar and by far the most prolific contributor to Diderot and d'Alembert's *Encyclopédie*, with 18,000 articles in it to his name, condemned support for the political economy of luxury because of its allegedly harmful effects on society, social responsibility, and the workings of government (Hoyt and Cassirer 1965: 49).

Saint-Lambert's support for the gaining of riches that contribute to the wealth of the state helps to identify the political nature of a luxury philosophy that entrusts private property contributing to the good of the community and to the well-being of all classes of citizens. One could argue historically that Rousseau's radical standpoint, which disagrees that there are assumed or set reasons as to why luxury must encourage the arts, and his declaration that knowledge of the social reality of luxury is not only socially constructed but also has a weakening effect on people, emerged for the very reasons outlined by Saint-Lambert when writing about people seeking to fulfill their desires: namely, that people's background assumptions about luxury, the arts, and the beneficence of government could no longer be taken for granted (1965: 217). As a result, they appeared in the foreground as debilitation and government unresponsiveness to the prosperity of the country, where their legitimacy and the expectation of social morality were challenged. The world of luxury had become modern because there was increasing skepticism about the legitimacy of governments that intensified the inequality of wealth and distributed exclusive privileges (Lough 1971: 352–4; Hont 2006: 381; Shovlin 2006: 122). According to economic historians Morrisson and Snyder, for instance, inequality in France in the eighteenth century was considerably higher than elsewhere in Europe (2000: 70). Similarly, in the luxury philosophy of Voltaire's 1736 poem "Le Mondain" (2011), there are no issues with the image of the popping wine cork for the benefit of wealthy citizens as an emblem of the early modern world of Europe—a world that was more and more populated by monopolies such as the East India Company instead of free trade (Erikson

2014). In the early modern world of Europe, therefore, there were no longer any secure, objective, background philosophical assumptions concerning, for example, the holding of public and private financial offices, which is also why serious debates about luxury could take place in poetry, in part as a defense of the use of verse for the discussion of ideas. To return to the issue of the relationships between ignorance and those who govern, the notion that government ill will was deliberately socially constructed rather than the result of government benign neglect of the governed appeared in social and political contexts, wherein basic categories of government behavior concerning the amassing of wealth were challenged and questioned. It was because people could no longer rely on their background understanding of the legitimacy of the love and seeking of wealth that the people who govern and those who were governed in the capital cities in particular were seen to be historically and socially contingent upon riches, power, and pleasure. "It is in the capital," remarked Saint-Lambert, that people "seek to fulfill their ... desires—to gain social prestige and to enjoy the pleasures of life" (1965: 217).

The Luxury of Appearances and the Civic Spirit

Saint-Lambert's work has not been as influential as it might have been, partly because it is challenging. In "Luxury," he presents a comparative perspective of luxury philosophy, the aim of which is to reconcile the existence of very rich people with a viewpoint on luxury philosophy on how people's love and seeking of wealth effect and shape the social life of wealthy people gathered in one place: the capital city. In fact, as noted, his view of the relationship between people and society is predicated upon the political economy of luxury. This theme is expressed through the comparison between people in society and the society of people who continually compare themselves to one another. Individuals endeavor to create meaning through unceasingly trying to establish the idea of their own superiority to shape the mental world they and others inhabit; these meanings become the basis of their love and seeking of wealth over time; and in turn this basis of people's love and seeking of wealth becomes a competitive social structure that causally determines the fashion for making wealth the measure of people's worth in social life. The chief illustration in Saint-Lambert's "Luxury" is his account of people trying to appear rich. At some stage individuals of all classes begin spending more money than they can afford and there arises a type of luxury Saint-Lambert (1965: 217) calls "the luxury of appearances." This spending is not confined to individuals of one class that they share with their families and friends. Saint-Lambert argues that the luxury of appearances is not confined to one class because every class considers itself poor if it does not revel in the immediate excess that arises from the love and seeking of wealth. Yet the way that individuals of whatever class are led to behaviors driven by desire that are the predetermined channels of "appearing rich" is very similar to what immediate excess does where the respect for wealth holds sway (Saint-Lambert 1965: 217). Saint-Lambert's luxury philosophy is complex because it is at once a radical view of the possibilities of deconstructing commerce, manufacture, and property and a counsel of caution that their progress creates a new type of wealth that belongs to ordinary people; a transformation wherein great riches no longer belong to ordinary people's social "superiors" but to ordinary people themselves who seek to become the equals of the nobles through imitating their lavishness. Saint-Lambert deconstructs how the nobles thought that the hierarchy which had raised them above ordinary people was collapsing, how they boosted their outlays to maintain their superiority, and how the imperative of the luxury of appearances became a burden for each estate and formed a danger to social morality. Certainly, Saint-Lambert recognizes that what masquerades as an inevitable fact about human arrangements such as the luxury of appearances is precisely driven by the human desire for gain, which can so easily deteriorate into extreme greed. However, an awareness of the dangers of the imperative of the luxury of appearances is necessary if people are to avoid desire becoming the ruling social passion and to maintain the disciplines and routines associated with the noble passions that make life possible and tolerable by controlling them. In short, when the luxury of appearances is taken to extremes, avarice pervades all emotions and enthusiasm for virtue disappears.

Saint-Lambert's political economy of luxury is intended to recognize the existence of people and their extreme cravings. Yet the general mood of Saint-Lambert's luxury philosophy is, much like Rousseau's (1987a), if from a very different perspective, dominated by fears of the disappearance of virtue (1965: 218). People rejoice in their capacity for the most extreme sense of property in the interests of securing a socially meaningful and "intense passion" that "burns out the soul and extinguishes its light" (Saint-Lambert 1965: 218). As Saint-Lambert suggests in "Luxury," people almost prefer corruption to government taxes because the former offers comfort through the procuring of immense sums of money without taxation. As Saint-Lambert contends, people require the security of their passions and their rewards to be maintained, if their world of luxury is to have any sense of honorable, and sometimes criminally dishonorable, legitimacy. People need the riches of their lives to be explained and justified by their perceived and real social "influence," by their ability to free themselves from all government constraints. I have argued in this chapter that this longing for gain is predicated upon the work of desire, hence the significance of Saint-Lambert's political economy of desire and conception of a lifeworld constructed by noble and ignoble passions. The trend of Saint-Lambert's argument about the necessity of excess to secure a meaningful and intense form of social passion is necessarily cautious, but to recognize this outcome is simply an interpretation rather than a value judgment. Saint-Lambert's political economy of desire and philosophy of luxury, of excess, and of the constant seesawing between the meaningfulness and meaninglessness of luxury, contributes further support to the view that the luxury of appearances is the counterpart to the simultaneous development within people's consciousness of the burden of the disappearance of virtue: a conclusion that raises interesting questions for the somewhat optimistic view on luxury of Hume (1987: 270), wherein luxury motivates people to work hard, to pursue law-abiding business with integrity, and to satisfy their natural rather than their unnatural desires. For Saint-Lambert, and in contrast to Hume, the burden of the luxury of appearances cannot be easily or long endured without the concurrent disappearance of virtue.

The implications of this disappearance of virtue for Saint-Lambert's luxury philosophy appear to be highly significant for what he calls "l'esprit de communauté" (e.g., 1965: 208, 214), translated variously as the "patriotic," "public," or, as utilized below, "the civic spirit" (Lough 1971: 351; Hont 2006: 381, 2008: 283). The social world produces a range of systems of luxury and philosophy in response to the need for a social morality of virtue. These social realities are all valid insofar as they satisfy the necessities of philosophy and protect the individual from the disappearance of virtue. It is difficult then to make value judgments across historical cultures, such as the culture of ancient Rome, given its specificity wherein the government "inculcated unrest and a turbulent spirit in the Romans," making war a necessity for them and for keeping "alive their moral strength and their fanatical love of country" (Saint-Lambert 1965: 210). The problem of the civic spirit is a specific issue for Saint-Lambert, especially in his luxury philosophy, and he was perfectly aware of the intellectual damage his philosophical, political, and economic understanding of luxury could cause for governments and citizens alike. For instance, he rejects one solution to the lack of civic spirit that was developed by some governments and citizens in which what is protected is the property of only a minority of citizens, the maintenance of only a part of the country, and the advantage of the minority. While the former defends the property of some citizens over time, the proper role of government is to protect the property of all citizens, with its key aim being the maintenance of the whole country and to the advantage of the majority. The maintenance of only part of the country and to the advantage of the minority is the policy of people sacrificing the well-being of one class of citizens to the well-being of another; maintaining the property of only a minority of citizens is the narrative of governments that neglect the whole of society. Saint-Lambert rejects this exclusionary political policy as class war, on the grounds that sacrificing the well-being of any citizen to the well-being of another is just another manifestation of luxury (1965: 214). There are no neat answers to the problems raised by the history of governments attempting to further the civic spirit and patriotism in their citizens and simultaneously "keeping alive and even stimulating their love of property, their desire to increase their possessions and to enjoy them" (Saint-Lambert 1965: 214).

Saint-Lambert's luxury philosophy has to confront a basic and difficult problem. The problem of a meaningful form of excess is solved in Saint-Lambert's luxury philosophy by claiming that luxury is a necessary condition of social existence. Without a social morality of virtue, social life would be impossible. But would any social morality of virtue or quality or quantity of luxury do? His position is an argument for governments concerning themselves with the way in which their citizens wish to meaningfully achieve riches and to delight in them in society. Social excess requires a social world that legitimizes luxury and that is also mindful that the means of acquiring riches must contribute to the prosperity of the state, and even how they are loved must be useful to it. Saint-Lambert believed that each property, inclusive of luxury property, must contribute to the benefit of the community, something that would be appropriate to give class society political coherence and cohesiveness. Luxury is a noble contributor to communal well-being because its adherents are the citizens of all classes and therefore it has a necessary function in society. Luxury is fundamental to the passions that are required for devotion and loyalty to the civic spirit and to the well-being of the community encouraged by the state. The work of philosophers must be enthusiastic about luxury because their ideas about citizenship and ambition, love of glory, and honor must not only be shared by the mass of citizens but, crucially, subordinated to the civic spirit which alone keeps the passions within respectable bounds. Yet Saint-Lambert's luxury philosophy cannot easily escape from the conclusion that people need a social morality of virtue because a social existence founded only on the love and seeking of wealth, based on continuous desire, would make people even more unjust than they already are and cause immense harm to all. Saint-Lambert's luxury philosophy struggles with a political economy of luxury of critical reflection and the possibility that the passions, if unleashed and not subordinated to the civic spirit, could destroy any social equilibrium.

Such a cautious position toward luxurious values in a potentially harmful and destructive world is troublesome, as Saint-Lambert recognizes. Although Saint-Lambert's luxury philosophy cannot present a general answer to the difficulties created by the possible lack of a civic spirit, he attempts to sketch out the conditions for a response in "Luxury." First, the question of citizenship can perhaps start to be answered more productively with a political economy of desire than with luxury philosophy, since the political economy of desire is not far removed from citizenship—it is an attempt to spell out what drives the human systems of government and nationhood, wealth, and industry in all their messy details. A political economy of desire—Saint-Lambert's language follows that of desire by employing "civic spirit" as a generic term for stimulating luxury without harmful effects—can produce what he calls a "desire for wealth and its enjoyment" (1965: 215) that does not entail the sacrificing of the well-being of one citizen to the well-being of another. By this he means a vision of civic spirit and of the political economy of desire that is derived from people's moral experience rather than deductively from abstract principles associated with, for example, Plato (2007) philosophical idea of the good and of the state as perfect, eternal, and changeless forms existing outside space and time. Second, Saint-Lambert argues that through this methodology people can inductively identify some signs of the civic spirit in the everyday world of government and the functioning of society. Saint-Lambert's argument points to a realm of moral experience and luxurious values that stand beyond or outside the everyday workings of good government. Take his argument from distinctions of birth. Some events concerning the rich and influential in history are thought to go beyond the realm of ordinary human moral experience. Events like the growing uneven distribution of wealth and the lavish display of abundance appear to challenge the adequacy of people's routine sense of fairness and proportionality. Such events entail far more than people seeking out the pleasures of social life, for the growing uneven distribution of wealth is an outrage to people's moral sense and experience; it is also a violation of the social order that leads to a rising awareness of the distinctions of birth disappearing (Saint-Lambert 1965: 219). This sense of people's outrage at the loss of good social tone and moral puzzlement at the loss of manners is also indicative of the limitations of Saint-Lambert's conception of the civic spirit. To argue that the lavish display of abundance by the rich was a social product of eighteenth-century France may be socially correct, but it is hardly appropriate or convincing to argue for maintaining the distinct characteristics of the different estates. Because ordinary people have no discernable means of resistance appropriate to wealthy people intent on lavish display, they experience a moral need for a higher order of values founded upon social justice and balance. People feel compelled to describe the decline of the spirit of each estate within a paradigm that allows for the existence of and care for the marks of people's stations. Saint-Lambert treats these situations as indications of the possibility of the loss of the civic spirit in an everyday world wherein people no longer feel any loyalty to the social order. In "Luxury,"

Saint-Lambert argues that the luxury of appearances depends for its effects upon a sense of obligation; the luxury of appearances as a result can make people question their station, indeed take them out of their desire to fulfill the obligations of their own station (1965: 219). The luxury of appearances is thus bound up with the moral experience of the civic spirit in everyday life, and the civic spirit is, in part, the moral experience of reminding oneself and others of the obligations of each social station. However, these moral experiences also provide a window on a world that is beyond obligation and social stations or outside the civic spirit, an overview of a larger whole perhaps devoid of marks of social distinction. In a world where care for the marks of people's social stations is seemingly all-important, there is still always the possibility of the "common people" rejecting such reasoning (Saint-Lambert 1965: 219).

Such an alternative to the maintenance of the civic spirit is obviously unappealing to Saint-Lambert. Nevertheless, he writes about the need to avoid a world that is beyond obligation and social stations and about the possibilities of the loss of the civic spirit with conviction and eighteenth-century charm. The argument for the importance of values that stimulate luxury without harmful effects to give meaning to the problems of early modernity is certainly compelling. One difficulty with this argument is that in early modern society the luxury of appearances often appeared to stand between people as an audience and the possibility of moral experiences of the reality of social class. In a literal sense, the luxury of appearances was and is a sociocultural institution that processes and coordinates sociocultural messages of pleasure and excess from people's environment. It is perhaps only in retrospect that the growing uneven distribution of wealth and the luxury of appearances have assumed a definite quality of burden for each estate because their significance has been shaped by over two centuries of research and debate (see, e.g., Jennings 2007). The perceived dangers of such a burden to social morality in the same period has not yet been researched or debated by contemporary luxury philosophy to such an extent. If we turn to the problem identified by Saint-Lambert (1965: 219) of people no longer wishing to fulfill the obligations of their station and their neglect of their external appearance, we are retrospectively conscious of the fact that the luxury of appearances constructed a set of manners that served to remind people of their obligations. But, as Saint-Lambert's anxieties about the common people and their imputed lack of reasoning indicate (1965: 219), it became clear to him that the nobility, the magistrates, and the ministers of religion must make a continual impression on the senses of the common people and to use their eminent marks of distinction to herald their own sovereignty. "The external appearance" of such people, writes Saint-Lambert, "must indicate power, goodness, seriousness, saintliness, whatever is or should be characteristic of a member of a certain class, of a citizen occupying high position" (1965: 219). Furthermore, had the use of wealth not awarded the magistrate with the train of a young noble? Had the use of wealth not awarded the soldier with the luxuries of life and flamboyant dress? Yet, because the use of wealth sometimes awarded the priest with the appearance of debauchery or intemperance and the ordinary citizen with the entourage of high station, it also became possible for the common people to regard those who were ostensibly chosen by birth to lead them without a sense of awe (Shovlin 2006: 135). In this case, the concern is less to make a political judgment about the proper attributes of each estate and more a concern to use this understanding of the use of wealth as an illustration of how the luxury of appearances constructs and simulates the reality of social class. In the early modern world of Europe, it was difficult to act outside of the general social order or to think politically toward understandings of the use of wealth in the social world because it was heavily mediated by the luxury of appearances. In this sense, the common people lived either in a world of wealth or within sight of a world of wealth, where their worldly responses to wealth and to their duties were constructed for them (Saint-Lambert 1965: 219). The possibility of the common people rejecting such reasoning became more remote and indeterminate as the luxury of appearances obscured immediate and heartfelt responses to the world of wealth by the sociocultural construction of an everyday life founded on comfort rather than considerations of utility.

The problem of the civic spirit in political philosophy is a well-established problem (see, e.g., Kellow and Leddy 2016). Saint-Lambert's is an important argument that has its origins in the issue of governments defending the property of citizens in France in the eighteenth century. The question of government objectives and the maintenance of society to the advantage of the majority meant that, for Saint-Lambert, governments must foster the civic spirit and patriotism in their citizens; a general problem of government that also entailed governments simultaneously keeping alive and even energizing people's love of property and their desire to increase their wealth and to take pleasure in them. This legacy was further compounded by the political economy of desire clashing with the civic spirit when Saint-Lambert insisted that the political economy of desire must be acquiescent to government, which must concern itself with how its citizens wish to obtain riches and to enjoy them; in short, Saint-Lambert argued that governments must have a distinct impact on citizens' means of securing possessions, which themselves must contribute to the wealth of the state, and even how they are enjoyed must be useful to it.

These traditional problems of the civic spirit took a variety of new directions under the impact of early modernity. To the traditional arguments of the political economy of desire and of the civic spirit, early modern political theory recognized the complex processes by which the reality of the political economy of desire was not constructed by the civic spirit but by what Hume called that "quick march of the spirits, which takes a man from himself" (1987: 270). With what Hume names the "spirit of the age" (1987: 271), people were living in a period in which, with the rise of the arts, "the minds of men," being "roused from their lethargy," were turning "themselves on all sides," and carrying "improvements into every art and science." People enjoying "the privilege of rational creatures" are incorporated into the world of culture as subjects of the moral experience of the political economy of desire, and "the pleasures of the mind as well as those of the body" are elaborated and reinvented as a refined component of the arts in early modern society (Hume 1987: 271). The challenge to Saint-Lambert's fear of the common people rejecting his reasoning is to what extent moral experiences of the political economy of desire are possible upon which a desire for wealth and its enjoyment that does not entail the sacrificing of the well-being of one citizen to the well-being of another could be successfully created and preserved. Thus, the early modern challenge to the passions and their rewards associated with luxury may be more profound than traditional forms of the civic spirit. One can argue that Saint-Lambert's notion of the civic spirit was more concerned with the first two stages of the debate—what might be called the civic spirit concerning property and the good of the community, and the political economy of desire regarding the civic spirit—and less engaged with early modern questions about the civic spirit which take account of the mediation of the reality of social class by the culture of the luxury of appearances.

Appraisal of Key Advances in Luxury Philosophy and Controversies

Saint-Lambert's luxury philosophy achieved a remarkable summation, balance, and coherence in direction and offers a considerable range of applications that have as yet to be taken up by other luxury philosophers wholeheartedly as a comprehensive approach to the question of whether luxury is harmful or beneficial (Lough 1971: 351; Hont 2006: 379). First, the basis of his comparative luxury philosophy was his approach to the philosophical, political, and economic aspects of luxury. Whereas the tradition of Hume had been to examine luxury as "a word of uncertain signification" in "a good as well as in a bad sense" (1987: 268), Saint-Lambert examined the constitution and maintenance of everyday understanding of the far from mundane world of luxury and its effects. Saint-Lambert also departed from the Rousseauist tradition because he rejected Rousseau's effort to have people avoid the evil consequences of luxury through an imagined return to a primitive state. Saint-Lambert was not wholly concerned with classical periods or preoccupied with proving that luxury is harmful to society, but more with the role of political economy in constructing and sustaining a meaningful world wherein luxury and morality, society, and politics might coexist in harmony (Hont 2006: 381). Saint-Lambert's notions of luxury and extravagance are not grounded in a critique of self-indulgence or affluence because his principal question is: what passes for "luxury" in society?

Second, Saint-Lambert's interest in the centrality of luxury to people's love and seeking of wealth in human society should be noted. Generally speaking, from the publication in 1752 of Hume's "Of Refinement in the Arts" (1987) to the 1765 publication of Saint-Lambert's "Luxury" (1965), work on the continental philosophy of luxury (as against work on the analytic philosophy of luxury such as Hume's), was marginal to mainstream analytical philosophy, and there was no attempt to provide a general or synthetic contribution to the continental philosophical study of luxury and people's love and seeking of wealth. Saint-Lambert brought luxurious phenomena back to the center of continental philosophical attention by showing how luxury was fundamental to the processes of constructing real and symbolic worlds founded on nonessential expenditures. In the 1750s, Rousseau's and Hume's luxury philosophies paid little attention to the political economy of luxury, which was seen to be relevant but not vital to the problems of early modern society. Rousseau's 1755 "Discourse on Political Economy" (1987b), for instance, scarcely mentions the concept of luxury while Hume's "Of Refinement in the Arts" states emphatically that luxury is "a *philosophical* question, not a *political* one" (1987: 280; original emphases). The principal exception to this neglect of the political economy of luxury is to be found in the earlier practical work of Jean-Baptiste Colbert (1661–83), the French First Minister of State from 1661 until his death under the rule of Louis XIV (see, e.g., Cole 1939). Saint-Lambert saw Colbert as a fellow political economist in, for example, favoring the promotion of factories that produced luxury textiles which were necessary for the support and adornment of the populations of rural areas (1965: 224; Hont 2006: 382). Such factories, argued Saint-Lambert, would respond to people's love and seeking of wealth and further their well-being. Although the roots of luxury philosophy in Colbert and Saint-Lambert were very different, their approach to luxury and to people's love and seeking of wealth represented an adherence to and development of Colbert's essentially mercantilist principle that the wealth and the economy of France should serve the state (Saint-Lambert 1965: 214; Trout 1978). Both Colbert and Saint-Lambert challenged conventional continental philosophical perspectives on the political economy of luxury by suggesting that, contrary to Rousseau for instance, all forms of people loving and seeking wealth have social, moral, and, crucially, virtuous dimensions.

Third, it is possible to suggest therefore that Saint-Lambert brought about a reintegration of continental luxury philosophy and the question of citizenship. From the perspective of the twenty-first century, it is difficult to realize that eighteenth-century continental luxury philosophy was grounded in a debate with, and adaptions from, questions of citizenship (see, e.g., Wells 1995;

Hammersley 2015). Eighteenth-century continental luxury philosophy was critically concerned with the role that governments had in encouraging the desire on the part of their citizens to accumulate wealth. Saint-Lambert's views on luxury and equality, power, nationhood, and happiness were profoundly influenced by the question of the comforts and pleasures of the majority of citizens (1965: 205). Yet, Saint-Lambert's understanding of citizenship would not have developed without his readings of the classics concerning, for instance, Sparta, the prominent city-state in Laconia in ancient Greece, and through which readings he learned that the desire to obtain wealth was not always harmless (1965: 213). Saint-Lambert's analysis of the importance of the civic spirit in everyday life represents an effort to understand the roots of the moral experience of luxury through the combined lenses of philosophy, politics, and economics.

Finally, Saint-Lambert's work is a synthesis of luxury philosophy and the question of citizenship in the sense that he was committed to understanding the relevance of luxury to the human condition and the moral and political dilemmas of early modern society (Hont 2006: 379). Within this synthesis of political and continental philosophical perspectives on luxury, Saint-Lambert's conception of the various influences on the social order played a central role (Shovlin 2006: 135). Within Saint-Lambert's discourse of citizenship, he was concerned with the problem of explaining the relationship between the marks of people's social station and the nature of people's feelings of loyalty to the extant social order. If people no longer wished to fulfill the obligations of their social station, for example, how could the luxury of appearances and the manners that served to remind everyone of such obligations continue to exist? Saint-Lambert transformed this question of citizenship into a powerful luxury philosophy that is concerned with how the eighteenth-century social world of the nobility, the magistrates, the ministers of religion, and the common people could be led or rationalized. For his part, Saint-Lambert envisaged a renewed enlightened monarchy and nobility as the guardians of national pride and the civic spirit: "The nobles," in particular, he wrote, "will inspire men with love of country and all the feelings of virtuous and uncompromising honor" (1965: 226). This was a vision that Saint-Lambert continued to promote for the rest of his life in texts such as his 1797–1800 *l'Analyse Historique de la Société*

(Saint-Lambert 2018; see, also, Bandau 2017: 208). Undoubtedly, it was a vision that, once the French Revolution of 1789 was under way, obliged Saint-Lambert, as a member of the nobility, to withdraw from public life until 1800. His discussion of how the luxury of appearances of the monarchy and the nobility made an impression on the common people's senses of nationalism and the civic spirit was one facet of this larger vision, which was to understand how the eighteenth-century social world of the monarchy and the nobility, of patriotism, of virtue, and of honor was made and how it appeared not as a historical and social construction but as natural and comprehensible in the years prior to the French Revolution.

References

Bandau, A. (2017), "Jean-François de Saint-Lambert and His Moral *conte* 'Ziméo' (1769) in the Context of Abolitionist and Imperial Activities," in D. Tricoire (ed.), *Enlightened Colonialism: Civilization Narratives and Imperial Politics in the Age of Reason*, 205–26, Cham: Palgrave Macmillan.

Cole, C. W. (1939), *Colbert and a Century of French Mercantilism*, New York: Columbia University Press.

d'Alembert, J.-B. (1995), *Preliminary Discourse to the Encyclopedia of Diderot*, trans. R. N. Schwab, Chicago: University of Chicago Press.

Erikson, E. (2014), *Between Monopoly and Free Trade: The English East India Company, 1600–1757*, Princeton, NJ: Princeton University Press.

Hammersley, R. (2015), "Concepts of Citizenship in France during the Long Eighteenth Century," *European Review of History*, 22 (3): 468–85.

Hont, I. (2006), "The Early Enlightenment Debate on Commerce and Luxury," in M. Goldie and R. Wokler (eds.), *The Cambridge History of Eighteenth-Century Political Thought*, 379–418, Cambridge: Cambridge University Press.

Hont, I. (2008), "The 'Rich Country–Poor Country' Debate Revisited: The Irish Origins and French Reception of the Hume Paradox," in C. Wennerlind and M. Schabas (eds.), *David Hume's Political Economy*, 243–322, Abingdon: Routledge.

Hoyt, N. S. and T. Cassirer, eds. (1965), *Encyclopedia: Selections—Diderot, d'Alembert and a Society of Men of Letters*, Indianapolis, IN: Bobbs-Merrill.

Hume, D. (1987), "Of Refinement in the Arts," in E. F. Miller (ed.), *Essays: Moral, Political, and Literary*, 268–80, Indianapolis, IN: Liberty Fund.

Jennings, J. (2007), "The Debate about Luxury in Eighteenth- and Nineteenth-Century French Political Thought," *Journal of the History of Ideas*, 68 (1): 79–105.

Kellow, G. C. and N. Leddy, eds. (2016), *On Civic Republicanism: Ancient Lessons for Global Politics*, Toronto: University of Toronto Press.

Kors, A. C. (1976), *D'Holbach's Coterie: An Enlightenment in Paris*, Princeton, NJ: Princeton University Press.

Lough, J. (1971), *The "Encyclopédie,"* New York: David McKay.

Mandeville, B. (1989), *The Fable of the Bees*, ed. P. Harth, London: Penguin.

Morrisson, C. and W. Snyder (2000), "The Income Inequality of France in Historical Perspective," *European Review of Economic History*, 4 (1): 59–83.

Plato (2007), *The Republic*, trans. D. Lee, London: Penguin.

Plutarch (2008), *Greek Lives*, trans. R. Waterfield, Oxford: Oxford University Press.

Rousseau, J.-J. (1968), *Politics and the Arts: Letter to M. d'Alembert on the Theater*, trans. A. Bloom, Ithaca, NY: Cornell University Press.

Rousseau, J.-J. (1973), *The Confessions*, trans. J. M. Cohen, London: Penguin.

Rousseau, J.-J. (1987a), "Discourse on the Sciences and the Arts," in *Basic Political Writings of Jean-Jacques Rousseau*, trans. D. A. Cress, 1–24, Indianapolis, IN: Hackett.

Rousseau, J.-J. (1987b), "Discourse on Political Economy," in *Basic Political Writings of Jean-Jacques Rousseau*, trans. D. A. Cress, 111–40, Indianapolis, IN: Hackett.

Saint-Lambert, J. F. (1765), "Lux," in D. Diderot and J.-B. d'Alembert (eds.), *Encyclopédie, ou, Dictionnaire raisonné des sciences, des arts et des métiers, Volume 9*, 760–71, Neufchastel: Samuel Faulche & Cie.

Saint-Lambert, J. F. (1965), "Luxury," in *Encyclopedia: Selections—Diderot, d'Alembert and a Society of Men of Letters*, trans. N. S. Hoyt and T. Cassirer, 203–32, Indianapolis, IN: Bobbs-Merrill.

Saint-Lambert, J. F. (2014), *Les Saisons*, ed. S. Inoué, Paris: Classiques Garnier.

Saint-Lambert, J. F. (2018), *Œuvres Philosophiques, Vol. 4: Contient la Suite de l'Analyse Historique de la Société*, London: Forgotten Books.

Shovlin, J. (2006), *The Political Economy of Virtue: Luxury, Patriotism, and the Origins of the French Revolution*, Ithaca, NY: Cornell University Press.

Shovlin, J. (2008), "Hume's *Political Discourses* and the French Luxury Debate," in C. Wennerlind and M. Schabas (eds.), *David Hume's Political Economy*, 203–22, Abingdon: Routledge.

Smith, L. V. (2023), *French Colonialism: From the Ancien Régime to the Present*, Cambridge: Cambridge University Press.

Trout, A. (1978), *Jean-Baptiste Colbert*, Boston, MA: Twayne.

Voltaire. (2011), *Le Mondain*, Paris: Atelier du livre.

Wells, C. C. (1995), *Law and Citizenship in Early Modern France*, Baltimore, MD: Johns Hopkins University Press.

Wokler, R. (2012), "The Enlightenment Hostilities of Voltaire and Rousseau," in R. Wokler (ed.), *Rousseau, the Age of Enlightenment, and Their Legacies*, 80–7, Princeton, NJ: Princeton University Press.

4

Karl Marx: Luxury Is the Opposite of the Necessary

Biographical Details and Philosophical Context

Karl Marx was at the center of European political and intellectual life in the nineteenth century. There was enthusiasm for his work among revolutionaries and activists, including philosophers and other fledgling communist intellectuals. Furthermore, it is notable that twentieth-century philosophers, who sought to recreate the modern world of advanced capitalism as socialism and communism, looked to Marx for a philosophical critique of history and the social sciences. His writings offer many points of contact with modern philosophical debates, not least the debates about luxury philosophy.

Born in 1818, in the Rhineland region of Prussia (Germany), Marx graduated in law and philosophy from the universities of Bonn and Berlin, the latter in 1841, subsequently embarking on a career as a radical journalist, before moving on to Paris in 1843 and, later, to Brussels and London. He was, for much of his adult life, an independent scholar and political activist, and, like many of the key European philosophers of his day, was influenced by radical politics. For example, in 1843, Marx wrote "On the Jewish Question" (1994a), in which he defended Jewish emancipation, emphasizing the limitations of "political" as against "human" emancipation; Marx followed this publication with "A Contribution to the Critique of Hegel's Philosophy of Right: Introduction" in 1844, which contains a critical account of religion, together with some prescient remarks about the emancipatory potential of the proletariat (Marx 1994b). He died in London in March 1883.

If Marx's work is to be categorized for the purposes of his inclusion in *Luxury Philosophy*, then "critical philosophy" is the most appropriate slot rather than economics or political theory, history, sociology, journalism, or revolutionary socialism. The *Economic and Philosophical Manuscripts of 1844* (Marx 1961), the *Grundrisse* or "Notebooks" (Marx 1993), and *Capital* Volume I (Marx 1976), which are Marx's most famous and arguably his best works featuring luxury philosophy, are studies in critical philosophy par excellence. However, Marx's work draws upon a wider range of sources than this label might suggest, addressing issues and contributing to debates removed from conventional philosophical paradigms. Moreover, even at his most economically technical, philosophical moments, Marx was always alive to the events in his own historical milieu, and always keen to bring his philosophy to bear upon these events. In particular, Marx, like many European critics, was influenced by the impact of the then emergent capitalist mode of production during the nineteenth century, and the related problem of the remorseless pursuit of profit, which he began to address in his analyses of the extraction of surplus value from the exploited working classes. Along with other intellectuals, Marx actively resisted what he considered the immorality of nineteenth-century capitalism. Marx's reflections on the issue and on the role of moral criticism are notably bolder than those of others. What people learned from moral criticism was historical critique, he argued. That is, they learned of the interconnectedness of their own lives with those of others and how this shapes their ways of making sense of the world of contemporary capitalist society, their opportunities, and the moral constraints they must circumnavigate. They learned that the meaning and morality of their actions are derived not from morality itself but from the place their ideology—their set of beliefs or philosophies—assumes in a constantly shifting and sometimes unpredictable economic and sociopolitical whole. It is this sense of historical critique that Marx attempts to convey in his philosophical works related to luxury.

Philosophical interest in Marx's work on luxury has grown, largely as a consequence of a developing concern with issues of luxury and automation, luxury and fashion, and the role of luxury in the fate of the Paris Commune, the French revolutionary government that seized power in Paris from March 18 to May 28, 1871, issues about which Marx says a great deal. There is unmistakable evidence of a Marx influence within luxury philosophy, specifically in the continental philosophical tradition. Much of the reception of Marx's work on luxury in the English-speaking world is shaped by the contributions of luxury philosophers such as Aaron Bastani. Bastani engages with a number of Marx's texts and offers his own critical exegeses and development of them in his work *Fully Automated Luxury Communism: A Manifesto* (2020).

Luxury Philosophy and Contributions

Economic and Philosophical Manuscripts of 1844

Marx's first major work featuring luxury philosophy, the *Economic and Philosophical Manuscripts of 1844* (hereafter *Manuscripts*; 1961), contains the clearest demonstration of Marx's theory of alienation (the process through which people suffer a loss of control over their interactions with nature and their fellow human beings), and his philosophical humanism (a philosophical stance that emphasizes the individual and social potential and agency of human beings, whom Marx considered the starting point for moral and philosophical inquiry). However, the *Manuscripts* remained unpublished until 1932, when they met a subdued reaction. Indeed, it was not until the 1960s that the *Manuscripts* became obtainable in numerous languages. The *Manuscripts* contains a preface and three manuscripts. They are important because they present Marx's primary disagreement with the governing convention in political economy, defined by Marx in *Capital* Volume I as covering the work of those political economists since the time of William Petty (1623–87) the English political economist, physician, scientist, and philosopher, who "investigated the real internal framework … of bourgeois relations of production" (Marx 1976: 174–5). Nevertheless, Marx concentrates mainly on the writings of Adam Smith (*c.* 1723–90), the Scottish philosopher and founding father of political economy, of which Smith's 1776 *The Wealth of*

Nations (2003) is the pivotal text, but also David Ricardo (1772–1823), author in 1817 of *On the Principles of Political Economy, and Taxation* (2015) and, along with Smith, seen by Marx as one of the great representatives of political economy. Marx also uses socialist sources to summarize the terrible conditions borne by the working class.

The first manuscript discusses the wages of labor and the position of capital, its push for profit, its rule over labor, the rent of land, and the growth of modern landed property. The last section of the first manuscript contains an explanation of Marx's concept of alienation in the labor process. He portrays four features of alienation, starting with the fact that the product of labor is antagonistic toward the producer as something alien, as something owned and controlled by employers. The worker is moreover alienated from the process of production, for work is forced labor over which the worker has no control, leading to the worker's loss of self. The third component is alienation from human essence or species-being. For Marx, what makes people's human essence can only be discerned through their species-being or their creative social activity and its ensemble of relations. Production is an important characteristic of what it is to be human, but when the production process is alienated, people are alienated from their essence. Consequently, a fourth kind of alienation happens: the alienation of people from each other and from nature. Marx concludes that as private property is based on alienated labor, the emancipation of society from private property is conceivable only through the emancipation of workers.

The second, short manuscript deliberates on social relationships in private property and protests that workers are turned into commodities and into psychologically and physically desensitized beings.

The third manuscript debates the relationship between private property and labor, with Marx depicting for the first time the relationship between capital and labor as a "contradiction," as "a dynamic relationship moving inexorably to its resolution" (1961: 98). Regarding property and the advent of future communism, Marx examines the historical expansion of communism from the rudimentary communism of sixteenth-century movements to modern communism that struggles to succeed private property and unshackle human sensibility. He also emphasizes the need for equality of respect between men and women. The *Manuscripts* continues with analyses of need, production, and the division of labor. Marx remarks that while the division of labor and exchange are considered by political economists as designating the social character of economics, actually they disclose a contradiction—the control of society by unsocial, specific interests. He also comments on the destructive power and misleading effects that money can have on human relationships.

The concluding part of the third manuscript is Marx's critique of the work of Georg Wilhelm Friedrich Hegel (1770–1831), the German philosopher who had a profound influence on Marx. Marx's critique concentrates on Hegel's 1807 *The Phenomenology of Spirit* (2019), an exposition of how knowledge is produced, but he also references Hegel's 1812–16 *The Science of Logic* (2015), the work wherein Hegel outlined his vision of reasoned judgment. The third manuscript is partly an appreciation of the writings of Ludwig Andreas von Feuerbach (1804–72), the German anthropologist, philosopher, and author in 1841 of *The Essence of Christianity* (2008) and, for Marx, the conqueror of Hegel's idealism, which is the view that reality is equivalent to mind, spirit, or consciousness. Marx then critiques Hegel for performing a double error. The first is dealing only with thought categories, so that alienation simply becomes a problem within thought to be determined only within consciousness. The second is envisaging the categories of the objective world as spiritual entities, thus staying within the sphere of abstract thought, so that the recognition of alienated relationships is itself alienated from sensuous reality. Marx contends that the humanism developed from Feuerbach's philosophy surmounts the drawbacks of Hegel's idealism without falling into a basic materialism that is preoccupied by materiality, material processes, and how these contribute to forming society. Notwithstanding these objections, Marx commends Hegel for understanding that there is a method of discovering the truth of ideas by discussion and logical argument and by considering ideas that are opposed to each other. This is a method that Hegel and Marx conceive of as the dialectic of negativity, as the moving and producing principle; a principle for envisaging the self-creation of people as a process and for identifying alienation and its supersession. Finally, Marx recognizes that Hegel understands labor as the self-confirming essence of human life, and also acknowledges that the "objective" being can be appropriated only through the supersession of its alienation.

For the above reasons, the *Manuscripts* is partially informed by and in debate with the work of political economists such as Ricardo, who would remain a central reference point and intellectual adversary in many of Marx's economic writings. For the Marx of the third manuscript, the analyses of political economists consider mere human existence as the overall criterion since it is appropriate to the masses. Political economists alter workers into insensate beings lacking all needs, while they alter their own activity into a pure abstraction from all activity. To such political economists, consequently, argues Marx, "every *luxury* of the worker seems to be reprehensible, and everything that goes beyond the most abstract need—be it in the realm of passive enjoyment, or a manifestation of activity—seems ... a luxury" (1961: 118; original emphasis). Ricardo, for example, "recommends thrift and execrates luxury;" he "recommends thrift to produce *wealth* (i.e., luxury)" (Marx 1961: 119; original emphasis). Yet, according to Marx, Ricardo's political economy is "hypocritical in not admitting that it is precisely whim and caprice which determine production" (1961: 120). Ricardo overlooks, writes Marx, the "refined needs; that there would be no production without consumption; ... that as a result of competition production can only become more extensive and luxurious"; and "that it is use that determines a thing's value, and that fashion determines use" (1961: 120). "Ricardo," argues Marx, "wishes to see only 'useful things' produced but ... forgets that production of too many useful things produces too large a *useless* population" (1961: 120; original emphasis). And, finally, Ricardo, says Marx, forgets that "extravagance and thrift, luxury and privation, wealth and poverty are equal" (1961: 120).

"Needlessness as the principle of political economy" is, for Marx, "*most brilliantly* shown in its *theory of population*. There are *too many* people. Even the existence of men is a pure luxury; and if the worker is '*ethical*,' he will be *sparing* in procreation ... The production of people appears in the form of public misery" (1961: 121; original emphases). "Industry speculates on the refinement of needs," suggests Marx but it "speculates just as much on their ... artificially produced crudeness, whose true enjoyment, therefore, is *self-stupefaction*—this *seeming* satisfaction of need—this civilization contained *within* the crude barbarism of need; the English gin-shops are therefore the *symbolical embodiments* of private property. Their *luxury* reveals the true relation of industrial luxury and wealth to man" (1961: 122; original emphases). The influence of political economists such as Ricardo on Marx, if only as an intellectual opponent, is evident. And, though problematic in many respects, in Marx's view, Ricardo's political and economic theories and findings, not least his commitment to a "bourgeois" or pro-capitalist position, have important implications for luxury philosophy. The key achievement of the *Manuscripts* for Marx's luxury philosophy is, first, Marx's positing of a critique of political economy's disdain for workers who choose luxury over thrift; second, Marx's critical analysis of political economy's mechanistic and theoretically reductionist account of population wherein even the existence of people is characterized as a luxury; and, finally, Marx's development of a conception of real and artificial needs, with the latter exemplified by workers drinking gin to achieve the "luxury" of self-stupefaction that was a key feature of British nineteenth-century industrial society.

Grundrisse

Next, in 1857–8, came the *Grundrisse* (1993). Written by Marx for reasons of self-illumination, the manuscript, which had been misplaced, was finally published in German in 1938 and 1939 and as a user-friendly edition in 1953. The *Grundrisse* is a prototype for *Capital* and contains seven notebooks in draft that have been arranged into four sections, including the introduction, chapters on money and capital, and a closing section devoted to French political economists such as Claude-Frédéric Bastiat (1801–50), the writer and prominent member of the French Liberal School. The *Grundrisse* offers an abundance of material that extends over 800 pages investigating the theories of, for example, Pierre-Joseph Proudhon (1809–65), the French political philosopher, economist, and critic of private property (see, e.g., Proudhon 1994).

The introduction to the *Grundrisse* is significant because it is there that Marx discusses his dialectical method, which applies to the study of historical materialism, Marx's theory of historical change, the rise of class societies, and the way people labor together to make their livelihoods. Marx's dialectical method claims to reflect the real world created by people and is thus a method by which they can examine social and economic behaviors. Still exhibiting the influence of Hegel, Marx also compares his own superior dialectical method with the mediocre method of political economy and considers this through different moments of production, distribution, exchange, and consumption. Marx also delineates his interpretation of what he thinks comprises an individual.

The chapter on money contemplates economic crises, value, price, and different analyses of money in its diverse forms. The chapter on capital has sections that reflect on the production process of capital, the concepts of surplus value and profit, the circulation process of capital, the way surplus value turns into surplus capital, the earliest accumulation of capital, theories of surplus value, and the transformation of surplus value into profit. In another section, Marx appraises the concept of alienation, and so confirms a connection with the humanism articulated by him in the *Manuscripts* of 1844. The *Grundrisse*'s significance also arises from its considerations of the world market and the state, the international division of labor and machines, wherein Marx thinks through how automation can be employed to release people from work. Lastly, the manuscript is vital for showing how Marx engages in his own work process, in contemplating and appraising his own concepts, and presenting an evaluation of those self-same concepts and the claims of others.

The *Grundrisse* is more obviously economic than the *Manuscripts* of 1844 and picks up on a central theme of luxury philosophy, gold, and silver (Marx 1993: 169, 216, 230–1). In the *Grundrisse*, Marx argues that people need to examine the consumption of gold and silver, the consumption of which develops only in inverse proportion to their costs of production. This is what Marx does, establishing in particular that the consumption of gold and silver develops "in proportion with the growth of general wealth, since their use specifically represents wealth, excess, luxury, because they themselves *represent* wealth in general" (1993: 169; original emphasis). Political economy encourages people to think of gold and silver as money, Marx argues, but people discover a different aspect to them if they understand that gold and silver are consumed more in proportion as wealth rises. Gold and silver are not given to people simply as money. Indeed, when the supply of gold and silver abruptly enlarges, even if their costs of production or their value does not proportionally decrease, they find an increasing market which retards their devaluation. However, as a particular commodity, money can be transformed out of its form as money into that of luxury objects, gold and silver jewelry, or, for example, transformed from silver money into silver plate and vice versa or, alternatively, as money, gold and silver "can be *accumulated* to form a *treasure*" (Marx 1993: 216; original emphases). For instance, since ancient times, gold and silver have always given people a way of recognizing religious and regal privileged beings in the world and they thereby "give" people a world of gods, kings, queens, and, for example, Egyptian pharaohs such as Tutankhamun. Reinterpreting the traditional conception of wealth as the abundance of valuable financial assets or physical possessions which can be converted into a form that can be used for transactions, Marx then considers the multiple ways in which the world of wealth appears for people by way of their accumulation and their activities designed to display their capacity for overabundance. Moreover, Marx argues that this same world of wealth, as a strange yet special thing, underlies the use of gold and silver to supply gifts for temples and their gods and makes possible not only the financing of public works of art but also a sense of security in situations of severe necessity.

Later in the distant past, Marx suggests, the work of accumulation becomes political as the rise of the state treasury and the banking system challenges the role of the temple. Simultaneously, private individuals begin to accumulate gold and silver for several reasons, including for conveying wealth into safety from the whims of the outside world in a palpable form wherein it can be buried, for secrecy, and for protection in circumstances of economic and sociocultural terror or military conflict. But, says Marx, a considerable part of gold and silver are removed from circulation as decorative and flamboyant objects of luxury in developed societies. As representatives of wealth, it is exactly gold and silver's retention without abandoning them to circulation and using them for specific needs, which is evidence of the wealth of individuals. In this way, suggests Marx, monetary wealth becomes the gauge of the worth of individuals, who are themselves driven to display gold and silver as representatives of their own private wealth. Thus, the display of gold and silver, whether in antiquity or in modernity, has less to do with gold and silver as money and more to do with what Marx calls their "*glitter*." It is, Marx argues, "a premeditated point," with the point being that gold and silver are "*not* used as money; here the form antithetical to circulation is what is important" (1993: 231; original emphases).

Even as he contemplates the glitter of gold and silver, however, Marx adds a biting commentary on the project of political economy, by critiquing its efforts to show that picking the lice out of a person's hair is somehow productive labor, particularly in his discussion of luxury production and consumption (1993: 273). Marx warns against the efforts of political economists, arguing that they reduce economic activities to their producers, such as the workers in luxury shops (1993: 273). This is crucial because such reductionism displaces questions concerning the people who consume such luxury goods and services and, at the same time, undermines political economy's own precise criticism of such people; people who Marx, later in the *Grundrisse*, calls a "*surplus population*" of "idlers" which does not work but whose task is to consume refined luxury products (1993: 608; original emphases). In contrast, for Marx, the practices of workers in luxury shops raise political and economic questions whose answers must be resolved without recourse to the claims of political economy if reductivism is to be avoided. In addition, Marx asserts that political economy cannot find solutions to these political and economic questions concerning productive and unproductive luxury workers as they reduce such workers to the status of slaves working to enlarge the capital of their master. Marx takes a different view. He believed that modern luxury production and its producers, which for Marx meant working-class production and producers, are indeed productive "as far as they increase the capital of their master" and, from a critical philosophical perspective, "unproductive as to the material result of their labor" (1993: 273). This paved the way, in Marx's view, for what may be termed a coalition of disinterest between "productive" luxury workers and capitalists. As Marx indelicately put it: "In fact, of course, this 'productive' worker cares as much about the crappy shit he has to make as does the capitalist himself who employs him, and who also couldn't give a damn for the junk" (1993: 273). Moreover, Marx argued that people could not ignore the findings of his own critical philosophy, as more abstract and intellectualist philosophies of political economy tended to do. The "true definition of a productive worker," wrote Marx, "consists in this: A person who needs and demands exactly as much as, and no more than, is required to enable him to gain the greatest possible benefit for his capitalist" (1993: 273).

Substantively, Marx's investigation of gold and silver, luxury production, and luxury consumption stresses two key points. First, he seeks to emphasize that gold and silver are not just money but representations of wealth in the world. Within the context of modernity, gold and silver are thus necessary proof of the wealth of individuals; indeed, gold and silver are the measure of the worth of individuals. The other side of this assertion is that the ownership of gold and silver by individuals necessarily entails the display of gold and silver to the world; people's ownership of gold and silver involves them in the world of display through spectacle and parade, through swagger and affectation, and they are always already engaged in it, so much so that gold, silver, and the world of display should be deemed elements of a system of visual representation predicated on private wealth. Second, following on from this, Marx's conception of gold, silver, luxury production, and luxury consumption is profoundly critical. Whether discussing productive and unproductive labor, political economy, or workers in luxury shops, he is always concerned with revealing their interrelatedness to questions concerning gold and silver within the world of modern capitalism.

For Marx, the modern world as it is revealed through life with gold and silver is no longer the rural world of agriculture. It is industrial; a practical world of manufacture which people in nineteenth-century England, for example, scarcely had a grasp upon, literally as well as metaphorically, and which they did not, in the first instance, "know" in a conceptual or intellectual manner (Thompson 2013). The realm that they lived in and through was not one that could any longer be described as agrarian, for instance. It was a disorienting yet practical realm centered no more around the natural circumstances of agriculture's own production within itself but, instead, centered around what was felt by many farmers and farm laborers to be unnatural circumstances that subsisted as an independent industry distinct from agriculture; a realm of disconnectedness that people "knew" in the form of the feeling they had for an entire multifaceted collection of newly emergent interconnections and for their capacity to understand how industry not only exists but is also pulled into the realm of the circumstances of agricultural production. Marx identifies this shift as fundamental, suggesting that "what previously appeared as a luxury is now necessary, and that so-called luxury needs appear e.g., as a necessity for the most naturally necessary and down-to-earth industry of all," agriculture (1993: 527–8). This "pulling away of the natural ground from the foundations of every industry," for example, suggests Marx, is the "transfer of its conditions of production outside itself" (1993: 528). Marx also believed that people were beginning to live in an era wherein this "pulling away" was becoming a generalized setting. Thus, Marx's investigations of the lived world of modern industry were not simply descriptions of "the transformation of what was previously superfluous into what is necessary, as a historically created necessity," but equally a critique of "the tendency of capital" as a whole and how the "general foundation of all industries comes to be general exchange itself, the world market, and hence the totality of the activities, intercourse, needs etc. of which it is made up" (1993: 528). From the point of view of Marx's luxury philosophy, this shift to general exchange is clearly indicated by his bold statement that "*Luxury* is the opposite of the *naturally necessary*" (Marx 1993: 528; original emphases) and his intensive exploration of the system of necessary needs, which are those of individuals themselves reduced to natural subjects. For Marx, the "development of industry suspends this natural necessity as well as this former luxury—in bourgeois society," but "does so only in *antithetical form*, in that it itself only posits another specific social standard as necessary, opposite luxury" (1993: 528; original emphases).

Capital Volume I

Marx's *Capital* Volume I of 1867 (1976) also builds upon and takes issue with the historical beginning of the capitalist mode of production, with capitalist individuality, greed, and the urge for luxurious self-enhancement. *Capital* Volume I is, needless to say, Marx's famed examination of the capitalist mode of production, subtitled *A Critique of Political Economy*. It was not translated from German into English until 1887. *Capital* Volume I is also a continuation of Marx's 1859 work, *A Contribution to the Critique of Political Economy* (1971), and but one part of a larger project that comprises *Capital* Volumes I, II, and III (Marx 1976, 1981, 1984).

Capital Volume I is divided into eight parts comprising the following headings: Part 1: Commodities and Money; Part 2: The Transformation of Money into Capital; Part 3: The Production of Absolute Surplus Value; Part 4: The Production of Relative Surplus Value; Part 5: The Production of Absolute and Relative Surplus Value; Part 6; Wages; Part 7: The Process of Accumulation of Capital; Part 8: So-Called Primitive Accumulation.

Part 1 analyzes the commodity because it is the most basic form wherein the wealth of capitalist society appears. Marx highlights that capital is a world of appearances, arguing that it is through his dialectical method that he will enter these appearances to disclose the inner essence of capital and uncover its laws of motion. Studying the commodity permits Marx to demonstrate that it has a use-value and an exchange-value and that capital is the rule of exchange-value over use-value. This allows Marx to advance his investigation from the commodity to money, which functions as the universal form of exchange in a society founded on commodity production and exists as the money-form of value. This process, suggests Marx, is obscured by "commodity fetishism," a fetishism that "attaches itself to the products of labor as soon as they are produced as commodities, and is therefore inseparable from the production of commodities" (1976: 165): in short, the labor producing the commodity becomes hidden from sight and the commodity itself acquires a life of its own, apparently empty of social content.

Such mystification of the real relations of production intensifies when Marx ponders the transformation of money into capital in Part 2 and scrutinizes the sale and purchase of labor power. Marx maintains that in the domain of circulation labor and capital appear to challenge each other on a just and equivalent foundation. However, to determine the real relations that rule the processes of the system involves entering what Marx calls "the hidden abode of production" (1976: 279). Consequently, Marx makes his chief finding of the secret of the source for profit-making and the production of surplus value: that a commodity is in fact labor power, which is a source of value and which produces more value than it has itself.

In Part 3, Marx reflects on surplus value production in its absolute form and establishes how capitalists try to increase it by lengthening the working day. Notably, Marx uses government records on the circumstances in factories to uncover the exploitation that was suffered by workers. Marx also shows the working day to be a site of ongoing class struggle between capital and labor around the question of the extraction of surplus value. In Part 4, Marx studies surplus value in its relative form, where the unpaid surplus labor of workers is extracted through intensifying work to make the workers work harder during a shorter time period, which includes issues of the division of labor and the application of machinery. In Part 5, Marx contemplates these processes through analyses of the relation between variable capital, living labor power, and constant capital, dead labor, or machinery. Part 6 is focused on the role of wages within capitalist production while Part 7 thinks through the process of accumulation, which capitalists must continually participate in if they are to endure the never-ending pressure of competition that they impose on each other in the search for surplus value. Part 8 reflects on the expulsion of the agricultural population from the land or what Marx calls "primitive accumulation" (1976: 873), which he depicts as being gruesome and fierce. This process brought about the shift away from feudal relations of production to the new social relations of capitalist and worker, which characterized the new capitalist mode of production.

Marx's exploration of capitalism in *Capital* Volume I is one of the most innovative ever written. It is permeated with a dialectical understanding of conceptual reality, shows a scholarly knowledge of political economy across various philosophical positions, and understands the historical development of humanity, all reinforced by evidence acquired from the philosophers he was criticizing himself. Employing state sources that he revealed to be censuring the system they were meant to maintain, together with his use of literary and artistic works to improve and exemplify his contentions, *Capital* Volume I is unrivaled and remains a significant challenge to those who would propagate or act in the interests of capitalist ideology today.

Marx's condemnation of the capitalist system and its ideology in *Capital* Volume I additionally considers the capitalist mode of production and questions the work of capitalists, whose historical development blends individualism, greed, and the drive for luxurious self-enhancement in a distinctive way. Capitalists posit a peculiarly radical conception of the predominance of the passions: the instinctive, emotional, primitive drives in people (including, for example, lust, anger, aggression, and jealousy) which people must contain, direct, develop, and reroute to be possessed of wisdom (Meyer 2000). Indeed, capitalists effectively suggest that almost everything people are and do, as people, can be explained in these terms. Marx finds this problematic. It renders the notion of the passions unintelligible beyond the realm of capitalist production, Marx argues (1976: 741).

In the first instance, any meaningful conception of the passions necessitates a notion of instinctive drives, but such instinctive drives presuppose a prior engagement with and belongingness not to capitalism's production of a world of luxurious amusements but to humanity's production of a world of socialized people. To engage the passions, capitalists must always already experience their position within the world as a meaningful site of speculation tied to the credit system, they must have thousands of sources of unexpected enrichment upon which to base their instinctive drives, and they must have taken-for-granted means of extravagance and prosperity at their disposal. None of these sources of speculation and credit can themselves be engaged as instinctive drives, however, at least not in the final instance, precisely because they are merely sources of speculation and credit. They are simply a business necessity. Second, people's instinctive drives are not just rooted in the world of luxury; they take root in other worlds, such as that of labor, worlds where people can also speak meaningfully of the passions. Individual capitalists who indulge in luxury have limited recourse to the passions because luxury enters into their world merely as one of "capital's expenses of representation" (Marx 1976: 741). Capitalists get wealthy at the same speed as they force out labor power from others, thus obliging workers to reject all the enjoyments of life. To be true to the passions would entail capitalists acting without concern for business expenditures, transforming their capital, themselves, and their circumstances in wasteful and profligate ways; ways which are not only contrary to the self-control and nervous calculation required to accumulate capital but also develop within capitalists what Marx calls "a Faustian conflict between the passion for accumulation and the desire for enjoyment" (1976: 741).

Lastly, Marx's notions of productive and unproductive workers, which he renders as one worker producing capital and the other not, are used to add weight to the above arguments, at the same time building in another argument, that the work of productive workers is necessarily a component in the self-valorization process of capital whereas the work of unproductive workers is not (1976: 1045–6). One worker producing capital and the other not, which in its collective form people know as the annual product, also root people in the world of consumption and revenue, a world wherein, according to Marx, a "large part of the annual product which is consumed as revenue … does not re-enter production as its means, consists of tawdry products (use-values) designed to gratify the most impoverished appetites and fancies" (1976: 1045). Furthermore, to the extent that the issue of productive labor is concerned, the character of these luxury objects is irrelevant. This kind of productive labor produces use-values and objectifies itself in artifacts that are intended only for unproductive consumption. Restoring the more traditional senses of workers, production, and capital, and at the same time noting their reality, Marx views such luxury objects critically and philosophically because "they have no *use-value* for the process of reproduction" (1976: 1045; original emphasis). And he relates it to the fact that, somewhere, such luxury objects have to be consumed un-reproductively. Political economy's theoretical disposition to find it impossible to articulate "a single sensible word on the barriers to the production of luxuries" and think "even from the standpoint of capitalism itself" is one clear example of the irrational relationship between workers, production, and luxuries under capitalism, for Marx, for example (1976: 1045). Hence, the irrational relationship between workers, production, and luxuries under capitalism implies a certain unreflective and even simple-minded disposition toward the process of reproduction. For the process of reproduction is the realm of progress and checks on progress, inasmuch as this is already decided by the natural growth of the population. The process by which the natural growth of the population might be stalled by the disproportionate rerouting of productive labor into un-reproductive luxury objects is therefore one wherein the means of subsistence or production will not be reproduced in the needed quantities. "In that event," writes Marx, "it is possible to condemn the manufacture of luxury goods from the standpoint of capitalist production" (1976: 1046). Yet, as Marx notes, "luxury goods are absolutely necessary for a mode of production which creates wealth for the non-producer and which therefore must provide that wealth in forms which permit its acquisition only by those who enjoy" (1976: 1046). Certainly, for Marx, in the "*actual* process of reproduction," and "considering only its *real* moments—there is a vast difference which affects the formation of wealth, between labor which is engaged on articles essential to reproduction and labor concerned purely with luxuries" (1976: 1046; original emphases),

Appraisal of Key Advances in Luxury Philosophy and Controversies

Marx's luxury philosophy attains an extraordinary consistency in direction and a substantial variety of uses as a wide-ranging method for the critique of political economy. First, the basis of Marx's humanistic critique of political economy in the *Manuscripts* is, among other important topics, his approach to the critique of the political economy of luxury. While the convention of Ricardo had been to consider workers, their needs, and their pleasure from the perspective of frugality and the loathing of luxury, Marx considered the composition of wealth and political economy's hypocritical understanding of the impulses of the world of production. Marx not only critiqued but also controversially diverged from the traditions of political economy, because he made clear distinctions between luxury production, luxury consumption, and use-value. He was not primarily concerned with political economy's theoretical principles of population (i.e., that there are too many people in the world), but with its role in constructing workers as unethical if they were unsparing in their procreation and in political economy's apparent support for a miserable and meaningless world of self-stupefaction achieved through drinking gin. Marx's ideas of people and workers are not based on political economy's uncritical notions of ethics and procreation, production, and industry since his main question is: What masquerades as "luxury" in so-called civilized societies predicated on private property?

Second, Marx's concern in the *Grundrisse* about the importance of gold and silver to any luxury philosophy of human society must be mentioned. On the whole, prior to Marx's writings in the *Grundrisse* in 1857–8, the critique of the political economy of gold and silver was negligible to radical political economy, and there had been no real effort to supply an overall or synthetic contribution to the critical political and economic investigation of gold and silver. Proudhon's 1884 *What Is Property?* (1994), for example, only offers brief discussions of the role of gold in society. Marx brought gold and silver back to the core of critical, political, and economic consideration by demonstrating how gold and silver were central to the processes of consumption, production, and, significantly, to the creation of symbolic worlds wherein gold and silver are transformed from tangible objects into intangible representations of wealth. In the 1850s, critical political and economic theories paid little interest to gold and silver beyond their monetary forms, which were seen to be pertinent to the problems of production, consumption, and value in an increasingly marketized society. Commoditization and monetization were seen as inevitable consequences of modern political and economic development. The major exception to this relative disregard of gold and silver is to be discovered in Marx's writings on luxury objects. Marx saw gold and silver jewelry, for instance, and its accumulation to form a treasure, as a form of recognition; a form of recognition that included the veneration of religious and royal privileged beings in the world rather than merely as an idea of wealth as the profusion of precious monetary possessions or physical belongings. For Marx, people's wealth and its accumulation to form a treasure is often converted into activities intended to display people's facility for excess. At the root of the critique of political economy in Marx is a different, not to say controversial, approach to gold and silver that presents an understanding of them not simply as monetary wealth but as extraordinary objects, as offerings to temples and gods, and as the basis for the funding of public works of art. As a critic of political economy, Marx contested established viewpoints on commoditization by proposing that all types of activity designed to display gold and silver have social and historical, economic, and political dimensions.

Third, it is possible to submit then that Marx produced a critical reinterpretation of political economy and gold and silver. From the standpoint of the early twenty-first century, it is difficult to understand that political economy was not founded in a debate with, and adjustments from, for example, the glitter of gold and silver, but with luxury production and consumption. Political economy was decisively involved with the economic activities of producers, such as the workers in luxury shops. Political economy's interpretations of luxury production and consumption, the practices of workers, and their changing standing were deeply influenced not by the glitter of gold and silver but by the idea that luxury and other workers must devote themselves to the expansion of the capital of their masters. Similarly, Marx's comprehension of the agricultural roots of industry and manufacture in nineteenth-century England would not have matured without his contributions to the philosophical appreciation of luxury. Marx's evaluation of luxury signifies an attempt to comprehend the origins of the glitter of gold and silver and the experience of luxury as the opposite of the naturally necessary through the lens of the critique of the political economy of luxury.

Fourth, as detailed above, predominant throughout Marx's *Manuscripts* and the *Grundrisse* in particular, human needs are invoked and comprehended as important social forms. Marx examines social production and concludes that all societies have to satisfy what he names their natural needs for food, clothing, and shelter. However, because capitalism is predicated on private property, workers cannot satisfy their natural needs without selling their labor power. Natural needs are also mediated by the value of labor power, which is determined by the socially necessary labor time needed for workers to reproduce themselves. But the wages that workers obtain can be above or below the level of reproduction, contingent on class struggle. It is at this point that natural needs take on the social form of what Marx, as examined earlier concerning the *Grundrisse*, describes as necessary needs, which are the needs of people when they are reduced to natural subjects (1993: 528). Thus, if the wages obtained by workers are more than the value of labor power, workers' necessary needs increase. This, as considered previously, permits a new form of luxury needs to come into being as a necessity to be satisfied even within agriculture (1993: 527–8). Equally, workers can be compelled back onto necessary needs or, if they cannot sell their labor power, compelled back onto natural needs. Natural needs consequently take the social form of necessary needs, which, in turn, take the form of luxury needs.

For Marx, luxury needs at any one time can, with social development and improved wages, become necessary, while necessary goods can become luxury goods. Likewise, dependent upon social development, necessary needs can become natural needs. New needs are socially formed through advances in the production process, and these emerge on the market in the form of luxury needs. Hence, the collective manifestation of need takes two forms: social and true social need. The former emerges on the market as effective demand, while the latter remains concealed as a possible level of need that people could satisfy if prices, and their own wages and living situations, were different. According to Marx, then, the market and political economy do not acknowledge true social needs. Indeed, in the *Manuscripts*, Marx reminds Ricardo that refined needs emerge not only because of competitive and increasingly extensive production but also because of competitive and increasingly extensive luxurious consumption (1961: 120). As people enter the market as a commodity to satisfy their natural needs, instances of human needs appear either in an alienated form as egoistic needs or as instants of self-valorization. Such activity can present a danger to capitalism when human need takes the form of radical need. As a result, Marx's study of forms of need discloses the internal link between these phenomena and the considerable implications of his theory of needs; a substantial and significant theory that cannot be explored here owing to its scale, scope, and complexity (however, see, e.g., Heller 1974; Chitty 1993; Berry 1989, 1994). Marx refused any favoring of universal or particular ideas of needs, preferring in its place an emphasis on interaction between the universal and the particular. For him, needs can be universal, but only through people interacting with others and the natural world. Yet, universal needs and their satisfaction can only be formed within the context of a specific mode of existence, which itself can take various forms. Therefore, the interaction of universal and particular, of the alienated and the truly human, continually resonates within and against the capitalist system. For people, the potential for subservience to a wretched level of need-satisfaction exists together with the potential for pleasure. New technological developments such as artificial intelligence (AI), gene editing, food and solar power technologies, for instance, writes Bastani (2020), offer increased time off from necessary labor, and the chance for people to become rich and complex in needs and their satisfaction, to construct a society beyond capitalism and scarcity, and to enter a world of freedom, luxury, and pleasure, just as they also offer the chance for humiliating labor and unemployment. For these reasons, Marx's theory of necessary, luxury, and refined needs in the *Manuscripts* and the *Grundrisse* especially, underlines the optimistic instants within the negative expressions of people's contradictory development in their interaction with others and the natural world. Consequently, for Marx, a movement beyond capitalism into a domain where human needs are satisfied can become a genuine possibility.

Lastly, Marx's writings on luxury in *Capital* Volume I are a synthesis of the critique of political economy and the issue of the passions in the sense that he was dedicated to appreciating the importance of the critique of political economy to the human condition under capitalism and the quandaries of people's instinctive drives in modern society. Within this synthesis of emotional and critical perspectives, the concept of luxury as a primitive drive played a principal role. Inside the discourse on the passions, Marx is involved with the question of elucidating the contradiction between the capitalists' passion for accumulation and the longing for pleasure. Similarly, if Marx's distinctions in *Capital* Volume I between productive and unproductive workers producing luxury objects entail the disproportionate redirecting of productive labor into un-reproductive luxury objects, how can political economy not understand that the means of subsistence or production will not be reproduced in the required amounts? Marx transformed this question of production into an authoritative critique of political economy that is concerned with how the social world involving the making of luxury goods can be justified or legitimated, even from the viewpoint of capitalist production. Marx's discussion of luxury goods is one facet of his greater project. Marx's overall aim was to comprehend how a social world established on the capitalist mode of production is made, how it creates wealth for non-producers, and how it appears normal and rational to provide that wealth in forms which allow its acquisition only by those "idlers" who do not labor but whose task it is to consume refined luxury products.

References

Bastani, A. (2020), *Fully Automated Luxury Communism: A Manifesto*, London: Verso.
Berry, C. J. (1989), "Need and Egoism in Marx's Early Writings," in M. Cowling and L. Wilde (eds.), *Approaches to Marx*, 122–34, Milton Keynes: Open University Press.

Berry, C. J. (1994), "The Historicity of Needs," in C. J. Berry, *The Idea of Luxury: A Conceptual and Historical Investigation*, 177–96, Cambridge: Cambridge University Press.

Chitty, A. (1993), "The Early Marx on Needs," *Radical Philosophy*, 64: 23–31.

Feuerbach, L. A. (2008), *The Essence of Christianity*, trans. G. Eliot, Mineola, NY: Dover Publications.

Hegel, G. W. F. (2015), *The Science of Logic*, trans. G. di Giovanni, Cambridge: Cambridge University Press.

Hegel, G. W. F. (2019), *The Phenomenology of Spirit*, trans. T. Pinkard, Cambridge: Cambridge University Press.

Heller, A. (1974), *The Theory of Need in Marx*, London: Allison & Busby.

Marx, K. (1961), *The Economic and Philosophical Manuscripts of 1844*, trans. M. Milligan, Moscow: Progress Publishers.

Marx, K. (1971), *A Contribution to the Critique of Political Economy*, trans. S. W. Ryazanskaya, London: Lawrence and Wishart.

Marx, K. (1976), *Capital Volume I*, trans. B. Fowkes, Harmondsworth: Penguin.

Marx, K. (1981), *Capital Volume III*, trans. D. Fernbach, London: Penguin.

Marx, K. (1984), *Capital Volume II*, trans. D. Fernbach, London: Lawrence and Wishart.

Marx, K. (1993), *Grundrisse*, trans. M. Nicolaus, London: Penguin.

Marx, K. (1994a), "On the Jewish Question," in J. O'Malley (ed., trans.), *Marx: Early Political Writings*, 28–56, Cambridge: Cambridge University Press.

Marx, K. (1994b), "A Contribution to the Critique of Hegel's Philosophy of Right: Introduction," in J. O'Malley (ed., trans.), *Marx: Early Political Writings*, 57–70, Cambridge: Cambridge University Press.

Meyer, M. (2000), *Philosophy and the Passions: Toward a History of Human Nature*, trans. R. F. Barsky, University Park: Pennsylvania State University Press.

Proudhon, P.-J. (1994), *What Is Property?* trans. D. R. Kelley and B. G. Smith, Cambridge: Cambridge University Press.

Ricardo, D. (2015), *On the Principles of Political Economy, and Taxation*, Cambridge: Cambridge University Press.

Smith, A. (2003), *The Wealth of Nations*, London: Penguin.

Thompson, E. P. (2013), *The Making of the English Working Class*, London: Penguin.

5

Emmanuel Levinas: A Philosophy of Voluptuosity

Biographical Details and Philosophical Context

Emmanuel Levinas, one of the most significant philosophers of the twentieth century, lived the life of an urban naturalized French academic, interrupted by his capture by the Nazis and imprisonment in Fallingbostel, a labor camp for officers, at the beginning of 1940. Levinas was born on January 12, 1905, to a middle-class family in the city of Kaunas in Lithuania; his father owned a bookstore. After his experiences as an émigré (to Karkhov, in Ukraine) in 1914 and his family's return to Lithuania in 1920, Levinas devoted himself to philosophy, finishing his studies at the University of Strasbourg (France) in 1928. He was married in 1932, and, as an adopted French citizen, served in the French military as an officer from 1939. After the Second World War, from 1947 onward, Levinas lectured at the Collège philosophique and became director of the École normale israélite orientale in Paris. Levinas taught philosophy at the Université de Poitiers from 1961 to 1967, at the Université de Paris, Nanterre, from 1967 to 1973, and at the Université de Paris IV-Sorbonne from 1973. Levinas's three important books featured in this chapter, *Existence and Existents* (1988), *Time and the Other* (1987), and *Totality and Infinity: An Essay on Exteriority* (1969; hereafter *Totality and Infinity*), appeared between

1947 and 1961 and, along with his many other books, essays, and interviews detailed below, slowly made him famous.

Prior to the rise of Adolf Hitler's National Socialist regime in 1930s Germany, Levinas traveled in 1928–9 to the University of Freiburg to study with Edmund Husserl (1859–1938), the Austrian-German philosopher and mathematician who established the school of phenomenology (e.g., Husserl 2017). He also attended the seminars of Martin Heidegger (1889–1976), the German philosopher known for his contributions to phenomenology, hermeneutics, and existentialism (e.g., Heidegger 1962). Levinas published his 1930 thesis in French (Levinas 1995), but additionally, in 1931, co-translated Husserl's Sorbonne lectures, *Cartesian Meditations: An Introduction to Phenomenology* into French (Husserl 1966). Publishing a philosophical analysis of "Hitlerism" in 1934 (Levinas 1990a), Levinas also published in 1935 an original essay in hermeneutic ontology (the branch of metaphysics that deals with the nature of being), *On Escape* (2003a). After the Second World War, Levinas published *Discovering Existence with Husserl* (1998a). However, in 1957 he delivered the first of many subsequent Talmudic readings at the Colloque des intellectuels juifs de langue française in Paris (see, e.g., Levinas 1990b, 1990c, 1999b). Levinas's numerous other principal publications include *Outside the Subject* (1993) and *Beyond the Verse* (1994a); *In the Time of the Nations* (1994b); *Proper Names* (1996); *Otherwise than Being or beyond Essence* (1998b); *Of God Who Comes to Mind* (1998c); *Entre Nous: On Thinking-of-the-Other* (1998d); *Alterity and Transcendence* (1999a); *God, Death, and Time* (2000); *Is It Righteous to Be? Interviews with Emmanuel Levinas* (2001); *Humanism of the Other* (2003b); and *Unforeseen History* (2004). Levinas died on December 25, 1995, in Paris.

Despite the great volume and range of Levinas's work, it is best understood in this chapter on his luxury philosophy as a response to a single question, the question of what might be called "being luxurious" (for a Heideggerian response to this question see, e.g., Armitage 2020). The question of being luxurious has two dimensions. First, what does it mean for people or any other entity to be? Although this is a classic Heideggerian (1962) philosophical question, Levinas (1988) argues that Heideggerian philosophy has long taken the answer to the question for granted: *Dasein* ("being-there") evades the being that is disclosed in its moods in the face of death. Second, the question of what it means to be luxurious presupposes a prior question: how is it that people understand what it means to be luxurious given their discovery that their own being is a burden? What enables being luxurious to have meaning for people, or be given to them, at all, when they experience being as anguish and despair, nausea, and shame? This problem of people being unable to hide from themselves, or the discovery that their selves are riveted to their being, involves an investigation into people experiencing "voluptuosity" (beings in pursuit of the surpassing of their own being through sensual pleasure)—that is, beings or entities that are distinguished by their ability to comprehend, if not fully understand, being luxurious (Levinas 1969, 1987, 1988).

Levinas's main accounts of voluptuosity are presented in *Existence and Existents* (1988), *Time and the Other* (1987), and *Totality and Infinity* (1969). These three volumes are works on transcendence, being, responsibility, and justice. That is, they describe major phenomena that form part of everyday life (e.g., human embodiment) and extraordinary experiences of existence; these phenomena are subjected to an ever-deepening interpretation regarding their fundamental modes of being luxurious. Levinas's 1947 text, *Existence and Existents* (1988: 35), interprets voluptuosity as a radically temporal and futural entity, whose way of being luxurious involves essential ties to the pursuit of an ever-richer promise. First, people have a desire, or are "hungry"; they find themselves in the position of pursuing an ever-growing hunger. This hunger is made manifest to people in many ways but chiefly through the fact that it constantly pulls away from their own being. People are unable to orient themselves and gain control over their existence in such a situation; instead, they must assume the task of existing on the basis of having no goal. Second, in terms of having no end in view, people understand themselves and their surroundings in this condition as the experience of voluptuousness. Third, thanks to these dimensions of desire, people launch forth into an unlimited, empty, vertiginous future, a "there" or "world" within which entities can become consumed or "temporalized" for people as having various sorts of significance. Voluptuosity is principally being luxurious in the world—that is, people do not remain in the luxurious beyond, but return to themselves and to the world as engaged participants in a realm of "meaning" which no object fills or even stakes out and within which they encounter all sorts of "satisfaction" in a univocal and present world of luxurious beings.

Existence and Existents offers an initial and incomplete account of voluptuosity. As it stands, it consists of an interpretation of voluptuosity as a spatiotemporal form of being luxurious in the world. Levinas had also hoped to show, however, that spatiotemporal pursuit is the horizon for being luxurious—that is, people's spatiotemporal pursuit of an ever-richer promise enables them to understand what it means to be luxurious. This would undercut the Heideggerian assumption that being-there and being luxurious are equivalent to evading the being that is disclosed in its moods in the face of death. The being that is disclosed in its moods in the face of death is only one mode of being, inclusive of being luxurious, which is made available by only one dimension of spatiotemporal pursuit in the present. Other modes of being and being luxurious include an ever-growing hunger, the being experiencing a hunger that pulls away from it or goalless ends and being luxurious in the world (the being luxurious of voluptuousness). Levinas planned to use this and related analyses in a deconstruction of the Heideggerian metaphysics of futural time, to prepare for a new and richer interpretation of being luxurious.

However, Levinas did not so much abandon the project of *Existence and Existents'* account of voluptuosity as perhaps deciding that it was dominated by his ambiguous relation to the Heideggerian tradition (Bernasconi 1988). Levinas's later work, *Time and the Other* (1987: 85–8), from 1947, turns to more social and mystical evocations of what he calls "the feminine Other" in which being luxurious comes to have meaning for people experiencing voluptuosity as the "pathos" of "the fact of being two" (Levinas 1987: 86). In *Time and the Other* Levinas dubs this feminine Other "a mode of being that consists in slipping away from the light" (1987: 87). In this half-light, being luxurious and voluptuosity come into their own within a unique existential site or event. The task of people is to recognize that this existential site and condition of voluptuosity is a way of fleeing before light and understand that "[h]iding is the way of existing of the feminine" Other (Levinas 1987: 87).

Starting with *Time and the Other*, Levinas increasingly emphasizes feminine "alterity" (people's perception in other people of an irreducible otherness), stressing that people must postulate "the Other's alterity as mystery, itself defined by modesty" (1987: 87). In *Time and the Other*, Levinas adopts the word "alterity" to name this event (1987: 87). Parallels between this notion and alienation, as well as Levinas's talk of "eros" (1987: 88), led him to speculate about a "phenomenology of voluptuousness" (1987: 89). Yet, Levinas's relation toward voluptuousness is perhaps better characterized not only as one concerned with "the exceptional role and place of the feminine," with "the absence of any fusion in the erotic," but also with voluptuousness as "the very event of the future, the future purified of all content, the very mystery of the future," which, for him, explains its "exceptional place" (Levinas 1987: 89–90).

Levinas's most extensive thoughts on voluptuosity, in his magnum opus of 1961, *Totality and Infinity* (1969), do not present a systematic doctrine, but circle around several topics of enduring concern. He explores many facets of the life of desire for the Other, or the story of its manifestations and concealments in the form of voluptuosity; he understands being luxurious itself as the unfulfilled (and unfulfillable) feminine Other existentially, in a dynamic of mysterious withdrawal and modest exposure. Levinas names people's contemporary understanding of the phenomenology of eros and shows that this feminine understanding is an "incessant recommencement of virginity," something untouchable (Levinas 1969: 258). His search for an alternative relation to being luxurious leads him to investigate fecundity and the category of the child (1969: 267–9). Levinas also explores subjectivity in eros (1969: 270). Much of this mature work is, therefore, devoted to transcendence, to a theory of knowledge that is concerned with being luxurious beyond the limits of experience and hence essentially unknowable (1969: 274–7), especially that of "the ontological signification of voluptuosity and the irreducible categories it brings into play" (1969: 276).

Luxury Philosophy and Contributions

Five Aspects of Voluptuosity

Levinas's luxury philosophy is not interested in people in general, but only as far as they are voluptuous—that is, only as far as they are open to being luxurious. This accounts for a particular vagueness in *Totality and Infinity*'s interpretation of some aspects of people's existence: he does not intend to produce a complete study of the origin and development of human cultures, political systems, and societies, but only a description of people's existence that is sufficiently rich to make manifest their spatiotemporality as the horizon for their understanding of being luxurious. Nevertheless, at least five aspects of voluptuosity as presented in *Totality and Infinity* have important implications for understanding luxury in culture, politics, and society.

The first aspect is the priority of desire over need. One of Levinas's main goals in *Totality and Infinity* is to show that people are primarily in the world by means of desire, in a broad sense, rather than by means of beliefs and philosophies, concepts, or propositions about need. Levinas shows this, as he does in *Existence and Existents*, by way of an interpretation of the everyday experience wherein people come into contact with voluptuosity as a hunger that pulls away from their being. People's relation to other entities is one that is "situated beyond satisfaction and nonsatisfaction," and their way of being luxurious can be understood as a way of being that "does not coincide with an unsatisfied need"; these words are meant to indicate that people relate to things and to people as the Other predominantly by letting "the idea of Infinity" accomplish it in desire, and only secondarily by forming propositional and other beliefs about need (Levinas 1969: 179; original capitalization of the "I" of Infinity here and hereafter). Philosophical assertions about need thus always depend on people living in the world in a relationship with the Other; the truths of need presuppose a primordial truth, in the sense of the idea of Infinity, that always accompanies people being luxurious in the world. For luxury philosophy, this would imply that interpersonal relations and cultural, political, and social structures should essentially be understood not in terms of people's needs, wants, and demands, or other notions such as satisfaction and nonsatisfaction, but in terms of how people reveal their desire for the Other in and through a form of desire that "no voluptuosity comes to fulfill, nor close, nor put to sleep" (Levinas 1969: 179).

The second aspect concerns the feminine. When Levinas turns to the question of who is engaged in desire in the phenomenological world of eros, he shows that voluptuosity is the feminine; in other words, the feminine is a "*regime* of tenderness" (Levinas 1969: 256; original emphasis). Phenomena such as tenderness, frailty, and vulnerability do not show that voluptuosity is fundamentally an inferior attribute; instead, it "manifests itself at the limit of being and non-being" or a mode of the feminine "where being dissipates into radiance" (Levinas 1969: 256). Levinas shows this initially by demonstrating that the individual voluptuous person is, in fact, "dis-individualizing" and "relieving itself of its own weight of being"; their everyday experience intrinsically involves references to other voluptuous people who are fellow producers and consumers of that hunger which pulls away from being in the form of a "flight into self in the very midst of its manifestation" (1969: 256). Thus each voluptuous person necessarily interprets themself in relation to the Other, and constantly has a sense of otherness or foreignness—that is, their status in relation to other voluptuous people is one of "extreme fragility" (Levinas 1969: 256). Levinas's analysis of the feminine in *Totality and Infinity* therefore specifically undercuts the "anthropocentrism" and "subjectivism" of Heidegger's philosophy, as inaugurated by Heidegger in *Being and Time* (1962) (Levinas 1969: 11).

The third aspect relates to the femininity of the caress. As deeply sensible beings, people share the caress and contact with the other members of their community of sensibility such as their lovers. Since the caress transcends the sensible rather than remaining within it, the "caress consists in seizing upon nothing," upon "soliciting what ceaselessly escapes its form toward a future never future enough, in soliciting what slips away as though it *were not yet*" (Levinas 1969: 257–8; original emphases). With this expression of the femininity of the caress that is a search for the invisible, which is the very expression of love, Levinas points to people's inability to speak of love and to satiate themselves through it: the caress not only aims beyond people as existents, as beings driven by desire, but also at "what *is not yet*," which is the feminine (Levinas 1969: 258; original emphases). For Levinas, the caress, a "less than nothing" that anticipates the future in the present is a profanation, a "dimension of absence" (1969: 258) that refers to being luxurious: "In the caress," Levinas writes, "the body ... denudes itself of its very form, offering itself as erotic nudity" while vacating "the status of an existent" (1969: 258).

The fourth aspect concerns the relationship between the ideas of voluptuosity as erotic desire and profanation. Voluptuosity within the context of the femininity of the caress, for example, is at once "impatient" and "surprised by its end, for it goes without going to an end" (Levinas 1969: 260). For Levinas, voluptuosity as profanation is the discovery of "the hidden as hidden"; the voluptuosity of the femininity of the caress is an extraordinary relation, a conjuncture, and a contradiction because, within it, "the discovered does not lose its mystery in the discovery, the hidden is not disclosed" (1969: 260). "The profanation-discovery," writes Levinas, "abides in modesty, be it under the guise of immodesty: the clandestine uncovered does not acquire the status of the disclosed" (1969: 260). Yet discovery is a violation "that does not recover from its own audacity—the shame of the profanation lowers the eyes that should have scrutinized the uncovered" (1969: 260). Voluptuosity as erotic desire and nudity "says" the inexpressible: hiding while exposing, the silence of the inexpressible is that ambiguous confusion between speech and the renunciation of speech, between the meaning of language and the "meaninglessness" of human desire and yearning. When voluptuosity profanes, therefore, it is an "*intentionality without vision*," without light or signification (Levinas 1969: 260; original emphases). The femininity of the caress expresses a refusal to express; it is a disturbing experience driven by the prevarication of the voluptuous. Consequently, while the voluptuosity of the femininity of the caress is characterized by Levinas as "pure experience," he describes profanation as "the revelation of the hidden as hidden" (1969: 260) which establishes a model of being luxurious in the world that is irreducible to intentionality.

The final aspect of voluptuosity is that the bond founded between lovers is contrary to the social relation. Levinas's descriptions of voluptuosity as erotic desire and of voluptuosity's spatiotemporality are reserved for his account of the barring of the third party from the intimacy; it is a double loneliness, a sealed society, which is nonpublic (1969: 265). The feminine or Other is a society deprived of language (wherein the future and "what *is not yet*" is decided) and a community *of "the sentient and the sensed"* (in which the Other is confirmed as sentient) (Levinas 1969: 265; original emphases). The "I" and the Other have an identical objective content or feeling that establishes love and voluptuosity as spontaneous forms of consciousness; the future and what is not yet combines with the "I" and the Other to confirm each Other as sentient. Levinas proposes that voluptuosity as erotic desire is within, intersubjectively organized, wherein the Other is both "I" and detached from

"I." The future and what is not yet is thus settled through the separation of the Other in the middle of this community of confirmation, sentience, and feeling, through a process in which the voluptuous in voluptuosity becomes "freedom untamed" or profanation (Levinas 1969: 265). The future and what is not yet can also serve as a source of nonpossession—for nonpossession of the Other escapes the dialectic of slave and master whose existence can be understood as the extinguishing of voluptuosity. Yet, the impersonality of voluptuosity stops people as lovers from taking their relation as a complementarity because voluptuosity aims not at the Other but at their voluptuosity, what Levinas calls the "voluptuosity of voluptuosity" or "love of the love of the other" (1969: 266). Thus, love pursues the infinite future through "I" voluptuously relishing in the voluptuosity of the Other.

Trans-Substantiation, Fecundity, Transcendence

However, in this supreme conjuncture of identification, in what Levinas calls "*trans-substantiation*" (1969: 266; original emphases), the "I" and the Other in relationship, although not amalgamated in voluptuosity in erotic desire, have the means to beget a child. As Levinas remarks, "the relation with the child—the coveting of the child, both other and myself—takes form in voluptuosity" and is "accomplished in the child" (1969: 266). For Levinas, this is a "new category" since it places people as lovers "before what is behind the gates of being" and, of course, behind the gates of being luxurious, before "the nothingness of the future buried in the secrecy of the less than nothing" (1969: 266). The profanation that disrupts this secrecy discovers the child through the transcendence of trans-substantiation wherein "I" am in the child as an Other. The child is the parents, who rediscover themselves as the sentient "I" and the Other in the child's materiality and gesticulations. Nevertheless, the child is also a stranger who belongs to the parents because the child is them and yet is estranged from them. The child is the parents' being, their labor, reinstated to existence as an Other human being. All the same, the meeting with the Other, affirmed as the sentient feminine, is needed in order that the future of the child, "coveted in voluptuosity," occurs (Levinas 1969: 267). Similar to Levinas's then new idea of infinity, the relation with the future of the child Levinas calls "fecundity" (1969: 267–8) because it signifies the future of the child and the future of the parents. For the parents, the future of the child is the future of an Other which entails, for them, a new journey that is discontinuous from their past and from their voluptuosity, which endures as pure desire in pursuit of its own transcendence.

Levinas's analyses of fecundity are followed by his discussions of subjectivity in eros (1969: 270–3). This essay is in part an exploration of voluptuosity as the imbrication of the lover and the beloved, particularly through a revaluation of their dichotomy as at once unification and separation. However, for Levinas, to develop an analysis beyond fecundity is to analyze voluptuosity as the transfiguration of the subject who hereafter "owes their identity to the passivity of the love received" (1969: 270). According to Levinas's interpretation, to understand voluptuosity is to understand the subject as "passion and trouble," as "constant *initiation* into a mystery rather than *initiative*" (1969: 270; original emphases). The subject in voluptuosity thus discovers itself once more as the self of an Other. The subject's affiliation with the sensuousness and sensitivities of the Other is one wherein the self is continually in ascendance: the subject's passion and trouble, as Levinas puts it, is their "being moved," their "effemination," which the "heroic and virile I will remember as one of those things that stand apart from 'serious things'" (1969: 270).

"Transcendence and Fecundity" (Levinas 1969: 274–7) is Levinas's final discussion of voluptuosity in *Totality and Infinity*; his mature thought continues his thorough-going critique of various phenomena such as "the philosophy of the biological" (1969: 276). The philosophy of the biological, in the Levinasian sense, is a way of thinking that fails to ask questions beyond those concerned with the human body as a mechanism. The philosophy of the biological represents the human body in terms of "finalism" and gives the "dialectic of the whole and the part" a central position; however, the philosophy of the biological either takes "the vital impulse" of human beings for granted or does not grasp that it is something that "propagates itself across the separation of individuals" (Levinas 1969: 276). Thus, the philosophy of the biological does not recognize that the trajectory of the vital impulse is discontinuous; at the same time, the philosophy of the biological not only misses the fact that this trajectory already presupposes intervals of sexuality but also fails to understand that the vital impulse contains within it a specific form of dualism in its articulation. On the psychoanalytical level, Levinas's critique of the philosophy of the biological translates into a rejection of the Austrian neurologist and founder of psychoanalysis Sigmund Freud's (1856–1939) approach to human sexuality. This is because, for Levinas, Freud's (2002) understanding of human sexuality "reduces it to the level of the search for pleasure" at the expense of ontology (Levinas 1969: 276).

What Levinas calls "the ontological signification of voluptuosity" refers to the irreducible classes of voluptuosity employed without ever being even thought of by the philosophy of the biological (1969: 276). By the ontological signification of voluptuosity Levinas means not just people giving themselves pleasure, but a way of reasoning with and conceiving of being luxurious on the basis of it. The ontological signification of voluptuosity is an experience that remains unknown by the philosophy of the biological when, in fact, it is a key source of the erotic that can be examined as fecundity and also "breaks up reality into relations irreducible to the relations of genus and species, part and whole, action and passion, truth and error" (Levinas 1969: 276). What the philosophy of the biological overlooks is that the ontological signification of voluptuosity indicates that, in their sexuality, people enter into relations with the Other; when approached in this way, being luxurious is the entering into relations "with an alterity of a type unforeseeable in formal logic" (Levinas 1969: 276).

Levinas sees the ontological signification of voluptuosity at work in the relation of the I and the Other that is never transformed into "mine" as well as in "the pathos of voluptuosity which is made of duality" (1969: 276). For instance, in one of Levinas's references to voluptuosity, he declares that it is neither "knowledge nor power" (1969: 276). In other words, the phenomenon of voluptuosity is the manifestation of the "I's" relationship with an Other human being, or the feminine, which is repeatedly retreating into its own mystery. For Levinas, this relationship with the unknown offers insight into the roots of people's relations with each other; it is a complex view that tries to account for the distinctive absence or absent presence that is voluptuosity.

The most original aspect of Levinas's account of the ontological signification of voluptuosity is his understanding of it in regard to the relationship established between lovers and being luxurious. The ontological signification of voluptuosity is not simply its lack of knowledge and power or an interpretation of love without initiative; it is the Other affirmed as sentient. The ontological signification of voluptuosity relates to being luxurious in such a way that its meaning lies less in people's sexuality than in the fact of their plurality of being, of their existence as such. People must learn to experience this meaning of being luxurious as an "I" and realize that their subjectivity stems from a mysterious erotic relation that cannot itself be understood outside the terms of the ontological signification of voluptuosity.

For these reasons, Levinas offers no plan of action to combat the philosophy of the biological through the ontological signification of voluptuosity. He limits himself to suggesting that people may be able to make small gains in their practical understanding of fecundity; perhaps they can appreciate the ontological signification of voluptuosity without succumbing to an understanding of the world predicated on power (Levinas 1969: 277). Such gains may hold open the possibility of a future ontological category of paternity that would return the I to the self through the child without notions of property ownership, control, and domination. To suppose that people *have* their child is merely to continue along the path that does not recognize the ontological signification of voluptuosity—thus there is much people can do by accepting that they *are* their child, who, while being a stranger to them and therefore Other, is also an Other that people can affirm as sentient. To end this section, only the acknowledgment that the child "*is* me," is "a relation of the I with a self which yet is not me," can people transcend the I and the philosophy of the biological (Levinas 1969: 277; original emphasis).

Appraisal of Key Advances in Luxury Philosophy and Controversies

Levinas's Influence

Levinas's influence on contemporary luxury philosophy is multiform. His writings on voluptuosity have become important points of reference for continental philosophers and feminist theorists in the United States, Australia,

France, and the UK; they have also affected disciplines such as luxury theory. Here it is possible to do no more than sketch some of the most significant appropriations of Levinas's thought concerning voluptuosity, particularly as they relate to luxury philosophy.

Totality and Infinity, along with *Existence and Existents*, had an impact on continental philosophers from the 1960s onward—notably on their English translator, the American philosopher Alphonso Lingis, who drew on Levinas's vocabulary of voluptuosity in his phenomenology of libido within various French existential theories (Lingis 1986a). Like other continental thinkers such as Levinas, Lingis attempts to understand the dynamics of human erotic care in terms of human voluptuosity and sensuality, and stresses that human beings cannot be understood as if they lacked tenderness. However, Lingis differs from other continental philosophers of the sensual in that he emphasizes the notion of libidinous human compassion and underlines that human identity is possible only within the context of vulnerability and weakness. For Lingis, Levinas's position does not so much fall prey to the problems of understanding human erotic excitement as perhaps to those of not accentuating enough how the voluptuous impulse is a kind of human freedom "untamed," an "animal freedom in the tumult of caprice and sensuality" (1986a: 65). For these reasons, Lingis highlights a continental philosophy of erotic voluptuousness focused on the quality or condition of difference inherent in the Other's skin and touch wherein "something else is divined—the alterity of the Other in the guise of passivity and susceptibility, ripples of torment and pleasure that die away in the exposed substance" (1986a: 65).

Thus, the 1980s saw the flourishing of Lingis's thought concerning a voluptuous sensuality that craves to connect, to sense as harmony and gratification, the unfamiliar in an Other's gratification. The influence of Levinas's earlier thought concerning voluptuosity is clear in Lingis's emphasis on goalless sensuality over directed sensuality and in his opposition to notions of the voluptuous sensual subject as anticipating an end to its internal, private realm of anguished pleasure (Lingis 1986a: 65). Lingis develops these insights into a philosophy of voluptuosity centered on the practice of abandonment within a craving, whereas Levinas's appreciation of abandonment never explored it as an autonomous sphere of craving, and, in his later years, Levinas tended to withdraw from writing about the world of voluptuosity.

A translator and student of Levinas, Lingis has thus developed Levinas's account of voluptuosity as lawless, electrified, fitful, as moving as a descent into a netherworld of erotic anxieties, bewilderment, uncovering, and defenselessness (1986a: 65–6). This discovery of voluptuous descent makes Levinas a major figure in Lingis's *Libido* and in his many other interpretations of existential theories, including *Excesses: Eros and Culture* (1984), *Phenomenological Explanations* (1986b), and *Deathbound Subjectivity* (1989). Levinas's influence is clear in the work of Lingis on voluptuosity as a form of complicity between two people that has no undertakings and no purposes. For Lingis, erotic voluptuousness is the instance of intimacy, the space of contact with the Other in their helplessness, mortality, and uncertainty. The experiential confirmation of alterity, voluptuous enjoyment is a craving, a pleasure, and a desire as well as a mode of obscurity, astonishment, and futurity. Voluptuous abandon consequently disrupts the time of people's endeavors and purposes, opening upon the endlessly "recommencing time of fecundity—the existential structure at the base of the idea of infinity" (Lingis 1986a: 68). In voluptuous fervor people's sensibilities shift to maintain and contentedly uphold the sensuality and the suffering of the Other whose face is effaced in bodily passion. At the heart of this "ex-perience," writes Lingis, an experience unaware of itself, abandoned to the Other, "the discontinuity of fecundity" (1986a: 69–70) wherein people's being comes to be with an Other identity, is fulfilled, as in the loving and voluptuous care of the parents for the child wherein the infantile identity of the child first ascends.

Levinas's luxury philosophy concerning voluptuosity has also appealed to feminist continental philosophers. In "Feminism and the Other," for example, the American continental philosopher Tina Chanter proposes that Levinas's interpretation of being luxurious in the world could help people to understand that "the relation of love is the movement of eros, a movement which takes place both as voluptuosity and as fecundity" (Chanter 1988: 43). After Levinas's own adventures in voluptuosity and fecundity, his thought is appealing to feminist continental philosophers because it is in the *difference* between these two terms, voluptuosity, and fecundity, that the prevarication of the feminine is created. Levinas's luxury philosophy of voluptuosity has therefore continued to attract feminist continental philosophers because (at least in *Totality and Infinity*, he stresses the importance of the feminine in voluptuosity and in fecundity in the world, and because his thought about the feminine with eros describes the asocial relation between lovers. For these reasons, and because of his influence on feminist continental philosophers such as Chanter, Levinas may be understood as an important source of the luxury philosophy of voluptuosity and fecundity and of their manifestation within the relation of love. As a narrative that reveals the unique characteristic of voluptuosity, Levinas's history of being luxurious can also function as a powerful tool for understanding voluptuosity as a return to self; in this respect, Levinas's thought about voluptuosity functions to highlight the relation of the One with an Other. The Levinasian notion of "voluptuosity of voluptuosity" (1969: 266) can then serve the purposes of a radical interpretation of love of the love of the Other in the name of a love that is preoccupied with loving the love the beloved bears the self, with a love that is additionally engrossed in a love of the self in love and thus with a return to the self.

Chanter's continental philosophy in "Feminism and the Other" (1988) and elsewhere, such as her edited collection *Feminist Interpretations of Emmanuel Levinas* (2001), and her monograph *Time, Death, and the Feminine: Levinas with Heidegger* (2002) is one of the most original of the radical appropriations of Levinas on voluptuosity that began in the United States in the 1980s. For Chanter, Levinas's main importance lies in his characterization of the voluptuousness of love as an entity that does not go beyond the Other, but specifically reflects the I itself. Chanter argues that this characterization implies that voluptuosity is "the relation that exists between lovers; and fecundity is the other side of this relation" (1988: 44). For Chanter, "Levinas is pointing to a fundamental ambiguity; the relation between lovers is characterized by femininity. It goes toward infinity while at the same time it is marked by a return to self" (1988: 44). The nature of voluptuosity is continuously a return to self; the lover loves the beloved but also itself in love. Chanter applies this characterization to fecundity; by understanding that fecundity signifies "a *transcendence of the self*," people can begin to appreciate that which goes beyond the transcendence of language (1988: 45; original emphases). Thus, in the complacency of voluptuosity, "the femininity of lovers returns to the self and it transcends every return to self, transcendent ... in fecundity ... [and] in the inadequacy of the lover's caress, which would reach for, without ever being able to hold onto, the otherness of the Other" (Chanter 1988: 51).

Cathryn Vasseleu's (1998) work can also be seen as having similar interests to Chanter, although Vasseleu's concern is as much with vision as it is with touch. Vasseleu's continental philosophy can be seen as a creative combination of Luce Irigaray (1930–), the Belgian-born French feminist, philosopher, psycholinguist, psychoanalyst, and cultural theorist who examines the uses and misuses of language in relation to women, and Maurice Merleau-Ponty (1908–61), the French phenomenological philosopher, influenced by Edmund Husserl and Martin Heidegger, and Levinas. From Levinas, Vasseleu adopts the concept of voluptuosity, which she describes as relating to "a being enthralled by the impossible" (1998: 38). From Levinas's history of being luxurious, Vasseleu embraces the idea that voluptuosity is indissociable from abandonment, or an abandonment of sociability, and that voluptuosity is a passage from physicalness into the invisible in favor of a formless and inexpressible community. Vasseleu also makes use of Levinas's account of human erotic love, a love that happens in the dark, outside of rational sociality, changing intelligibility into passion and darkness. In Vasseleu's analysis, voluptuosity has a specific sense: voluptuosity is a break, or a pause in the time of being, and its inexpressibility is a unity counter to any social relation. Voluptuosity in this sense is an asocial relation that negates all plans, all thematization of the world (Vasseleu 1998: 113). This analysis is inspired by Levinas inasmuch as it highlights the tensions within voluptuosity, which, according to Vasseleu, is a commencement without memory, a commencement which knows no Other.

Levinas's conception of voluptuosity has thus been taken up by Australian continental philosophers such as Vasseleu in search of an understanding of the abandonment of the familiar. For Vasseleu, *Totality and Infinity* teaches that voluptuosity and Levinas's conception of it stem from an abandonment of the familiar that is also a risking of people's existence in their affirmation of an Otherness that will never be apparent to consciousness (1998: 116). For Vasseleu, this implies, among other things, that voluptuosity "is a re-turning to a state of movement," and that people's wavering corporeality should be understood as a kind of swaying "between matter and light" (1998: 116). According to Vasseleu, Levinas progresses beyond the night to a desire for an unchallengeable, incomprehensible, ever-changing light. Vasseleu's appropriation of Levinas is not unlike that of Lingis's and Chanter's, except that she seeks to emphasize the miracle of light. Vasseleu holds that the role of continental philosophers is not to shun the natural and the intelligible but, following Plato (2007), to foster conversation about people's amazement before them, an amazement that is related to the human subject; this translates into a Levinasian philosophy of "love as a desire for the abyss" (Vasseleu 1998: 116).

Points of Controversy

The debates concerning Levinas's luxury philosophy are colored by the controversial topic of his understanding of people in relation to the determination and differentiation of sexual being. There is a wide variety of opinions on whether Levinas's philosophical thought concerning voluptuosity has sexist and political implications (for a range of views, see Chalier 1991; Ainley 1996; Sandford 2004).

For some continental philosophers, Levinas's luxury philosophy is simply the philosophical codification of a reactionary sexist political position. Simone de Beauvoir (1908–86), the French existentialist philosopher, feminist activist, and author of *The Second Sex*, originally published in 1949, in which she provided an early analysis of Levinas's *Time and the Other* as frequently concerned with nothing other than what men decide (de Beauvoir 2011: 29, 42, 43). Men see women as sexed beings. For men, women are sex in the absolute. De Beauvoir's intent is not only to expose Levinas's flawed determination and differentiation of women regarding men, but to dispute his account of the supposed male relation to women; Levinas's analysis of women as the inessential in front of the essential male must be challenged in the sociocultural field at large. For Levinas, de Beauvoir writes, man "is the Subject; he is the Absolute. She is the Other" (2011: 29). Even Levinas's most exalted ideas are a maneuver conducted within an established game of alterity, a set of possible sociocultural stances toward the being of two separate species of the same type. For instance, de Beauvoir reads Levinas's distinction between the masculine and the feminine as a way of obscuring sexual differences.

De Beauvoir's analysis of *Time and the Other* points out, for example, that Levinas's explanation of the differences between the sexes parallels the language of many of his sexist contemporaries, whose own alterity is such that they "forget" that the feminine is also a woman who has consciousness for herself (2011: 43). For de Beauvoir, the elucidation of alterity, the feminine, and voluptuosity in *Time and the Other* is a call for "a man's point of view" that ignores "the reciprocity of the subject and the object" (2011: 43). When Levinas "writes that woman is mystery," de Beauvoir remarks, "he assumes that she is mystery for man. So this apparently objective description is in fact an affirmation of masculine privilege" (2011: 43).

Equally, for Luce Irigaray (1991, 1993), Levinas's luxury philosophy is one that must be questioned in terms of its ethical perspective concerning voluptuosity because it leaves the feminine Other "without her own specific face" (Irigaray 1991: 183–4). "On this point," Irigaray writes in her essay "Questions to Emmanuel Levinas," Levinas's "philosophy falls radically short of ethics" (1991: 183–4). Irigaray presents a feminist examination of Levinas's *Totality and Infinity* wherein the feminine is continuously described by Levinas as the Other of men, an Other which, contrary to Levinas's own stated philosophical viewpoint in *Totality and Infinity*, reduces the feminine to the Other of the same. Irigaray's aim is to uncover Levinas's apparent lack of concern with the possible alterity of woman-for-herself and to contest the idea of woman merely as the Other of the same; in questioning Levinas's philosophical discourse of the caress, Irigaray argues that his luxury philosophy downgrades the body of the Other, of woman, for the objective of men's own becoming, thus transfiguring the body of the Other into the temporality of men. Interrogating Levinas's conception of sexual difference, Irigaray specifies the conditions for the ardent exchange where the woman would be a desiring subject as well. For example, Irigaray's essential condition is that of a maternal genealogy wherein the daughter could position herself in her identity regarding her mother.

Irigaray's interpretation of *Totality and Infinity* notes, for instance, that Levinas's explanation of the maternal ought to have a divine aspect, and that it should not be demoted to the purely sensuous, leaving the divine to the genealogy of the father. For Irigaray, the elucidation of woman in *Totality and Infinity* lacks the divine, which for her is associated with the issue of women's general identity in the symbolic order: women lack a mirror for developing into women. Irigaray's emphasis on the divine is an additional methodology whereby she can conceive of the need for a symbolic redeployment, so that women, like men, might be both body and soul. What Irigaray is pursuing is a world of voluptuosity without exchange, without conditions, and without explanations. It is a world of voluptuosity that is beyond the predictable, the computable, and, especially, the measurable. Voluptuosity, then, as the primary or fundamental and matchless moment of love, as a unique form of wonder, awe, and veneration, and also as a risk without future assurances or defense.

In contrast, in "Questions to Luce Irigaray," Kate Ince (1996), the British feminist philosopher, argues that, despite Levinas's perceived conceptual shortcomings, his luxury philosophy concerning the feminine and voluptuosity has more to add to Irigaray's undertaking of an ethics of sexual difference than Irigaray herself seems to believe. The descriptions of the fervor of voluptuosity provided in *Totality and Infinity* are important, argues Ince, because, notwithstanding their sexist associations, they mark out a passage between the sensible and the transcendental, and also because they are consistent with Irigaray's call for the fusion of the body and the soul. Irigaray's call rightly treats such a passage as one that has not yet been directed into the reproduction of the child. However, for Ince (1996: 140), Levinas's *Totality and Infinity* also implies that such a passage or what might be called the event of oscillating feminine erotic difference, while lacking a feminist gesture, does initiate an alterity into its discourse of voluptuosity and being luxurious. A strong example of this type of argument is provided by Ince, who concludes that the evocation of voluptuosity by Levinas can therefore be interpreted as an indication of the divine and the equally fecund ardent relationships to which Irigaray's work itself points to.

Another controversial reading of Levinas's work on voluptuosity moves away from the preoccupation with the determination and differentiation of sexual being and toward a philosophical understanding of luxury (e.g., Armitage 2022). Such an interpretation neither uses Levinas's commentaries on sexuality to reject his luxury philosophy, nor dismisses his remarks on being as irrelevant; it seeks to find food for independent thought in Levinas's luxury philosophy and in the implications of his work for art history. The suggestion is that, within art history, luxury and voluptuosity are seldom stated in single works of art by name; Levinas's attraction for art historians is shown in two paintings that do reference luxury, the Golden Age Dutch artist Jan Steen's *Beware of Luxury* (1633) and the Symbolist stateless artist Giovanni Segantini's *The Punishment of Luxury* (1891). This view comprehends Steen's and Segantini's ideas of luxury and voluptuosity as explainable through Levinas's phenomenological accounts of art, knowledge, and ontology. An original reading, the argument is that luxury and voluptuosity can be understood not as aesthetic categories but as features of Levinasian desire and happiness, need, the untouchable in human contact, and as the future in the present. For a Levinasian reflection on the broader philosophical implications of why luxury and voluptuosity are not frequently mentioned by artists and writers on art history, what is required is an ongoing stress on their importance for an appreciation of being luxurious within seventeenth-century, nineteenth-century, and contemporary art; this vision presents a challenge to conventional understandings of contemporary American artists' work, such as that of Jeff Koons, as a means to radicalize an element of contemporary art history.

Applying Levinas's luxury philosophy in this way is equally controversial on the level of questioning his analysis of the relationship between luxury and voluptuosity. In this reading, Levinas's preoccupation with the question of being luxurious and voluptuosity, while intellectually inspiring, is also questionable because, it is proposed, luxury and voluptuosity must be understood as an encounter with a continuum.

In contrast to Levinas's argument, this contention holds that his work on the philosophical explanation of the relationship between luxury and voluptuosity is actually debatable because it is quite possible to conceive of it in a way that is far from his somewhat traditional ideas of luxury as enjoyment, pleasure, and happiness (on Levinas on luxury see Levinas 1969: 62, 103); it is thus suggested that such ideas, when applied to luxury and voluptuosity, can effortlessly slide into ideas of joylessness, displeasure, and unhappiness. Consequently, Levinas's analysis of luxury and voluptuosity as separate entities can, perhaps inadvertently, alert people to the need to view them differently; not only as a continuum but also as entities that raise tough questions for art history and for luxury philosophy.

Assessment

In conclusion, one method of contemplating Levinas's importance for luxury philosophy is to regard his work as dealing a blow to the contemporary image of the human condition of being luxurious, according to which human beings are secluded minds and sumptuous bodies, microscopic subjects who interact with other exterior subjects and objects through pictures of comfort and opinions concerning inessential pleasures. Levinas portrays people, instead, as luxurious beings who come into contact with their voluptuosity and their environs chiefly through desire. This could be interpreted as the irreducibility of human desire to human need.

Simultaneously, however, in any case in *Totality and Infinity*, Levinas fulfills certain ambitions of contemporaneity. He makes space for the contemporary demand for individual sovereignty and the contemporary view of humanity as free and yet in search of dis-individualizing human contact, rather than being limited by a fixed essence. Levinas's concept of voluptuosity manages to combine luxury with erotic desire by developing an explanation of the inexpressible.

Accordingly, Levinas's work on voluptuosity holds potential for people's understanding of luxury. His challenging accounts of voluptuosity have the ability to augment and transform orthodox conceptions of eroticism and desire.

When Levinas describes voluptuosity and the luxurious life he is concentrating on their profound sources—the relationship created between lovers that is contrary to the social relation, including the prohibition of the third party from the tenderness. This examination is more helpful as an evaluation of the twofold separateness of lovers than as a guide to society in general. Levinas never attempts to support his assessment that human relationships are grounded in the existence of being in love by conducting in-depth sociocultural investigations. His views on lovers being contrary to the social relation are perhaps too abstract to offer genuine insight into how luxury works and into the diverse varieties of possible human societies and cultures. It can be argued that continental philosophers such as Vasseleu have gone some distance toward applying Levinasian concepts to sociability. Nonetheless, Levinas's luxury philosophy tends to operate as an unfalsifiable framework rather than as a hypothesis that can be confirmed or contradicted by experiential investigations. As such, it should be regarded as a suggestive instrument for the clarification of luxury, but not as the last word.

The troubling sexist and political implications of some of Levinas's thought concerning voluptuosity should not be overlooked, but people must beware of appraisals such as those of Irigaray, which are complex yet problematic. Irigaray places Levinas's discussion of voluptuosity in its contemporary setting; this in itself is inoffensive and is even in keeping with Levinas's own view that human beings are situated and sociable. Such attempts are also useful in forewarning people of potential blind spots in Levinas's thinking about voluptuosity. Yet, when a feminist and political analysis such as Irigaray's is offered as an analysis without exchange, without terms, accounts, calculations, or measurements, it can itself become questionable; it excludes the possibility that Levinas's reflections on voluptuosity, situated though they are, may also have direct significance for people's understanding of love and for the truth of life for them. For example, it is possible that Levinas's view of human existence as fundamentally bound up with being luxurious simply is truer than the concept of luxury as merely something that is desirable but expensive or hard to obtain or do. It should be acknowledged that feminist analyses such as those of Irigaray also assume an understanding of being luxurious, and human beings overall. Whether or not people accept Levinas's explanation of voluptuosity, it deserves to be taken seriously as an effort to deepen their understanding of themselves.

References

Ainley, A. (1996), "The Feminine, Otherness, Dwelling: Feminist Perspectives on Levinas," in S. Hand (ed.), *Facing the Other: The Ethics of Emmanuel Levinas*, 7–22, London: Routledge.

Armitage, J. (2020), "Being Luxurious: On the Rolls Royce Ghost Black Badge and Beyond," in J. Roberts and J. Armitage (eds.), *The Third Realm of Luxury: Connecting Real Places and Imaginary Spaces*, 25–46, London: Bloomsbury.

Armitage, J. (2022), "Luxury, Voluptuosity, Levinas: On Jan Steen and Giovanni Segantini," *Luxury: History, Culture, Consumption*, 9 (1): 59–80.

Bernasconi, R. (1988), "Foreword," in E. Levinas, *Existence and Existents*, viii, Dordrecht: Kluwer.

Chalier, C. (1991), "Ethics and the Feminine," in R. Bernasconi and S. Critchley (eds.), *Re-reading Levinas*, 119–29, Bloomington, IN: Indiana University Press.

Chanter, T. (1988), "Feminism and the Other," in R. Bernasconi and D. Wood (eds.), *The Provocation Of Levinas: Rethinking the Other*, 32–56, London: Routledge.

Chanter, T., ed. (2001), *Feminist Interpretations of Emmanuel Levinas*, University Park: Pennsylvania State University Press.

Chanter, T. (2002), *Time, Death, and the Feminine: Levinas with Heidegger*, Stanford, CA: Stanford University Press.

de Beauvoir, S. (2011), *The Second Sex*, trans. C. Borde and S. Malovany-Chevallier, New York: Vintage Books.

Freud, S. (2002), *Civilization and Its Discontents*, trans. D. McLintock, London: Penguin.

Heidegger, M. (1962), *Being and Time*, 7th edn, trans. J. Macquarrie and E. Robinson, New York: Harper & Row.

Husserl, E. (1966), *Méditations cartésiennes: Ecartesianische Meditationene, introduction à la phénoménologie*, trans. G. Peiffer and E. Levinas, Paris: Vrin.

Husserl, E. (2017), *Ideas: General Introduction to Pure Phenomenology*, trans. W. R. B. Gibson, Eastford, CT: Martino Fine Books.

Ince, K. (1996), "Questions to Luce Irigaray," *Hypatia*, 11 (2): 122–40.

Irigaray, L. (1991), "Questions to Emmanuel Levinas," in M. Whitford (ed.), *The Irigaray Reader*, 178–89, Cambridge: Blackwell.

Irigaray, L. (1993), "The Fecundity of the Caress: A Reading of Levinas, *Totality and Infinity*, 'Phenomenology of Eros,'" in L. Irigaray (ed.), *An Ethics of Sexual Difference*, trans. C. Burke and G. C. Gill, 185–217, Ithica, NY: Cornell University Press.

Levinas, E. (1969), *Totality and Infinity: An Essay on Exteriority*, trans. A. Lingis, Pittsburgh, PA: Duquesne University Press.

Levinas, E. (1987), *Time and the Other*, trans. R. A. Cohen, Pittsburgh, PA: Duquesne University Press.

Levinas, E. (1988), *Existence and Existents*, Dordrecht: Kluwer.

Levinas, E. (1990a), "Reflections on the Philosophy of Hitlerism," trans. S. Hand, *Critical Inquiry*, 17: 63–71.

Levinas, E. (1990b), *Difficult Freedom: Essays on Judaism*, trans. S. Hand, London: Athlone.

Levinas, E. (1990c), *Nine Talmudic Readings*, trans. A. Aronowicz, Bloomington: Indiana University Press.

Levinas, E. (1993), *Outside the Subject*, London: Athlone.

Levinas, E. (1994a), *Beyond the Verse*, trans. G. D. Mole, Bloomington: Indiana University Press.

Levinas, E. (1994b), *In the Time of Nations*, trans. M. B. Smith, Bloomington: Indiana University Press.

Levinas, E. (1995), *The Theory of Intuition in Husserl's Phenomenology*, 2nd edn, Evanston, IL: Northwestern University Press.

Levinas, E. (1996), *Proper Names*, trans. M. B. Smith, London: Athlone.

Levinas, E. (1998a), *Discovering Existence with Husserl*, ed., trans. R. A. Cohen and M. B. Smith, Evanston, IL: Northwestern University Press.

Levinas, E. (1998b), *Otherwise than Being or beyond Essence*, trans. A. Lingis, Pittsburgh, PA: Duquesne University Press.

Levinas, E. (1998c), *Of God Who Comes to Mind*, trans. B. Bergo, Stanford, CA: Stanford University Press.

Levinas, E. (1998d), *Entre Nous: On Thinking-of-the-Other*, trans. M. B. Smith and B. Harshav, London: Athlone.

Levinas, E. (1999a), *Alterity and Transcendence*, trans. M. B. Smith, London: Athlone.

Levinas, E. (1999b), *New Talmudic Readings*, trans. R. A. Cohen, Pittsburgh, PA: Duquesne University Press.

Levinas, E. (2000), *God, Death, and Time*, trans. B. Bergo, Stanford, CA: Stanford University Press.

Levinas, E. (2001), *Is It Righteous to Be? Interviews with Emmanuel Levinas*, ed. J. Robbins, Stanford, CA: Stanford University Press.

Levinas, E. (2003a), *On Escape*, trans. B. Bergo, Stanford, CA: Stanford University Press.

Levinas, E. (2003b), *Humanism of the Other*, trans. N. Poller, Urbana: University of Illinois Press.

Levinas, E. (2004), *Unforeseen History*, trans. N. Poller, Urbana: University of Illinois Press.

Lingis, A. (1984), *Excesses: Eros and Culture*, New York: State University of New York Press.

Lingis, A. (1986a), *Libido: The French Existential Theories*, Bloomington: Indiana University Press.

Lingis, A. (1986b), *Phenomenological Explanations*, Dordrecht: Martinus Nijhoff.

Lingis, A. (1989), *Deathbound Subjectivity*, Bloomington: Indiana University Press.

Plato (2007), *The Republic*, trans. D. Lee, London: Penguin.

Sandford, S. (2004), "Levinas, Feminism and the Feminine," in S. Critchley and R. Bernasconi (eds.), *The Cambridge Companion to Levinas*, 139–60, London: Routledge.

Vasseleu, C. (1998), *Textures of Light: Vision and Touch in Irigaray, Levinas, and Merleau-Ponty*, London: Routledge.

6

Georges Bataille: Luxury as Expenditure

Biographical Details and Philosophical Context

Born on September 10, 1897 at Billom, Puy-de-Dôme, France, Georges Bataille had a disturbing childhood. His father was blind, syphilitic, and endured paralysis when Bataille was three years old. Raised by atheist parents, in his youth Bataille became a Catholic. Although he later scorned Christianity and his registration for the priesthood following his loss of faith in 1920, Christianity still gave a focus for a fundamental feature of his work on luxury: what notions of expenditure and principles of loss justify luxurious human activity in the modern world? Bataille's conversion to Catholicism accorded with the declaration of the First World War in 1914, two events that are connected in his luxury philosophy. Bataille did not see combat (he was called up, but demobilized following tuberculosis) but his character was forever stained by the experience of the war. Bataille researched medievalism at the École nationale des chartes in 1922 and was awarded a study grant in Spain where he saw the death in the bullring of the matador and torero Manuel Granero i Valls. Granero I Valls's death affected Bataille, fusing eroticism, luxury, and death in his mind and creating associations that captivated him.

Returning to Paris, Bataille worked as a librarian at the Bibliothèque nationale de France for twenty years. Simultaneously, he studied philosophy. A student of the exiled Russian existentialist and religious philosopher Lev Isaakovich Shestov (1866–1938), known for his critiques of rationalism and positivism, Bataille also read Friedrich Nietzsche, who was to become an influence on his luxury philosophy. Shestov presented a lesson to Bataille: it showed him that philosophy was helpful only when linked to bodily experience, and that development of corporeal sensory perception was as significant as development of the mind. A phase of volatility and dissolution in Bataille's personal life ensued, during which he came to interact with the Surrealists, whose sensibility he shared, but found the ambiance around the Surrealist Group repressive.

Bataille began to write in 1927 and his experience of intense feelings is obvious in his early work on luxury, as can be seen in such articles as 1933's "The Notion of Expenditure" (1985a), if not in his pseudonymously published first novel under the name of Lord Auch, *The Story of the Eye* (2001a). Concurrently, Bataille also aided in the production of the journal *Documents*, which was published until 1931, and for which he authored articles and became its co-editor.

Throughout the 1930s, Bataille's interest in luxury expanded into the subjects of anthropology and sociology and he attended the lectures of Marcel Mauss, the French sociologist and anthropologist who analyzed topics such as magic, sacrifice, and gift exchange in diverse cultures around the world (Mauss 2002). Bataille also became politically engaged, partaking in Boris Souvarine's Cercle communiste démocratique and contributing articles to its journal *La Critique sociale*, wherein he investigated for the first time in expanded form his thoughts about the notion of expenditure, the principle of loss, luxury, and on the menaces signified by the rise of fascism. He also became involved in an unsuccessful effort to construct a popular university and in 1935 established, with André Breton, the French writer, poet, and co-founder, leader, and principal theorist of surrealism, the anti-Popular Front group Contre-attaque.

In 1934, Bataille attended the Russian-born French philosopher and political leader Alexandre Kojève's (1902–68) philosophical lectures on Hegelian phenomenology, which gave him a new viewpoint on the possibilities of Hegel's philosophy. Additional chaos in Bataille's personal life led to the ending of his first marriage and a relationship with Colette Peignot, whose death in 1938 had a shattering influence on him.

In 1938, Bataille created the College of Sociology, an effort at an activist sociology in addition to Acéphale, a secret society determined on a journey beyond the bourgeois world, which also had the purpose of freeing Nietzsche from the misrepresentations spread about him by the Nazis.

A period of public activity closed with the arrival of the Second World War which saw Bataille retreating into himself. However, he went on to write one of his most thoughtful books, *Guilty* (2011), along with the erotic stories *My Mother, Madame Edwarda,* and *The Dead Man* (2012a). Compelled by illness to depart the Bibliothèque nationale, Bataille left for the French countryside and, in 1943, published his first considerable work featuring luxury philosophy, *Inner Experience* (1988), which, in part, investigated luxury as one of the existential problems of living in the modern world. Throughout the 1940s, Bataille submerged himself in a variety of projects, publishing poems in *L'Archangélique et autres poèmes* (2008), philosophical texts such as *On Nietzsche* (2016), *Méthode de méditation* (1947), and three works containing his luxury philosophy: *Theory of Religion* (1989a), the economic studies comprising extensive commentaries on luxury, *The Limit of the Useful* (2023), and *The Accursed Share: An Essay on General Economy, Volume I—Consumption* (1989b). In 1946, Bataille founded *Critique,* a journal dedicated to reviews of books in a variety of topics. He was its editor until his death and published many articles in it. In 1947, Bataille gave lectures at the Collège philosophique but had no steady employment and faced financial problems until 1949, when he became a librarian in Carpentras.

Through the 1950s, besieged by sickness but still prolific, Bataille published the novels *L'Abbé C* (2012b) and *Blue of Noon* (2012c), three books on art (the *Prehistoric Painting: Lascaux or the Birth of Art* [1955a], *Manet* [1955b], and *The Tears of Eros* [1989c], on eroticism in art) on top of two books including his luxury philosophy, the first a compilation of articles on literature, *Literature and Evil* (2012d), and the second, his vital study, *Eroticism* (1987). Bataille died in Paris in 1962.

Bataille had extensive interests and, apart from writing books in the areas of economic theory and art history, literature, and fiction, he also published works in the area of luxury philosophy, three of which, *The Accursed Share Volumes II and III* (1991a), *The Unfinished System of Nonknowledge* (2001b), and *The Limit of the Useful* (2023), were published posthumously. All these texts are dominated by a concern with the subject of luxury. They have to be seen against the backdrop of Bataille's times. Disturbed by childhood experiences and the First World War, Bataille's work on luxury is an effort to engage with the economic issue of the notion of expenditure, of whether it is feasible to exist in luxury by way of a principle of loss or whether the modern consciousness has attained such a condition of sickness that being luxurious is unfeasible. Bataille is thus within the context of Surrealist rebellion and was disgusted by a civilization that was to blame for the First World War. He thought that the tradition of French rationalist philosophy was incriminated in this disaster and was willing to look to Nietzsche and Hegel as philosophers who had a complexity and an intensity that could possibly contend with the economic crisis of the contemporary consciousness of expenditure on luxury as a principle of loss.

Luxury Philosophy and Contributions

Luxury as Expenditure and Experience

At the center of Bataille's concern with luxury is the character of humanity's shared existence and how people deal with what he called, in 1933, "The Notion of Expenditure" and "The Principle of Loss" as individuals (Bataille 1985a). How do people live and act with luxury in a social world dominated by processes of production and consumption? How do people cohabit with their fellow human beings when their consumption, in particular, according to Bataille, "must be divided into two distinct parts" (1985a: 118)? "The first, reducible part," wrote Bataille, "is represented by the use of the minimum necessary for the conservation of life and the continuation of individuals' productive activity in a given society; it is therefore a question simply of the fundamental condition of productive activity" (1985a: 118). Yet, the "second part," Bataille argued, "is represented by so-called unproductive expenditures: luxury, mourning, war, cults, the construction of sumptuary monuments, games, spectacles, arts, perverse sexual activity (i.e., deflected from genital finality)— all these represent activities which, at least in primitive circumstances, have no end beyond themselves" (1985a: 118). Bataille saves "the use of the word *expenditure* for the designation of these unproductive forms, and not for the designation of all the modes of consumption that serve as a means to the end of production" (1985a: 118; original emphasis). Such forms of expenditure thus "constitute a group characterized by the fact that in each case the accent is placed on a *loss* that must be as great as possible in order for that activity to take on its true meaning" (Bataille 1985a: 118; original emphasis). "This principle of loss," of "unconditional expenditure," which is counter to "the economic principle of balanced accounts," of acquisition and rationality, was a principle and a question that preoccupied Bataille (1985a: 118), as can be exemplified through numerous instances he provided from everyday life. Bataille had little interest in "being luxurious" (Armitage 2020), nor was he concerned about the character of individualized luxurious identities. Rather, what interested Bataille about jewelry such as a diamond necklace, for example, is that it "must not only be beautiful and dazzling," which makes the "substitution of imitations possible," but also that it represents the sacrifice of "a fortune," which is "necessary for the constitution of this necklace's fascinating character" (1985a: 119). What concerned Bataille was "the symbolic value of jewels" in dreams where diamonds denote excrement or in the unconscious where they are "cursed matter that flows from a wound" (1985a: 119): "they are," wrote Bataille, "a part of oneself destined for open sacrifice (they serve, in fact, as sumptuous gifts charged with sexual love)" (1985a: 119). "The functional character of jewels" thus necessitates what Bataille called "their immense material value and alone explains the inconsequence of the most beautiful imitations, which are very nearly useless" (1985a: 119). Luxurious existence was therefore only of interest initially to Bataille because of its sacrificial and sacred aspects. Humanist philosophies were foreign to Bataille's method of reasoning, for human beings live only in relation with others, as in competitive games, where loss generally is produced under multifaceted conditions. Human life is unable to bear solitary being: people are shaped as humans through, for instance, spending substantial sums of money on the sociocultural upkeep of their residences, on interacting with animals, equipment, and other people. Similarly, people often exist within structures founded not to live within but to challenge extant social limits: human energy is wasted to create sensations of confusion, bewilderment, and passion while reality is redefined through the "unproductive" initiative of an unconscious fascination with the threat of death. It not only means that any thought of transcendence is an illusion but also that the presence of competitions and the public distribution of prizes, of huge, excited, and often unimpeded crowds, entail the loss of money through betting. Bataille believed that it is vital to confront such sociocultural realities as the "*real* charge of the passions unleashed by competition" (1985a: 119; original emphasis), an existential reality that frequently leads to the inability to escape the certainty of one's destiny through losses disproportionate to one's means. As Bataille puts it: "these losses even attain such a level of madness that often the only way out for gamblers is prison or death" (1985a: 119). Seeking the causes for existence merely in productive expenditure has little meaning in the context of unproductive expenditure on immense competitive displays: horse races, for example, are, according to Bataille, "associated with a sumptuary process of social classification" (1985a: 119). The principal focus for Bataille's research into luxury is thus to comprehend how people are capable of living within and challenging the limits that life within societies inflicts on them and where the existence of, for instance, jockey clubs, "the ostentatious display of the latest luxurious fashions" at the races, and the complex of profligate expenditure signified by contemporary horse racing is the norm (Bataille 1985a: 119).

However, unlike a lot of philosophers absorbed in appreciating luxurious existence, Bataille was unconcerned with taking the perceived world as an object of study. Instead, he commenced with his own existence. Bataille did not examine given information with the aim of extracting a philosophy from it. His luxury philosophy arises internally and is projected externally. Philosophical consideration, novels, and poetic texts thus all become ways to survey the character of what Bataille called *Inner Experience* (1988) where, in a wide-ranging discussion on "The Torment" (1988: 33–61), for example, he writes that people's will for "the extreme limit is not disorder or luxuriance" because "the will for the extreme limit stops at nothing (we can't really attain it)" (1988: 50).

In employing his own experience as the methodological foundation of his luxury philosophy, though, Bataille was not capitulating to vain subjectivism. Bataille studied his inner experience only to understand the relation of his being with that of others. The information of Bataille's own life was of worth only as far as it was the greatest dependable and obtainable source available to him.

The Sacred and the Profane: Three Luxurious Forms of Nature

Bataille's appreciation of what established the fact of luxury in culture, politics, and society arose from the work of Émile Durkheim (1858–1917), the French sociologist and author of, among many other works, *The Elementary Forms of Religious Life* (2008). Bataille argued that luxury was a concept and a practice that, following Durkheim, took place in cultures, political systems, and societies that are organic wholes, whose features are different from the sum of their parts. Simultaneously, however, cultural, political, social, and luxurious beings are not to be seen as dissimilar things. Collective consciousness is a tangible reality as idiosyncratic as that of the people existing within it. To comprehend luxury within culture, politics, and society, consequently, it is necessary to comprehend the relation people have with them.

Bataille's reliance on Durkheim is observed in his examination of the sacred (see, e.g., Bataille 1985b). Acceding the distinction Durkheim made between the sacred and the profane, Bataille thought that the equilibrium between them had been ruptured in modern cultures, political systems, and societies increasingly replete with luxuries, wherein the sacred, and thus sacred ideas concerning luxury, fight to endure in a world subjugated by the profane, inclusive of the world of luxury.

The sacred is communication and Bataille perceived the possibilities of communication nowadays being ruptured by the supremacy of exchange-values. This has an influence at all levels of culture, politics, society, and, self-evidently, luxury. The sacred is an agreement between human culture, political systems, society, and the universe. This is given manifestation in such practices as ritual sacrifice. In his *Theory of Religion*, for example, Bataille writes of "The Consummation of Sacrifice," arguing that death clarifies the meaning of sacrifice through the reinstatement of "a lost value" and "through a relinquishment of that value" (1989a: 48). For Bataille, however, death is not inevitably connected to sacrifice because sacrifice may not be bloodstained. To sacrifice is, instead, "to relinquish and to give," to "pass from a lasting order, in which all consumption of resources is subordinated to the need for duration, to the violence of an unconditional consumption" (Bataille 1989a: 49). What is significant for Bataille is to "leave the world of real things" and to enter the world of sacrifice, which is a world of consumption that is concerned only with the moment (1989a: 49). Sacrifice is both gift and relinquishment, an offering that passes into the world of immediate consumption. To sacrifice is to partake of the sacred, to give, to offer beyond all utility. "This is so clearly the precise meaning of sacrifice," writes Bataille, "that one sacrifices *what is useful*; one does not sacrifice luxurious objects" (1989a: 49; original emphases). Sacrificing useful objects rather than luxurious objects thus helps to uphold the balance between the sacred and the profane by sanctioning an opening—consumption that is only concerned with the moment—to the excess outpouring produced by human activity. It is a transgressive act that serves to preserve the taboo that protects the world of luxurious objects from destruction. As cultures, political systems, societies, and luxuries develop, however, this compound interrelationship is broken and the uniformity of modern culture, politics, society, and luxury is instituted by a profanation.

This profanation can be investigated through what Bataille, in his *The Limit of the Useful* (2023) and *The Accursed Share Volume I*, describes as the "*restrictive* economy" (1989b: 25; original emphasis). This is typical of modern cultures, politics, societies, and luxury, and is founded on the need to decrease scarcity. It boosts the accumulation of wealth and luxuries at the cost of the cultural, political, and social communication that is the condition of the sacred. Bataille understood this as an illusion. Bataille considered the "history of life on earth" as "the effect of a wild exuberance" or "the development of luxury," as "a luxurious squandering of energy in every form!" (1989b: 33)—a form that was struggling to expend itself uselessly. Indeed, according to Bataille, there are three luxurious forms of nature, with the first being the "eating of one species by another" (the elementary variety of luxury; 1989b: 33). Eating, of course, begets death, which is the second of Bataille's three luxuries of nature, since death is not only lethal and expensive but also highlights the frailty and complexity of the animal body, a luxurious quality that is exuberant and intense. In this regard, the luxury of death is considered by people in the same way as that of Bataille's third luxury of nature, human sexuality, which is a negation of the self. "Under the present conditions" Bataille comments, "independently of our consciousness, sexual reproduction is, together with eating and death, one of the great luxurious detours that ensure the intense consumption of energy" (1989b: 35). With sexual reproduction, people sacrifice growth for themselves, multiply the number of people in the world, and transfer their consumption of energy to the impersonality of life. Sexuality is the luxury of individual people. For Bataille, sexual reproduction in people entails the giving of "life as one *gives to others*," in a rapid and wild squandering of energy resources, transmitted in a moment to the limit of possibility, which leads to the destruction of bodies "and ultimately connects up with the senseless luxury and excess of death" (1989b: 35; original emphases). However, for Bataille, when people extend themselves through labor and technology, there eventually comes a point when "the advantage of extension is neutralized by the contrary advantage," that of "luxury" (1989b: 35); extension continues to function, but what counts mostly is no longer to expand the productive forces but to squander their products luxuriously, to waste wealth, as when, following the Second World War, increases in the standard of living and increasingly unproductive services appeared, lessening the need for work in a climate where wages were increasing. For Bataille, people respond to the problem of the extension of economic growth beyond previously given limits, made possible by the development of labor and technology, by enacting that luxury that is the consumption, intensely and sumptuously, of the excess energy offered up by existence on planet Earth, a planet that is dominated by the solar energy of the sun and thus is the source of life's exuberant development (Bataille 1989b: 28–9). Humankind has progressively controlled this excess energy and its expression through work which, in modern cultures, political systems, and societies, provides the limit by which activity is assessed. This last signifies the victory of the profane, instituting the framework within which the restrictive economy controls activity. Counter to the restrictive economy, Bataille postulates the concept of the "*general* economy," which would reinstate the principle of generosity into human relations (1989b: 25; original emphasis).

In Bataille's view, the general economy is established by expenditure: the elated consumption of excess wealth through the festival, happiness, and recreation (1989b: 64). In modern cultures, political systems, and societies, the latter activities are "accursed," being given to people only as reward for their dedication to the principle of work (Bataille 1989b: 37–8). It is then no longer possible to experience unadulterated excess energy as effusion. Transgression, as the secret of the sacred, is controlled and relegated to a means of cultural, political, and social control. It can be preserved only in controlled pleasure (e.g., the all-inclusive luxury vacation), or in destructive activities, for instance, the Second World War (Bataille 1989b: 23–6).

For Bataille, the fundamental cultural, political, and social problem confronting humanity "*is not necessity but its contrary, luxury*" (1989b: 12; original emphasis). And this problem is the consequence not of luxury itself but of the fact that people have individualized it. People have persuaded themselves that luxury is something they can possess, that accumulates to them as individuals instead of belonging to humankind. This is the falsehood that shatters any sensation of accord people can attain with the universe and which, in previous times, was captured by the concept of the sacred.

Sovereignty, Eroticism, Nonknowledge

Consequently, luxury not only comes to decide the rank of the person who displays it but also becomes the only gauge of cultural, political, and social distinction or standing wherein, according to Bataille, wealth incites desire, but true luxury is the preserve of people who hold riches in disdain, uncaringly decline work, and enjoy the destruction of magnificence (1989b: 76–7). And servility in turn is inaugurated as the measure against which personal luxurious distinction acquires its value: Bataille points to the critique of luxury—"Protestant at first, then revolutionary"—which "coincided with a possibility of industrial development, implicit in the technical advances of the new age," and with the "largest share of the surplus … reserved, in modern times, for capitalist accumulation" (1989b: 107). Class distinction is established and so rank, or status, and not luxurious religious activities, sacrifices, and festivals comes to determine being. This results, for example, in Martin Luther (1483–1546), the German seminal figure of the Protestant Reformation, opposing the possibility of gaining heaven by making a profligate use of individual wealth. Later, John Calvin (1509–64), the French theologian, pastor, and reformer in Geneva during the Protestant Reformation, emphasizing the sovereignty of God and the authority of the Bible, withdrew value from meditative indolence, from flamboyant luxury, and from the types of charity that upheld non-productive poverty. Instead, value was given to the virtues that have their foundation in utility: the reformed Christian had to be modest, saving, diligent, enthusiastic in trade and industry and even had to help eradicate begging, which went against values whose standard was productive activity (Bataille 1989b: 123). Similarly, as documented in the work of Max Weber (1864–1920), the German sociologist, historian, jurist, and political economist, the spirit of bourgeois capitalist industry amounted to a censure of inactivity and luxury while confirming the value of enterprise and labor, the rational allocation of time, materiel, and resources to the development of the production apparatus (Weber 2002: 104; Bataille 1989b: 124, 137, 156). For Bataille, this spirit brings about the boundless development of industrious forces under capitalism and communism and in servility permeating each facet of culture, politics, and society (1989b: 159), so that even power comes to be used in servility in place of what Bataille (1991a) calls "sovereignty" or the refusal to submit to the useful in the name of "the ambiguity of pleasure and play" (Bataille 2018).

Sovereignty is a principle of life that takes moral form in human communication. It is present in the sanctification of the immediate and the human will to fulfill itself. Sovereignty embodies the spirit of becoming: recognition of the immediacy offered by life, together with a refusal to accept a degraded existence. But this is inconsistent, because the movement of human life works against the prospect of a sovereign existence. To endure in culture, politics, and society, people are compelled to accommodate their fellow beings and the world. This inaugurates an opening that cannot be cleared.

This opening means that people are incomplete beings whose existence is discontinuous, specifically, separated from other beings.

The existence of death discloses this opening and people's acknowledgment that they are limited beings. The principle of work and building for the future endeavor to repudiate death. Aching for the continuity they have lost by being born, people come to understand that, on the one hand, death commits aggression against them but, on the other, it reunifies them with the continuity of the world. It is in the understanding of death that human communication is originated. Certainly, in Bataille's view, in *Eroticism* (1987), sexual activity—particularly nonreproductive sexual activity—is of the highest importance. The sexual act joins life and death but also momentarily offers the possibility of resolving the disconnection between them (1987: 14). In eroticism, life momentarily bursts its limits, giving people the promise of an excessive abundance (1987: 231). But this promise takes form because of the consciousness people have of death, which, for the Bataille of *The Accursed Share Volumes II and III*, is the most luxurious form of life (1991a: 84–6). For Bataille, death is associated with eroticism, regarded as a confirmation of life. "It is easy," Bataille writes, "to turn away from the luxurious truth of death," yet, he asks, "How could we not be aware that death … constantly ensures the renewal of life?" (1991a: 84). In short, for Bataille, "life is the luxury of which death is the highest degree"; indeed, for him, "of all the luxuries of life, human life is the most extravagantly expensive" (1991a: 86).

Sexual congress is not just a visceral activity people need for the reproduction of the species but an activity that is essential for people's existence: it is a deeply felt cerebral act that arises as a will to experience a fundamental communication with the lover. It is the body wanting to surpass the limits inflicted on it by existence and the will to fuse with another human being even with the acknowledgment that this conflict is a danger to its own integral sensibility. The erotic act is a type of communication between life and death, involving an encounter with the luxuriousness of human life and with the loss of identity that death involves (Bataille 1991a: 85–6). The apprehension at the core of this conflict is what originates "the anguish without which a life devoted … to luxury would be less boldly luxurious" (Bataille 1991a: 86). For if it is a fact of human existence to be luxurious, "what," inquires Bataille, "to say of a luxury of which anguish is the product and which anguish does not moderate?" (1991a: 86).

Similar to erotic luxuriousness, the instinct to write literature originates from the need for communication. However, for Bataille, literature is an essential yet evil moral act (2012b: 3–4), this is, since the state of human existence is a guilt that is established through anguish and is a part of human nature that is produced by the reality of being born (2011: 123–6). People acknowledge their being as an absence and the authentic writer is the person who appreciates this. In his essay on Charles Baudelaire (1821–67), the French poet, essayist, art critic, and translator, in his *Literature and Evil*, for example, Bataille (2012d: 25–49) understands that the society wherein Baudelaire's 1857 poetic masterpiece, *Les Fleurs du Mal* (*The Flowers of Evil*), was written was capitalist society at full blast. Being was increasingly achieved through working for the increase of the means of production and through the absence of luxury. In fact, according to Bataille (2012d: 43–4), this "society was prepared to crush the luxury of the great even by terror." As in sacrifice, Bataille the writer is seeking to bring about harmony between a human existence progressively devoted to industrialism and reason, utility, and private interest, and the universe, which seeks the increase of productive forces for unproductive luxurious pleasure, for irrational values, and for uselessness (2012d: 44, 142). And, in poetry, which, for the Bataille of *The Impossible*, "opens the night to desire's excess," writing has the same quality of sacrifice or "the mad will to exceed the world" (1991b: 162–3). Poetry is the only option people have nowadays for an authentic experience of the sacred because it reveals the "power of the unknown, painted in blinding colors, in the image of a sun" (Bataille 1991b: 164). The acts of writing and reading are therefore, for Bataille, discreet and tied to what might be called the luxury of silence, a luxurious absence of language and awareness wherein truth is negated in an eventually uninhabitable sovereign space of nonbeing; the erotic silence of lovers, for instance, exceeds communication, exceeds philosophy, and is in fact an excessive gift that is concurrently the space between human experience and the universe. The luxury of silence, the gap between what is written and what is read, is what Bataille's *Eroticism* describes as "a language that equals zero, ... that equals nothing at all": in truth, it is a silence that takes people "out of the world" and thus presents an alternative to practicing the utilitarian self-interest that rules modern culture, politics, and society (1987: 264). Nonetheless, this is an inconsistency, for, if writing aims at immediate communication with the reader, the fact of writing prevents this immediacy because the reader can only encounter the text in circumstances the writer has not selected: the experience is forever mediated. Consequently, writing is a less authentic way of expression than sacrifice.

This understanding also conditions Bataille's grasp of truth. Bataille had a suspicion of Enlightenment assertions concerning truth as a principle for comprehension. For Bataille, knowledge had an aptitude for undercutting itself. Indeed, Bataille's (2001b) conception of "nonknowledge" is a challenge to developmental views of knowledge as leading to a superior knowledge since he argued that knowledge can also lead to ignorance and to the breakdown of knowledge. Moreover, there are conditions of being luxurious wherein lack of knowledge includes wisdom: people can "understand" through the serenity of the "vacancy" of meditative methods conducted in luxurious silence such as yoga—that group of physical, mental, and spiritual practices which began in ancient India and that aim to still the mind through detection of a detached witness-consciousness unaffected by the mind and everyday suffering—which, for Bataille, is a desirable state of being. Equally, for the Bataille of *The Unfinished System of Nonknowledge*, the practice of smoking tobacco is not just a languorous expenditure of fumes without any ability to produce knowledge, but includes wisdom reached through the elegance and lightness of smoke (2001b: 7). Here, "understanding" is a form of lightness, which, in the case of the serenity produced by smoking tobacco, leads to a sort of empty transparency that Bataille labels "a reef" (2001b: 7). Smoking tobacco is thus a meditative method to achieve a kind of elegance that, for Bataille, "settles beside this reef, underlines it, and presents it as a pretext for not going further" and is frequently a practice that is performed in a luxurious silence that is falsely equated with a lightness bordering on insignificance (2001b: 7). For Bataille, therefore, "truth" is to be discovered in the boundaries between knowledge and nonknowledge.

This belief influences the practice of writing about luxury. Bataille did not convince through argument but by fostering a relationship of personal involvement with readers, by inciting and confronting their self-satisfaction.

Life for Bataille is contradictory, an impossible mixture of diverse conditions of being from the necessary to the luxurious that lie at the center of human nature. Living with the consciousness that they are temporary beings who will die, people withdraw from this consciousness in fear. However, in escaping this consciousness and building for a future that will never arrive, people also have a need to destroy the works by which they struggle to attain a transcendence of death. This, as we shall see below, is also the foundation of the pursuit of luxury as an act of transgression that is vital to the arrangement of human culture, politics, and society. The conflict between the will toward order and the attraction of disorder is the reality that Bataille investigated through analysis of how consciousness of death influences human experience.

Bataille rejected the possibility of final knowledge of luxury or any other concept. People can never fully comprehend the world of luxury since life's condition is unavoidably unfinished. Human existence is an enigma that people cannot untangle but which they are fated to follow until their demise.

Appraisal of Key Advances in Luxury Philosophy and Controversies

Bataille was initially a minor luxury philosopher whose effect on French intellectual life was inconspicuous but important. Due to editing the journals *Documents* and *Critique* and as the inspiring figure in the groups Acéphale and College of Sociology, he came into interaction with some of the foremost figures of the interwar era. Bataille had many friends, and some enemies, among the writers and artists of the Surrealist groups, such as Michel Leiris and Roger Caillois, René Char, André Masson, and André Breton (who had an early conflict of temperaments with Bataille). Maurice Blanchot (1907–2003), the French writer, philosopher, and literary theorist, also remained a close friend of Bataille until the latter's death in 1962, whereas Jean-Paul Sartre (1905–80), the French Marxist philosopher and playwright, novelist, screenwriter, political activist, biographer, and literary critic, wrote a lengthy unfavorable review of Bataille's *Inner Experience* in *Cahiers du Sud* in 1943, labeling Bataille "A New

Mystic" (Sartre 2010) who presents himself as returning from an unidentified yet exalted expanse, having encountered there the enigmas of nonknowledge.

However, the crucial element in Bataille's luxury philosophy was the notion and problem of expenditure, which meant a great deal to him whether or not the concept had any "influence" on contemporary thought about luxury within anthropology or within Hegelian and Nietzschean continental philosophy (Kendall 2016). Most notably, Bataille was drawn by the aesthetic, political, and ethical implications of a political economy of luxury founded in a refusal of servile accounts of necessity. This was the voyage to the end of luxury of which he wrote about in the 1940s at the time of *The Accursed Share* (1989b).

The political economy of luxury of which Bataille imagined in the 1940s was sustained in the expenditure he later discussed, particularly with respect to the accursed share that is luxury, or that share of energy or wealth in excess of what is necessary for the stable maintenance of any organism or system (Bataille 1989b: 21): an approach to luxury that questions most resolutely what Bataille called the restrictive economy. In no sense did the followers of the restrictive economy, such as John Maynard Keynes (1883–1946), the English economist and philosopher whose ideas changed the post-Second World War theory and practice of macroeconomics and the economic policies of governments, recognize Bataille's questioning of expenditure, of excess energy and wealth, let alone his questioning of how such expenditure was to be spent: gloriously or catastrophically? Rather, they engaged in a discussion about the need for sovereign nations to restrict their own trade surpluses wherein Bataille is—as interlocutor on the accursed share or associate concerning the circulation of energy on the surface of the globe—never present (McGoey 2018). Yet, Bataille was unequivocal in making clear the character of this expenditure that had, by its nature, to be acknowledged as unceasing. It was founded as a mode of analysis and description, as Bataille put it, of the allocation, arrangement, and displacement of energy. The idea of this political economy of luxury is in the end the tracing of the always astonishing journeys of energy, which is also why it cannot be "restrictive."

Bataille's relationship with expenditure has been extensively acknowledged. It rests in a concern with cultural, political, and social beings, the problem of the consciousness of forms of luxury, and the physical and psychological exuberance that energy involves. A comparable interest in human existence as stemming from an act of expenditure that is fundamentally energy in motion is crucial to the less well-known work of Bataille on, for example, architecture (Hollier 1990), which is also fascinated by the limits of existence and the lure of luxury (see, also, Sharr 2016).

Luxury expenditure is often also indicated by restriction to narrow concerns about utility and functional efficacy and Bataille did not lack for a more general perspective. Bataille's political-economic analysis of luxury that moves from specifically narrowly restricted areas of luxury production and consumption to the circulation of energies generally is now well known. This reflects a readiness on Bataille's part to work beyond any single disciplinary framework, material resource, or type of energy.

Another more contemporary analyst of luxury production and consumption, or, more precisely, of excess, who is indebted to Bataille is the French sociologist Jean Baudrillard (1929–2007). Less interested in Bataille's conceptions of inner experience and theories of religion and more interested in his concept of general economy, Baudrillard suggests a transgression of capitalism through excess in his *For a Critique of the Political Economy of the Sign* (2019). Baudrillard's idea of symbolic exchange reads reminiscently of Bataille's (1985c) *Visions of Excess*, as it involves excessive forms of cultural, political, and social behavior (e.g., gift-giving and the wasteful expenditure of luxury and other goods), now associated with Bataille, and which promises to transgress the order of capitalist political economy. Based on his important text, *Symbolic Exchange and Death* (2016), Baudrillard's luxury philosophy is at odds with Bataille's since Baudrillard moved away from the theme of transgression and altered his understanding of excess. Bataille's ideas about the nature of excess are different to the way Baudrillard conceives of excess—as the Other to the system of capitalist political economy and as an indication of the extremes of the contemporary capitalist system itself. For Baudrillard, Bataille's idea of excess revealed a way of analyzing contemporary culture, politics, and society in terms of the implosion of meaning in the media, which had to be resisted through philosophical analysis of the disappearance, or, rather, of the excess of reality. Bataille would no doubt have responded to such claims with an essay on the excess of information as the abyss of nonknowledge. In it he would likely refuse to relegate his argument to the context Baudrillard would impose. In its place he would focus on Baudrillard's misunderstanding of the problem of communication as a philosophical issue of excess.

If Baudrillard's indebtedness to Bataille now seems at odds with Bataille's work on luxury and even a misunderstanding of it, it is nevertheless typical in that, along with that of many other philosophers, Baudrillard's texts have still functioned to outline the way Bataille has been received by later writers—by his critics and by his devotees—as a possibly anti-rationalist passionate outsider to French thought and a worthy provocateur, a cultural, political, and social critic, a continental philosopher, a literary commentator, a theologian, an anthropologist, and a political economist who is an important forerunner of the poststructuralist critical project of deconstruction. And it is concerning the latter that Bataille's reputation has usually been evaluated in writings by, among numerous other continental philosophers, Jacques Derrida and Roland Barthes, Julia Kristeva, and Michel Foucault, none of whom have written about Bataille's luxury philosophy, even though it is his luxury-related texts that have served to help mark Bataille out as a central figure in contemporary thought.

What unifies these writers is the will to disentangle the power relations that structure Western ideas outside of luxury philosophy. Yet, Bataille is an eminent figure not only in opening the way into such a project but also as a critic of the consistency of thought about luxury and the nature of luxurious subjects, thus supplying ammunition for a yet-to-be realized deconstructive impulse that might exemplify a poststructuralist approach to luxury. Undeniably, Bataille's thought about luxury is essentially open to any number of discourses, from Derridean deconstruction and Foucauldian poststructuralist discourse to possible departures from Baudrillard's provocative, even cynical, post-Marxist ideas concerning excessive consumerism, notions of seduction, reality, and the reproduction of signs.

One attraction to Bataille and to his notions of sovereignty and desire originates in the idea of the pursuit of luxury as an act of transgression (Armitage 2023). In this sense, Bataille opened up a fruitful theoretical trail to follow. Yet transgression can be considered in a different way to Bataille. It can be seen as an act that is fundamental to the pursuit of luxury within modern culture, politics, and society. It denotes the pursuit of sumptuous living and associated actions focused on the difficulties of human lives in search of luxuriousness throughout history. As such, it provides a key to comprehending how the pursuit of luxury as an act of transgression has taken the form it has and so offers a means by which to oppose the idea that the pursuit of luxury is unnecessary that lies at the core of much luxury philosophy (Armitage and Roberts 2016: 3–4). This provides the backdrop to a conception of the pursuit of luxury as the appearance of the will to transgress, which is understood as a will that is not only unfeasible ever to achieve but which also calls into question many suppositions contained within daily life. It supports a notion of the pursuit of luxury that affirms luxury as the provision of pleasure (indeed, in this text on Bataille, it can be seen that the pursuit of luxury is transgressive because it is also the pursuit of an infringement). This consideration of the use-value of understanding the pursuit of luxury as an act of transgression adopts yet also adapts Bataille, who saw transgression as being tied to an initial prohibition. Here, Bataille's understanding of cultural, political, and social relationships is consistent with a suggested shift in the explanation of the pursuit of luxury away from subjects related to affluent environs and toward the concept and acts of transgression. In this Bataillian interpretation, what is noteworthy about acts of transgression is not only that they are a shared dynamic that, far from being fulfilled in modern culture, politics, and society, are quickly disappearing: it is also that they point to an alternative explanation of the contemporary communal dynamic of human lives in modern culture, politics, and society wherein the disappearance of acts of transgression reappears as the search for luxuriousness. No longer part of the sacred, which the advancing drive of capitalism must destroy if it is to fulfill itself and which it is powerless to restrain, the pursuit of luxury as an act of transgression is an act of sovereignty, of human lives pursuing luxuriousness as a means of achieving independence and autonomy. This is because, in a post-Bataillian framework, the pursuit of luxury as an act of transgression, while not undermining the taboo but completing and reinforcing it, is a moral vision: the purpose of the pursuit of luxury as an act of transgression is to challenge the taboo of necessity, to ensure that it retains a dynamic force. The subduing of the sacred and the pursuit of luxury as an act of transgression in modern culture, politics, and society are thus problems of sovereignty, moral principles, and the interior relation of people to the subjects and objects of their desire.

The pursuit of luxury as an act of transgression is what matters especially to this Bataillian object of study, and this signifies a decisive difference with non-Bataillian methodologies, whose explorations are often instituted in an assumption of analytical philosophy and a will toward ultimate truth. This is exactly what a Bataillian perspective on those qualities possessed by subjects or objects that are expensive sees as being apprehensible as an act of transgression, particularly those that are established on, for instance, the erotic. Critically, a Bataillian standpoint believes that inner sovereign experiences can be identified if not fully unraveled, that nonknowledge can undermine the maintenance of the existing state of things. A Bataillian interpretation of taboo or the refusal to surrender to the useful sees cultural, political, and social relations as established in a movement that is unknowable as it remains beyond the idea of understanding and, while there can never be any likelihood of their being remade, research on the pursuit of luxury as an act of transgression can know lavishness and comprehend opulence as forces that challenge the ultimate taboo for the sovereign individual: the useful (Bataille 2023). It is thus the extravagant sovereignty at the heart of the existential disposition that provides the means for an appreciation of the pursuit of luxury as the appearance of the will to transgress, not an uncritical disengagement from the secret mysteries and delights of the human spirit. And it is the surpassing of the useful, not limits, that is the focus for change from a Bataillian position.

From this perspective, also, any idea that the Bataille of *The Accursed Share* (1989b) was in some way only concerned with a contemporary critique of the pursuit of luxury, expenditure, and excess would also be a misreading. This is an idea challenged by Michèle Richman (2021), who focuses on Bataille's consideration of the cultural, political, and social consequences of economic surplus since Paleolithic times. For Richman, if Bataille's thought is rooted in a critique of the Western tradition of luxury, this does not mean that he was concerned to challenge luxury itself. He was more interested in a universal history that, like the history provided by Ibn Khaldun (1332–1406), the Arab sociologist, philosopher, and historian, places luxury as a corruptive force at the heart of world history, thus disclosing the limitations of urban life, and particularly the role of luxury in undermining the health of the soul (Baali 1988). Competing for riches, argued Khaldun, sedentary urban people lose their previous nomadic group feeling, their cultural, political, and social solidarity, and, instead, descend into a corrupted world of luxury where their fighting spirit and, eventually, their whole body politic are sapped of their strength and stability (Richman 2021: 290).

While there exists a space between Bataille's luxury philosophy and the ideas about the nature of luxurious reality that are connected with poststructuralism, others, such as Mark Featherstone (2016), are concerned with Bataille's approach to the ethics or true logic of luxury. This concern with the profane world of luxurious things does not involve a distrust of metanarratives but an engagement with the moral center of luxury that founds an idea of human society that is constantly seeking to move beyond the material sphere into a theological or atheological space. The true luxurious life is sensed as beyond materiality, as characterized by intimacy with the world and offers a dissolution into a universal substance that exceeds individual self-identity. It might be true in Bataille's luxury philosophy too that it is possible to imagine a luxurious state wherein the world is devoid of human life, but this does not mean that life is just a number of boundless imaginative possibilities, fictions, and visions rotating on themselves. If there is no hope of human transcendence or redemption, this is because people are real beings who are confined to a limited framework that delineates their humanness. But as humans people are only a minor part of the potentiality of luxurious existence. The continuity of luxurious existence remains present all around them. People may not be able to imagine its varied and very real possibilities, but they do catch sight of it in those moments of suspension where they imagine the end of materialism and the emergence of a state of luxury beyond mere things. And people have a responsibility as humans to follow up such sightings, whether they lead to luxurious spaces of light or to luxurious spaces of darkness.

What one notices in Featherstone, and which one does not notice in poststructuralist and postmodernist work on Bataille's luxury philosophy, such as that of Jean Baudrillard, is a spirit of familiarity regarding mysticism and discretion concerning theology. Featherstone's text is perturbing but not wild; it is concerned with the fate of contemporary capitalism but does not bring notice to itself or announce that luxury is always beyond the profane world of things in a way that Bataille would have disapproved of.

Bataille is a self-effacing luxury philosopher. He made no declaration to be able to elucidate the experience or the world of luxury. Consequently, he is hard to categorize as a luxury philosopher. Yet even if, by bringing awareness to the idea of luxury as nonknowledge in, for example, the cases of yoga and smoking tobacco, he destabilized the pathway of pure knowledge of luxury and other concepts that Western thought has seen as the way to enlightenment, he still supported the importance of the personal and collective search for understanding luxury. In this sense, his method has much in common with Theodor W. Adorno's (2007) call for negative dialectics or nonidentity thinking which is discussed in Chapter 7.

References

Adorno, T. W. (2007), *Negative Dialectics*, trans. E. B. Ashton, London: Continuum.

Armitage, J. (2020), "Being Luxurious: On the Rolls Royce Ghost Black Badge and Beyond," in J. Roberts and J. Armitage (eds.), *The Third Realm of Luxury: Connecting Real Places and Imaginary Spaces*, 25–46, London: Bloomsbury.

Armitage, J. (2023), "The Pursuit of Luxury as an Act of Transgression: Bataille, Sovereignty, Desire," *French Cultural Studies*, 34 (4): 343–58.

Armitage, J. and J. Roberts, eds. (2016), *Critical Luxury Studies: Art, Design, Media*, Edinburgh: Edinburgh University Press.

Baali, F. (1988), *Society, State, and Urbanism: Ibn Khaldun's Sociological Thought*, Albany: State University of New York Press.

Bataille, G. (1947), *Méthode de méditation*, Paris: Fontaine.

Bataille, G. (1955a), *Prehistoric Painting: Lascaux or the Birth of Art*, Geneva: Skira.

Bataille, G. (1955b), *Manet*, Geneva: Skira.

Bataille, G. (1985a), "The Notion of Expenditure," in A. Stoekl (ed.), *Visions of Excess: Selected Writings 1927–1939*, trans. A. Stoekl, C. R. Lovitt, and D. M. Leslie, Jr., 116–29, Minneapolis: University of Minnesota Press.

Bataille, G. (1985b), "The Sacred," in A. Stoekl (ed.), *Visions of Excess: Selected Writings 1927–1939*, trans. A. Stoekl, C. R. Lovitt, and D. M. Leslie, Jr., 240–5, Minneapolis: University of Minnesota Press.

Bataille, G. (1985c), *Visions of Excess: Selected Writings 1927–1939*, ed. A. Stoekl, trans. A. Stoekl, C. R. Lovitt, and D. M. Leslie, Jr., Minneapolis: University of Minnesota Press.

Bataille, G. (1987), *Eroticism*, trans. M. Dalwood, San Francisco: City Lights Books.

Bataille, G. (1988), *Inner Experience*, trans. L. A. Boldt-Irons, Albany: State University of New York.

Bataille, G. (1989a), *Theory of Religion*, trans. R. Hurley, New York: Zone Books.

Bataille, G. (1989b), *The Accursed Share: An Essay On General Economy, Volume I—Consumption*, trans. R. Hurley, New York: Zone Books.

Bataille, G. (1989c), *The Tears of Eros*, trans. P. Connor, San Francisco: City Lights Books.

Bataille, G. (1991a), *The Accursed Share: Volumes II and III*, trans. R. Hurley, New York: Zone Books.

Bataille, G. (1991b), *The Impossible*, trans. R. Hurley, San Francisco: City Lights Books.

Bataille, G. (2001a), *The Story of the Eye*, trans. J. Neugroschel, London: Penguin.

Bataille, G. (2001b), *The Unfinished System of Nonknowledge*, trans. M. Kendal and S. Kendall, Minneapolis: University of Minnesota Press.

Bataille, G. (2008), *L'Archangélique et autres poèmes*, Paris: Gallimard.

Bataille, G. (2011), *Guilty*, trans. S. Kendall, Minneapolis: University of Minnesota Press.

Bataille, G. (2012a), *My Mother, Madame Edwarda, The Dead Man*, trans. A. Wainhouse, London: Penguin.

Bataille, G. (2012b), *L'Abbé C*, trans. P. A. Facey, London: Penguin.

Bataille, G. (2012c), *Blue of Noon*, trans. H. Mathews, London: Penguin.

Bataille, G. (2012d), *Literature and Evil*, trans. H. Hamilton, London: Penguin.

Bataille, G. (2016), *On Nietzsche*, trans. S. Kendall, Albany: State University of New York Press.

Bataille, G. (2018), "On the Ambiguity of Pleasure and Play," *Theory Culture & Society*, 35 (4/5): 233–50.

Bataille, G. (2023), *The Limit of the Useful*, trans. C. A. Knudson and C. Elliott, Cambridge, MA: MIT Press.

Baudrillard, J. (2016), *Symbolic Exchange and Death*, 2nd edn, trans. I. H. Grant, London: Sage.

Baudrillard, J. (2019), *For a Critique of the Political Economy of the Sign*, trans. C. Levin, London: Verso.

Durkheim, E. (2008), *The Elementary Forms of Religious Life*, trans. C. Cosman, Oxford: Oxford University Press.

Featherstone, M. (2016), "*Luxus*: A Thanatology of Luxury from Nero to Bataille," *Cultural Politics*, 12 (1): 66–82.

Hollier, D. (1990), *Against Architecture*, trans. B. Wing, Cambridge, MA: MIT Press.

Kendall, S. (2016), "Expenditure," in M. Hewson and M. Coelen (eds.), *Georges Bataille: Key Concepts*, 75–87, Abingdon: Routledge.

Mauss, M. (2002), *The Gift: The Form and Reason for Exchange in Archaic Societies*, Abingdon: Routledge.

McGoey, L. (2018), "Bataille and the Sociology of Abundance: Reassessing Gifts, Debt and Economic Excess," *Theory, Culture & Society*, 35 (4/5): 69–91.

Richman, M. (2021), "Palaeo or Neo? Bataille, Lévi-Strauss and the Rewriting of Prehistory," *Paragraph*, 44 (3): 280–95.

Sartre, J.-P. (2010), "A New Mystic," in J.-P. Sartre, *Critical Essays*, trans. C. Turner, 219–93, London: Seagull Books.

Sharr, A. (2016), "Libeskind in Las Vegas: Reflections on Architecture as a Luxury Commodity," in J. Armitage and J. Roberts (eds.), *Critical Luxury Studies: Art, Design, Media*, 151–76, Edinburgh: Edinburgh University Press.
Weber, M. (2002), *The Protestant Ethic and the "Spirit" of Capitalism and Other Writings*, trans. P. Baehr and G. C. Wells, London: Penguin.

7

Theodor W. Adorno: The Dual Character of Luxury

Biographical Details and Philosophical Context

Theodor Wiesengrund Adorno was born in Frankfurt am Main in Germany in 1903. A musician and composer at sixteen, at eighteen he was studying philosophy, music, and psychology at university, and publishing music criticism. Adorno's PhD on the phenomenology of Edmund Husserl (1859–1938), the Austrian-German philosopher and mathematician, appeared in 1924 before he moved to Vienna in 1925 to study composition. Returning to Frankfurt, Adorno withdrew his Habilitation dissertation on "The Concept of the Unconscious in the Transcendental Doctrine of the Soul," which manifested a Marxian influence that he retained throughout his career, and which focused on the relationship between the emergence and adoption of philosophical theories and cultural, economic, political, and social developments. Editing the musical journal *Anbruch* (*Dawn*) in the 1920s, Adorno encountered the Hungarian Marxist philosopher György Lukács's (1885–1971) *History and Class Consciousness: Studies in Marxist Dialectics* (1972) and befriended Walter Benjamin (1892–1940), the German Jewish philosopher and cultural critic, before completing his 1931 Habilitation on *Kierkegaard: Construction of the Aesthetic* (1989), which bears the traits of his mature work and the influence of Benjamin.

Adorno initially regarded the Nazis as a passing phenomenon, visiting Germany until 1937, while he was an "advanced student" at Merton College, Oxford. Moving to the United States in 1938, Adorno worked with the German philosopher and sociologist Max Horkheimer (1895–1973) as a member of the Institute for Social Research (ISR), living first in New York then Los Angeles between 1941 and 1949. Adorno wrote *Dialectic of Enlightenment* (1972) with Horkheimer, completed his *Minima Moralia: Reflections from Damaged Life* (1974) and *Philosophy of New Music* in 1949 (2006) on the work of Austrian-American composer Arnold Schoenberg (1874–1951) and Russian composer Igor Stravinsky (1882–1971), influencing the German novelist Thomas Mann's (1875–1955) 1947 novel *Doctor Faustus* (1996). Adorno was also a member of the group that wrote *The Authoritarian Personality* (1950) on antisemitism. Returning to Frankfurt in 1949, Adorno became a professor at the re-established ISR in 1956. In the 1960s, he was involved, along with his then academic assistant Jürgen Habermas (1929–), the German philosopher and social theorist, in *The Positivist Dispute in German Sociology* (1976) in which Adorno's opponents included the Austrian-British philosopher Karl Popper (1902–94). Throughout the 1960s, Adorno wrote his major works, *Negative Dialectics* (2007) and *Aesthetic Theory* (1997), and other, sometimes incomplete, projects. He died in Switzerland in 1969.

Such a biographical summary suggests the diversity of Adorno's work on aesthetics and cultural studies, musicology, psychology, sociology, and, as detailed below, luxury philosophy. His work is a critical approach to modernity, the historical period and cultural, political, and social norms, attitudes, and practices that arose following the seventeenth-century Renaissance and the eighteenth-century Enlightenment. However, locating Adorno in relation to contemporary luxury philosophy is difficult because his work derives from traditions of thought of which little is known in the English-speaking world. His early philosophy is, for example, concerned with German philosopher Immanuel Kant's (1724–1804) thought, seen through twentieth-century German neo-Kantianism, which sought to develop Kant's conception of moral philosophy. The question in that philosophy is how to establish a basis for claims to truth about the natural and social world, given Kant's claim that people can no longer assume that the world has a "ready-made" structure which exists independently of how it is apprehended. Like Martin Heidegger (1889–1976), the German philosopher known for his contributions to phenomenology, hermeneutics, and existentialism, the Adorno of the 1920s believed that a philosophy of timeless principles was no longer viable in modernity. This means that philosophy and sociology move into a new relationship wherein the division between the question of the social history of philosophical thought and its truth content can no longer be sustained. Adorno also rejected the Hungarian Karl Mannheim's (1893–1947) relativistic sociology of knowledge. By the 1930s, then, Adorno was convinced that a farewell to philosophical principles that transcend those in other disciplines should result in the abolition of philosophy as a foundational discipline, and in a relocation of philosophy in relation to, among other topics, luxury philosophy.

This leaves open the role of luxury philosophy. Throughout his career Adorno negotiated between Hegel- and Marx-influenced contextualization and historicization of luxury and other philosophies, and ideas about language and philosophy informed by the Jewish mysticism and pre-Marxist work of Benjamin. Adorno addresses the repressive nature of totalizing forms of thinking that often plays a different role in the philosophy of, for example, Jürgen Habermas and Michel Foucault, Jacques Derrida, and Jean-François Lyotard. Adorno's philosophical reflections thus offer a critical awareness of the specificity of modern cultural, political, and social life while refusing to abandon the notion of rationality, even as it analyzes the destructive effects of aspects of "Enlightenment" thinking on modern culture, politics, and society. Adorno is close at times to the pragmatism derived from John Dewey (1859–1952), the American philosopher who considered words and thought as tools and instruments for prediction, problem-solving, and action, thus rejecting the idea that the function of thought is to describe, represent, or mirror reality. For Adorno, truth is not about reality or grounding knowledge but about giving a philosophical voice to suffering, to the avoidance of pain, and to post-theological hope.

Luxury Philosophy and Contributions

Adorno's Attack on Veblen

In relation to luxury philosophy, Adorno's work can be approached as part of the critical tradition concerning, in this instance, the relationship between the American economist and sociologist Thorstein Veblen's (1857–1929) explanation and critique of luxury in his 1899 book *The Theory of the Leisure Class* (2007) and Adorno's understanding of luxury and luxury culture which he develops in his "Veblen's Attack on Culture" in *Prisms* (Adorno 1981) via the work of Sigmund Freud, Walter Benjamin, and Karl Marx. Adorno elaborates ways of thinking about luxury that distinguish it from meaningless ostentatious display and yet also takes account of the fact that such display takes place within sociohistorical contexts which often render luxury as a "singular instant" (Armitage 2021) of emancipation from the realm of utility and thus a phenomenological experience of luxury. Adorno questions the idea that "the enslavement to utility" (1981: 80) is appropriate to luxury philosophy, highlighting the resistance of autonomous subjects—products of the conjunction of history and the unconscious—to utility in terms of their desire to escape it. The main conceptual resources for his ideas concerning the phenomenon of luxury are, like those of many critical luxury philosophers, drawn from the work of Marx, Freud, and Benjamin, but Adorno understands these resources in the light of the aesthetic, which relies on anthropology and on autonomous subjects, particularly those who recognize that what is present in luxury is the possibility of a refusal to be co-opted by a functional culture, political system, and society.

The essential conviction of autonomous subjects is, as it is for Adorno, that the project of grounding a philosophical system which could undermine instrumental rationality, the diktat of means, and usefulness is doomed to failure. Adorno is led by this conviction to a concern with luxury, and to the idea, which becomes central to Adorno's thought, that luxury may in some respects tell people more about the nature of modern existence than philosophy. For autonomous subjects, this is because luxury's resistance to definitive interpretation reminds them of the inherently temporal nature of their capacity to grasp the world, and they are led by such ideas, as Adorno was, to a new evaluation of the significance of the view that a successful life is achieved not solely in pursuit of what is pleasant, practical, and purposeful. Luxury is also significant for Adorno because it is often irreducibly particular (e.g., a luxurious work of art, such as Gustav Klimt's *The Kiss* from 1907–8) and cannot be reduced to general explanatory concepts, though it may, for that very reason, give access to insights into cultures, political systems, and societies dominated by instrumental and utilitarian thinking not available to approaches based on general conceptions of knowledge of the necessary and the unnecessary. Adorno developed the implications of such critical ideas about luxury throughout his essay on Veblen.

Adorno does not offer a luxury philosophy in the sense that his nemesis Veblen does in his 1899 *The Theory of the Leisure Class* (2007), which attempts to map out a methodological framework for understanding how the refusal of instrumental rationality by means of luxury comes to be in modern cultures, political systems, and societies. Adorno's relation to luxury philosophy is more indirect and must be established in relation to works as diverse as, for instance, his study of *The Authoritarian Personality* (Adorno et al. 1950), his critique of positivism in Veblen's sociology (1981: 77, 88) and more generally (Adorno 1976), or his more immediately philosophical works, like *Minima Moralia: Reflections from Damaged Life* (1974) and *Aesthetic Theory* (1997). Adorno's work on achieving a successful life, for example, his critique of Veblen's understanding of culture as meaningless ostentatious display wherein there is no difference between luxury and ostentation, is an attempt to show how Veblen's theory of "the leisure class" (an "institution" that, according to Veblen, "is found in its best development at the higher stages of the barbarian culture" [2007: 7]) and its world deprives all but the most radical achievements and successes in life—that of autonomous subjects, whose abandonment of the conventions of instrumentalism make them resistant to immediate rationality—of their ability to bring about a critical stance toward existing luxurious reality. On the other hand, although his philosophical work on Veblen retains a Marx-oriented concern with the historical location of Veblen's anthropological convictions (Adorno 1981: 75, 83, 85, 89–90), Adorno also relies upon Marx's materialist inspired idea that luxury in the modern world should be despised because, according to a Marxian perspective on luxury (see Chapter 4), people do not willingly do something consciously irrational, wasteful, and superfluous (1981: 77–8). Despite the differences between the approaches of Veblen and Marx, with Veblen introducing a non-Marxian psychologism, for example (Adorno 1981: 77), they both involve a conceptual structure that takes us to the heart of Adorno's luxury philosophy.

In his work on Veblen, Adorno often refers to what might be called "utilitarian instrumentalism" as the target of his philosophical critique. By utilitarian instrumentalism I mean that, for Adorno (1981: 76), Veblen's broadly conceived Darwinian tradition of American pragmatism that gives primacy to the life of people in society as a struggle for existence or as a process of selective "adaptation" (one of Veblen's favorite concepts according to Adorno [1981: 76]) before deliberate wastefulness, and Veblen's tradition of utilitarian instrumentalism that emerged as a response to "unnecessary" leisure and culminates in what Veblen characterizes as a sort of irrationality. Adorno's objection to utilitarian instrumentalism stems from his belief that systematic philosophical thinking about luxury obscures the irreducible particularity of people being wasteful with themselves and their things. The crucial link which Adorno (1981: 78, 82, 85, 87) makes is between the principle of much modern systematic, rational, and utilitarian thinking about luxury and Marx's analysis of the luxury commodity forms' fetish character and subordination of use-value to exchange-value. In Adorno's German philosophical tradition, the conceptual basis of this link develops as a consequence of his rediscovery through Veblen of the critique of luxury, which influenced Adorno's thought on what Veblen considered the merely purposeless, the wasteful, the leisurely, the demonstration of people's own capacity to spend or because their business situation expects it of them.

Adorno's critique of luxury is not a systematic principle concerning Veblen's account of ostentation, yet it does entail that he challenge individual elements of Veblen's system involving the unnecessary, experience, and "conspicuous consumption," Veblen's (2007: 49–69) term for the consumer practice of buying and using goods of a higher quality, price, or in greater quantity than practical. Nevertheless, for Adorno, one of the main aims is to challenge Veblen's identification of luxury as a simple utilitarian instrumental status symbol or "evidence of wealth" (a term used no less than ten times in Veblen's *The Theory of the Leisure Class*) through the relations it has to other things such as transgression. Adorno's unsystematic principle is thus employed by him in his assertion that, contrary to Veblen, luxury is more than conspicuous consumption, leisure, and waste (Adorno 1981: 86). Adorno's critique of Veblen's account of luxury as mere ostentation and his unsystematic principle is an argument that leads to what might be termed Veblen's denial of luxury, because the existence of luxury has no value or significance in itself for him, its significance depending not on a critique of luxury but, rather, on chains of relations to other, "superfluous," "wasteful," things with a "necessary" connection to the "reality" that "the consumption of excellent goods is an evidence of wealth" made for this purpose (Veblen 2007: 53). Analogously, in Marx's theory of the luxury commodity, the value of a luxury object in capitalism is not its intrinsic use-value in terms of utility, efficiency, or rationality, but rather its exchange-value, which, in being determined by its relation to other exchange-values, might well involve voluntary expenditure on "pointless" waste (see Chapters 4 and 6).

Adorno regards Marx's claims about the nature of capitalism as the key to understanding the historical significance of Veblen's attack on culture and systematic utilitarian instrumentalism, which is for him perhaps the central expression of the essential nature of the modern denial of the existence of luxury. It is, though, at the same time important to remember that Adorno's criticisms of Veblen are directed against the latter's systematic attempt to present the whole of culture as sham and lies. According to Adorno, Veblen's system is based on the thesis that "Culture turns against utility for the sake of a mediated utility," which, for Adorno, implies that culture is "marked by the life-lie" (1981: 76). This, as stated by Adorno, leads Veblen to effectively deny people the possibility of even thinking that they might be capable of resisting the utilitarian rationality of an increasingly administered world. For Veblen, the awareness of the banalities of everyday life leads to the denial of luxury: not surprisingly, such an awareness ultimately leads to absolute rejection of the delusions of luxury, in which submission to the systematic pressure for self-preservation is articulated as nothing less than an aspirational cultural, political, and social philosophy. In the light of Veblen's modern denial of the existence of luxury, which functions for Adorno in terms of the promotion of irrational fears and malicious assumptions, and of Veblen's perhaps inadvertent account in *The Theory of the Leisure Class* of how capitalism creates a negativity that obscures the qualitative features of the world of luxury via the abstract representation of material things under the guiding principle of exchange-value (2007: 147), Adorno connects the systematic aspect of Veblen with actual negative processes which occur in the spread of the luxury commodity form across the globe through "cultural efficiency" experts such as Veblen (1981: 84). Rather than deny people the possibility of even thinking that they might be capable of resisting the utilitarian rationality of an administered world, Adorno argues that these negative processes actually obscure the underlying truth about modern cultures, political systems, and societies, rendering Veblen's judgments about "unnecessary" wasteful ornamentation inappropriate, whence Adorno's critique of Veblen in "Veblen's Attack on Culture" in 1967 when the essay was first published: "In Veblen's eyes … ornamentation becomes menacing" (1981: 79). However, this leaves Adorno with an initially paradoxical critical position, in which he renounces Veblen's negative claims and yet relies as the basis of his renunciation upon a negative characterization of luxury that results from the dominance of the commodity principle. This problematic dialectic between a kind of Marxian negativity and the critique of that same Marxian negativity recurs throughout Adorno's work on Veblen.

Adorno is concerned with how it is possible to articulate the truth about luxury in modern cultures, political systems, and societies. Must luxury philosophy renounce all claims to grasp the negativity of the processes that determine phenomena such as the threat to the existence of autonomous subjects? This concern is the source of Adorno's infuriation with Veblen's theory of the leisure class. Veblen claims that modern cultures, political systems, and societies are not and should not be characterized by the possibility of transgression, resistance, or dreams of emancipation but by the realm of utility, which he interprets through the role of culture in modern political systems and societies, where, according to Adorno, culture becomes for Veblen "the meaningless ostentatious display of the bankrupt" (1981: 83). In his work on luxury, Veblen suggests how the conception of culture can apply to ideas like those of a Darwinian struggle for existence, thereby revealing the reasons for Adorno's link between Veblen's conception of the leisure class, luxury, the beautiful, and ostentation. Indeed, for Adorno, Veblen's "discussion of beauty is very abstract because there is nothing beautiful in which the imminent movement of injustice can be eliminated. To be consistent, Veblen would have to advocate the abolition of art" (1981: 86). Veblen, however, has no interest in, let alone a response to, the negative luxury philosophy promoted by people like Adorno concerning the subject's capacity to resist being taken in by a functionalized society. Rather, Veblen proposes the idea of the leisure class as a class that does not think to resist the dictates of instrumental reason through luxury or by other means, inclusive of education and art. Adorno, unlike Veblen, thinks of the significance of the leisure class and luxury not as some kind of cultural, political, and social pretense but as radically meaningful, as an existential and conscious transgression against expectations to be reasonable in the modern era; he rejects Veblen's position, which he critically characterizes as utilitarian instrumentalism in his "Veblen's Attack on Culture."

Adorno's work is devoted to the idea of a conception other than that of the leisure class, which would be adequate to the situation where there no longer seems to be a way of definitively avoiding the rejection of a utilitarian orientation toward use. Adorno's key ideas about culture and about the importance of luxury for understanding modernity derive from his interpretation of this situation. Adorno claims, for example, that within and without the leisure class, luxury in modernity "has escaped the principle of unvarnished necessity" and has moved toward becoming "humane" (1981: 75), the absolute unity of luxury and culture, which is for him life in its immediacy to all those experiences of a human subject in a function-dominated world. Ideas like this about moving beyond Veblen's conception of the leisure class are also the source of Adorno's notion of luxury always having something human about it, in which a unique human life always has something luxurious that is beyond the realms of utility, efficiency, and purposefulness. Adorno articulates the particular issue that there is a structural affinity between the quality of a human life and the quality of luxury while claiming, in effect, to find a philosophical position that runs counter to that of Veblen, something Adorno also sees in terms of creating models of thought about luxury and human life which are adequate to the specificity of their object: the refusal of the human subject to be reduced to an existence that is no more than an efficient means to an end. The notions of luxury always having something human about it and of models of thought about luxury can be used to explain—if not always to justify—the often dense, exploratory nature of Adorno's own writing on luxury and human life, which prevents his discussions of the domination of instrumental reason, the good life, and utilitarianism being easily condensed to a series of essential precepts in his critique of Veblen.

The Dual Character of Luxury

Adorno employs notions of the kind outlined in a framework that associates the critical intent of his thinking about life and luxury with the idea of a more humane world as the means of breaking the culturally, politically, and socially destructive dominance of "the enslavement to utility" (1981: 80). However, in light of the "yearning to escape" the enslavement to utility delineated in "Veblen's Attack on Culture" (Adorno 1981: 80), Adorno believes in the possibility of radical cultural, political, and social transformation by means of such yearning among human beings. This means that Adorno becomes ever more critical of Veblen's characterization of luxury as mere ostentation under the repressive manifestations of modern capitalism. Certainly, Adorno's essential conception that the longing to escape the slavery of goals through luxury is the contemporary subject's reply to a world dominated by utility never changes. The ideas described above concerning luxury remain constant in Adorno's work on Veblen. But, throughout "Veblen's Attack on Culture," Adorno focuses more and more on what makes luxury a utopian power in modern cultures, political systems, and societies; a singular power often capable of generating resistance to expectations of submission and thereby revealing what he calls the "dual character" of luxury (Adorno 1981: 86), which permits human beings a singular experience because it is never wholly an instrument of efficiency, exchange, and profit.

One of the most important manifestations of Adorno's questioning of the modern ends–means–rationality of utility is his unswerving support for subjects with an oppositional attitude who, through luxury, long for the liberation of culture, politics, and society. Moreover, and although Adorno's "Veblen's Attack on Culture" was written in 1967, it is only recently, some fifty years later, it has begun to have a considerable influence on luxury philosophy, especially concerning the way Adorno characterizes luxury as a means of emancipation for those subjects who defend themselves against integration into a functionalized society and seek the emergence of autonomous and emancipated human beings. The cynical tone of Veblen's way of looking at luxury in *The Theory of the Leisure Class* is infuriating to Adorno, given Veblen's insistence that luxury is merely the product of hidden, repressed, and authentic interests in status. Indeed, the degree of unconcern Veblen evinces regarding modern forms of rationalized subjectivity and the possibility of their autonomy is remarkable. For Adorno, subjects with an oppositional attitude must rely on conceptions of luxury that separate themselves from Veblen's conception of ostentation. And this last is the source of Adorno's appeal to those people longing for the liberation of culture, politics, and society. For his modern luxury philosophy offers what might be called a singular instance of vision concerning people's experience of luxury and an insight into their own cultural, political, and social situations. This is because Adorno presents Veblen's description of luxury as only concentrating on one side of its "dual character": "that part of the social product which does not benefit human needs and contribute to human happiness but is instead squandered ... to preserve an obsolete system" (1981: 86). However, rationalized subjectivity and luxury in modernity are not described by Adorno as the triumph of instrumental reason over subjectivity or as systematic forms that crush subjectivity with the aim of dehumanizing it in the name of pervasive utilitarian rationality. Rather, Adorno regards the "other side" of luxury's dual character as "the use of parts of the social product which serve not the reproduction of expended labor, directly or indirectly, but of man in so far as he is not entirely under the sway of the utility principle" (1981: 86). The basis of Adorno's argument is a conception of luxurious subjectivity derived from luxury's unique way of opposing instrumental rationality, which he connects to the fact that luxury does not intend to be culturally, politically, or socially destructive let alone revolutionary. What happens with the concept of luxury in modern capitalism is already perceptible in the history of luxurious subjectivities who do not fight against the utilitarian world directly. In this history the luxurious identity of the subject is established through the possibility of withdrawing from the utilitarian world, not in the name of ending but in the name of escaping, if only for a singular instant, the slavery of goals required for self-preservation under the regime of utilitarian instrumentalism. Does this history obviate the point of existing as an individual luxurious subject with a luxurious lifestyle, because of the violence done by utilitarian instrumentalism to the luxurious subject? The processes of the history of luxurious identity are seen by Adorno as the source of the impulse of all those subjects who do not want to be absorbed into or defined by modern capitalism's utilitarian instrumentalist system, which suppose that luxury means freeing, emancipating, and releasing oneself from coercion rather than destroying utilitarian instrumentalism. The only way beyond such a situation for Adorno involves an appeal to the idea of the subjective experience of luxury. How this could take place is not left open: Adorno suggests that whereas luxury opposes society, it is nevertheless unable to assume a position beyond it; it achieves opposition only through identification with that against which it remonstrates.

Perhaps one of the most influential aspects of Adorno's support for subjects with an oppositional attitude is his critique of Veblen's attempt to dissolve the singular instance of luxury, in which conspicuous consumption, like the "fullness of life of the consumer" (Veblen 2007: 82) is seen as the basis of his philosophy, which, for Veblen, is in some measure the expression of human happiness, or at least a schematic effort to isolate the nature of contemporary luxury. This effort is epitomized for Adorno by Veblen's inability or unwillingness to recognize that happiness comprises the inherently mediated identity of luxury, which accords with happiness existing only when people have singularly and instantaneously eluded the process of a pernicious socialization—an argument that is relevant to the fact that the concrete form of people's happiness always contains in itself the general condition of society. Although Adorno's aim in supporting subjects with an oppositional attitude is to provide resources for establishing models of luxury that avoid the results of the dialectic of utilitarian instrumentalism, it is not clear whether the philosophical model he employs can lead to anything but the consequence that utilitarian instrumentalism is inherently based on a repressive or at best contradictory version of happiness that is determined for people by society, rather than also being potentially culturally, politically, and socially enabling and liberating. Adorno's approach in his work to the dilemmas evident in his support for subjects with an oppositional attitude are decisive in assessing his contribution to luxury philosophy.

Appraisal of Key Advances in Luxury Philosophy and Controversies

Adorno's support for subjects with an oppositional attitude is extremely critical of modern ends–means rationality, and its history of utilitarian instrumentalism. Yet the story described in the previous section is somewhat at odds with Adorno's desire elsewhere to avoid the procrustean effects of the abstractions of terms such as "luxury culture" or the "liberation" of politics and society. One of the central—thoroughly rational—claims of Adorno's "Veblen's Attack on Culture" is that his luxury philosophy opens up the concept of luxury without neglecting it as a means of emancipation for those subjects who defend themselves against integration into a functionalized society and who seek the emergence of autonomous and emancipated human beings (Adorno 1981: 86). But is the concept of luxury employed in Adorno's discussions of support for subjects with an oppositional attitude too crudely imposed on its subject matter? Adorno's support for subjects with an oppositional attitude also points to another potential weakness in Adorno's work on Veblen: it bases its account of the history of subjects with an oppositional attitude on an interpretation of luxury through *The Theory of the Leisure Class* but relies on the idea that luxury is a singular instance of emancipation to confirm that luxury can indeed be interpreted in this manner. In Adorno's contribution on Veblen, his work on luxury, his demystification of Veblen's idea that luxury is merely the product of hidden, repressed, and authentic interests in status, and his study of modern forms of rationalized subjectivity, Adorno develops means for adequately analyzing luxury as a singular instance of emancipation, a moment of vision, using resources from his own luxury philosophy. However, Adorno's aim is marked by tensions concerning his philosophical claims about luxury, and in his work on Veblen he sometimes regards luxury as a singular instance of emancipation as inherently unquestionable.

The problem faced by Adorno regarding luxury as a singular instance of emancipation is evident in the analysis of subjects with an oppositional attitude. If the would-be autonomous consciousness of people is actually constituted by Veblen's ostentation-determined forms of luxury, the task of the luxury philosopher is to reveal the damaging implications of such a conception of luxury. Adorno claims that this is best accomplished on behalf of those people longing for the liberation of culture, politics, and society by analyzing the production and nature of ostentatious luxury, such as the factors determining modern luxury, and the structure and the content of that modern luxury. In "Veblen's Attack on Culture" Adorno therefore argues that people's experience of luxury gives them an insight into their own cultural, political, and social situations: recall that Adorno presents Veblen's descriptions of luxury as only concentrating on one side of its dual character (Adorno 1981: 86). But just how debatable Adorno's endorsement of luxury as a singular instance of emancipation is becomes apparent if one considers Adorno's reflections not as a failure concerning the social product and human needs, happiness, and luxury, but, rather, as a failure to understand, or at least to explain, the sheer complexity of a singular instance of insight that, through squander, breaks through the fallen temporality of the everydayness of an obsolete system and that confronts people not with the prospect of emancipation but with their own, perhaps rationalized instead of authentic, and historical subjective temporality. Of course, it is an open question, which can only be answered within a singular instance of vision, whether, to what extent, in what dimensions, the cultural, political, and social implications revealed in modern luxury are also grasped by subjects. The paradigmatic divergence of these approaches results from tensions in Adorno's conception of the role of instrumental reason in luxury philosophy and his related reflections on the question of subjectivity.

Adorno's embrace of the singular instance of luxury as a form of emancipation, for example the resistance of subjects to the systems crushing their subjectivity, can be justified as far as the emancipation is a sort of investigation into what aspects of subjectivity are being dehumanized. Such an investigation requires detailed analysis of the relationship between utilitarian rationality and the cultural, political, and social forms of the kind that can be found discussed in Adorno's "Veblen's Attack on Culture." This sort of emancipation is necessarily resistant to Veblen's approach centered on that part of the social product which does not benefit human needs, because its object cannot be specified as, for example, human happiness: it is only when human happiness is located in what Adorno's *Negative Dialectics* calls a "constellation" that "illuminates the specific side of the object" (2007: 162), a constellation of contexts and practices, that it can give rise to insights into the cultural, political, and social roles of luxury. The "other side" of luxury involved in emancipation like this has proved to be a vital aspect of luxury's dual character in the use of parts of the social product that serve people as far as they are not entirely under the sway of the utility principle. However, Adorno also adheres to the problematic conception of luxurious subjectivity being derived from luxury's unique way of opposing instrumental rationality encountered above, which regards modern luxury as dominated and constituted not by revolutionary cultural, political, and social forms of luxurious identity but by conventional cultural, political, and social forms of luxurious identity produced by the exchange principle.

During the dispute with Veblen concerning the concept of luxury in modern capitalism, Adorno claims that the abstractness of the exchange-value of luxury commodities is connected *a priori* with the domination of the general luxury commodity over the particular luxury commodity (e.g., the domination of general luxury-branded commodities such as those produced by Louis Vuitton over specialized artisanal luxury commodities; 1981: 78, 80, 82, 85, 86, 87, 92). This domination includes any sort of luxurious identification with historically developed luxurious subjectivities, which subsume particular luxurious subjectivities under a general term, as well as emancipatory claims about the singular instance of luxury as an indirect fight against the utilitarian world. There is, though, an ambiguity in Adorno's conception of historically cultivated luxurious identities. The idea that there is a source of repressive luxurious identity common to the sphere of luxury or any other commodity exchange, and to conceptual thinking about luxury, relies on two different senses of luxurious identity, which Adorno conflates in "Veblen's Attack on Culture." The identification of, for example, a luxury commodity with all other luxury commodities, as an exchange-value, independent of its use-value, does involve the danger of devaluing the particular luxury commodity: this is why some subjects establish their luxurious identity through a withdrawal from this essentially utilitarian world of mass-produced luxury commodities in the name of escaping, if only for a singular instant, the slavery of exchange-value driven goals required for self-preservation under the regime of utilitarian instrumentalism. However, commodities in the cultural, political, and social worlds, including those bought as luxury commodities, can also be identified as a whole number of luxurious commodities, which may be particular to individual luxurious subjects, and which can only be assessed in particular terms in particular contexts. If the two senses of luxurious identity are indeed different, then the inherent link of the luxury (or any other) commodity structure to luxurious and all other forms of identity and their possibly damaging consequences cannot be upheld, and the totalizing aspects of Adorno's conception of luxury are unpersuasive. This does not mean, though, that the second sense of luxurious identity (which includes the aim of doing justice to luxury and other commodities that is one of Adorno's goals), cannot be used for critical purposes, for instance when the particular way a specific luxurious commodity is identified precludes the critique of utilitarian instrumentalism and thus the realization of its possibilities for luxurious subjects.

Is Adorno's suggestion in the dispute with Veblen that luxury involves a necessary link between identifying utilitarian instrumentalism and those subjects who do not want to be absorbed into or defined by modern capitalism's utilitarian instrumentalist system implausible? Or is Adorno's dispute with Veblen over luxury based on a series of misunderstandings and misinterpretations by Adorno? One of Adorno's targets (e.g., 1981: 76) is Veblen's apparent support for the enforced adaption of individuals to their environment, but Veblen (2007: 44) is, for example, equally concerned to attack what he sees as wives being forced to function as servants in households with a male head. Perhaps, then, Adorno's linking of the identification of utilitarian instrumentalism and those subjects who do not want to be absorbed into or defined by modern capitalism's utilitarian instrumentalist system could only be sustained if utilitarian instrumentalism were, as he seems to suggest (1981: 86, 92), itself subjected to the logic of identity inherent in the commodity structure of luxury and elsewhere, which produces the consciousness of the people in that culture, political system, and society, and therefore precluded the adoption of a critical philosophical perspective on luxury? However, this situation would render the position of the luxury philosopher who makes such claims about the effects of the commodification of luxury itself problematic, because of their lack of a location from which to judge those effects without also being subject to them.

Valid as they may be, criticisms of this kind can unfairly obscure the fact that Adorno's primary aim in "Veblen's Attack on Culture" is not methodological or conceptual but political. Adorno wishes to make what he sees as the violence forced upon subjects by utilitarian instrumentalism into a focus of reflection on human thought and politics concerning luxury. This is the violence that entails luxurious identities never experiencing political freedom, political emancipation, or even cultural or social releasement, an aim echoed in Adorno's demand to make the lessons of the subjective experience of luxury one of the foci of philosophies of modernity. Looked at in this perspective the subjective experience of luxury in culture, politics, and society does seem, despite the problem of how this is to be established, to be connected to the processes Adorno associates with "identity thinking" or the tendency of reason to objectify what it seeks to describe (1981: 86, 92). Adorno claims that the subjective experience of luxury, which opposes society, nevertheless confirms the philosopheme of pure identity as it is unable to assume a position beyond society, thus achieving a kind of rational opposition only through descriptive identification with that against which it remonstrates (1981: 90). Yet the fact that subjects with an oppositional attitude are developed in a modern consumer society with cultural and political traditions regarded by Adorno as second to none is a further reason to take his luxury philosophy seriously. Even if one rejects Adorno's assertion that the singular instance of luxury has irrefutably proved the possibility of a full life beyond conspicuous consumption, the challenge it poses to Veblen's consumer philosophy and to any other philosophy concerned with human happiness cannot be ignored. The decisive question is whether Adorno's model linking the structures of reason to the dominance of the exchange principle and the concomitant domination of people is adequate for interpreting the nature of modern luxury. Is luxury one of the keys to the essential character not only of happiness but also of modern political systems and societies that is merely disguised by the increasingly mediated forms of modern cultural identity?

The most sustained attempt to move beyond this view has been the work of Lambert Wiesing, who, eschewing the question of reason, writes that Adorno's

"Veblen's Attack on Culture" shaped the phenomenological description found in his *A Philosophy of Luxury* (Wiesing 2019: 5–6), which distinguishes luxury from meaningless ostentatious display. This shaping, which in Wiesing's interpretation of modern thought about luxury and its application in modern culture, politics, and society, gives rise to a special moment of emancipation from the realm of utility; and it relies, Wiesing maintains, upon a questioning founding conception of the phenomenology of luxury as an aesthetic experience of possession, which leads to the equation of the philosophical experience of luxury with the philosophical experience of art. Wiesing seeks to highlight the centrality of the notion of aesthetics, which underlies Adorno's conception of the autonomous individual subject who aims to defy, if not wholly escape, the slavery of utility. This change of orientation in the phenomenon of luxury does not preclude the political because the subject with a mind of their own can always refuse to conform to cultural expectations of restraint and reject co-option by a functional society through the presence of luxury. It is therefore possible to see that advances in, for example, the "rational" cultivation of education need not be shaped to "advances" in purposeful utilitarian instrumental rationality, as educational and political developments in democratic cultures, political systems, and societies can suggest. Wiesing associates his view of luxury with the growing subjective need for freedom from the diktat of means and usefulness, in which a successful life is achieved not in pursuit of what is pleasant, practical, and purposeful, but in pursuit of noninstrumental, nonutilitarian, and nonidentity thinking, of the kind of education that only the subjective aesthetic experience of luxury can provide (Wiesing 2018).

Wiesing's alternative has itself been criticized for its failure to acknowledge those conceptions of luxurious subjectivity in the anthropological tradition of Marcel Mauss and Georges Bataille which do not see it as being reducible to economic transgression or to philosophy (see Featherstone 2018). Adorno's own claims regarding luxurious subjectivity, in *Minima Moralia* (e.g., 1974: 119), that the individual luxurious subject is perhaps the only remaining locus of emancipatory possibilities in advanced capitalist cultures, political systems, and societies, therefore suggest an ambiguity in his work on luxury. On the one hand, Adorno insists on the pressure of the pernicious socialization and consciousness-forming objective general conditions that led, for example, to German fascism, which itself has a yet to be fully explored sociohistorical connection with luxury and luxury brands such as Hugo Boss (which produced Nazi uniforms) during the Third Reich (d'Almeida 2008); on the other, he can also suggest, within the context of advanced capitalism, that an oppositional attitude on the part of the luxurious subject provides resources for a reinforcement of its own self-awareness and self-confidence and thus also of its own luxurious selfhood. Adorno's work on the dynamic between the pressures exerted by modern cultures, political systems, and societies on their luxurious and other members and the philosophical response to those pressures suffers, then, from an unnecessarily metaphysical conception of the effects of the utilitarian instrumentalism which underlies the commodity principle. A conception of modern luxurious subjectivity that retains even a diminished role for the luxurious subject's autonomous individuality can, while still taking account of the effects of the pressures for conformity to utilitarian instrumentalism in modern cultures, make Adorno's work on luxury a more useful resource for luxury philosophy. Such a conception allows people to draw on the insights offered by the best of Adorno's explorations of modern political repression, notions of social happiness, and his criticisms of the deterministic, disabling, and anti-liberatory economic, political, and sociological traditions represented by, among many others, Thorstein Veblen, without falling prey to his exaggerations.

References

Adorno, T. W. (1974), *Minima Moralia: Reflections from Damaged Life*, trans. E. F. N. Jephcott, London: New Left Books.

Adorno, T. W. (1976), *The Positivist Dispute in German Sociology*, trans. G. Adey and D. Frisby, London: Heinemann.

Adorno, T. W. (1981), "Veblen's Attack on Culture," in S. Weber and S. Weber (trans. and eds.), *Prisms*, 73–94, Cambridge: MA: MIT Press.

Adorno, T. W. (1989), *Kierkegaard: Construction of the Aesthetic*, trans. R. Hullot-Kentor, Minneapolis: Minnesota University Press.

Adorno, T. W. (1997), *Aesthetic Theory*, trans. R. Hullot-Kentor, London: Athlone.

Adorno, T. W. (2006), *Philosophy of New Music*, trans. R. Hullot-Kentor, Minneapolis: University of Minnesota Press.

Adorno, T. W. (2007), *Negative Dialectics*, trans. E. B. Ashton, London: Continuum.

Adorno, T. W. and M. Horkheimer (1972), *Dialectic of Enlightenment*, trans. J. Cumming, New York: Seabury.

Adorno, T. W., et al. (1950), *The Authoritarian Personality*, New York: Harper.

Armitage, J. (2021), "Critical Theory and the Singular Instant of Luxury: On Contemporary Conceptions of Luxury Customer Experience," in P.-Y. Donzé, V. Pouillard, and J. Roberts (eds.), *The Oxford Handbook of Luxury Business*, 41–58, New York: Oxford University Press.

d'Almeida, F. (2008), *High Society in the Third Reich*, trans. S. Randall, Cambridge: Polity.

Featherstone, M. (2018), "The Utopianism of Luxury [book review of Wiesing, *A Philosophy of Luxury*]," *Cultural Politics*, 16 (2): 270–3.

Lukács, G. (1972), *History and Class Consciousness: Studies in Marxist Dialectics*, trans. R. Livingstone, London: Merlin Press.

Mann, T. (1996), *Doctor Faustus*, London: Vintage.

Veblen, T. (2007), *The Theory of the Leisure Class*, Oxford: Oxford University Press.

Wiesing, L. (2018), "Toward a Phenomenology of Luxury," *Cultural Politics*, 14 (1): 78–89.

Wiesing, L. (2019), *A Philosophy of Luxury*, trans. N. A. Roth, Abingdon: Routledge.

8

Roland Barthes: Luxury Mythology

Biographical Details and Philosophical Context

Roland Gérard Barthes (1915–80) was essential in positioning literary and cultural criticism upon a self-styled-scientific basis known as structuralism and, later, as poststructuralism. In *Writing Degree Zero* (2001), *Mythologies* (1993), *Elements of Semiology* (1984), and *The Fashion System* (1983a), Barthes formulated the principles of semiology, the science of signs, a structuralist methodology which implied the clarification of culture and communication.

Barthes was no academic system builder, preferring the practice of writing and teaching. His academic career was atypical given that his first publications appeared as monthly newspaper columns in *Les lettres nouvelles*, sooner than in academic journals and books. These short essays addressed topics that did not feature in the academia of the time, such as washing powder advertisements and novels, striptease and plastic. They formed the foundation for Barthes's 1957 book, *Mythologies* (1993), to which he inserted a philosophical essay, "Myth Today," thus giving it academic credibility, brimming with references. However, the book was written in a terse, neat, and unacademic writing style that contributed to its success with a broad audience seeking new critical pathways in the investigation of society and culture.

Nonconforming in dedicating himself to semiology when the topic went unrecognized in academia, Barthes also played no part in the linguistics of the 1950s which was dominated by functionalist models of language wherein problems of the signification and play of meaning in ordinary communication were subordinate to the causal relations between components in the language system. Nevertheless, this did not stop the functionalist Raymond Picard (1969) delivering an assault on Barthes's arguments and what Picard called the "New Criticism," accusing both of unimportance and recklessness (Allen 2003: 53–6).

Within sociology, the topic of popular culture was absent when Barthes was writing about myth and consumer culture. With hindsight, he has been recognized as one of the first post–Second World War philosophers to take popular culture earnestly and his *Mythologies* recognized as an originating text of cultural studies. Yet, in the 1950s, cultural studies did not exist, and academic sociology consequently ignored Barthes's examinations.

Elected to a position at the elite Collège de France in 1976 without a PhD, at the encouragement of Michel Foucault (1926–84), the French philosopher, historian of ideas, writer, political activist, and literary critic, Barthes's unconventional occupational path eventually led to a chair of literary semiology. A shy and reserved man who craved privacy and well-ordered routines, Barthes nevertheless went on to deliver many lectures and seminars at the Collège de France (e.g., Barthes 2011).

Barthes was born in Cherbourg, France, in 1915, one year before his father was killed in a First World War naval battle, leaving his mother to rear him and his younger half-brother in destitution. Contracting pulmonary tuberculosis at nineteen, Barthes spent the next twelve years physically incapacitated, in and out of miserable and insulating sanatoria, experiences that made him alert, thoughtful, and a critical interpreter of the codes and sign systems of the human world. Distrustful of the apparent transparency of cultural, political, and social life, Barthes was infatuated with the hidden meanings beneath surface appearances, with the syntax of power in human relations, and the "naturalization" of reality through the falsification of representation and meaning.

While Barthes held school-teaching appointments throughout these years, his physical condition was too uncertain to endure a conventional career. In convalescence in Paris in 1946–7, Barthes envisaged writing two books: first, an interpretation of the work of the historian Jules Michelet (1798–1874; Barthes 1987a), and, second, a work of philosophy on the character of writing in petit-bourgeois culture.

The second work became, in 1953, Barthes's first book, *Writing Degree Zero* (2001), a response to the French Marxist philosopher and novelist, political activist, and literary critic Jean-Paul Sartre's (1905–80) *What Is Literature?* (2002) wherein Barthes redirects such Marxist and existentialist theories of literature and commitment to the issues of appearance and reality, to how "ordinariness" is formed through sign systems, and to questions of language, style, and writing. Offering a philosophy of these last three terms, accompanied by a history of French literature since the eighteenth century, Barthes supports the writing of such contemporaries as Albert Camus while arguing that no form of writing can in the long run withstand assimilation by and into bourgeois culture.

In 1947, aged thirty-two, Barthes left Paris to become a librarian and teacher at the French Institute in Bucharest, Romania. However, in a clampdown on Western influence, the Romanian communist government ejected all Institute staff in 1949. Barthes left for Egypt, teaching at the University of Alexandria alongside Algirdas Julien Greimas (1917–92), the famous Lithuanian linguist, literary scientist, and semiotician.

Barthes returned to Paris in 1950, working as an assistant in the education office of the General Cultural Department in Paris and as a lexicographer at the Centre national de la recherche scientifique (CNRS). In 1955, Barthes moved to the sociology division of CNRS and became chair of the economic and social science division of the École pratique des hautes études where, in 1962, he was appointed director of study in the sociology of signs, symbols, and representations. In 1980, shortly after the publication of his *Camera Lucida: Reflections on Photography* (1981), Barthes died, after a van knocked him down in Paris.

Luxury Philosophy and Contributions

Barthes's Method of Luxury Philosophy

Barthes's heterogenous luxury philosophy was influenced by Sartre; Karl Marx (see Chapter 4); Louis Trolle Hjelmslev (1899–1965), the Danish linguist; and Ferdinand de Saussure (1857–1913), the Swiss linguist, semiotician, and philosopher. However, unsuited to intellectual followership, Barthes practiced an intellectual nomadism across ideas from linguistics, sociology, and literature, while reorganizing them and the study of popular culture.

Barthes's method of writing luxury philosophy involved making notes on index cards, filing and rearranging them until a structure—which had nothing to do with the philosophy of structuralism—arose through accumulation. Barthes's practice of reorganizing his material thus created new meanings in his writings through the influence of chance and contingency rather than through thorough research. With the exclusion of 1964's *Elements of Semiology* (1984), which is Barthes's attempt to lay the philosophical foundations for the kind of semiological work to be found in *Mythologies*, he never positioned himself concerning existing philosophies or ideologies such as structuralist philosophy. Nevertheless, Barthes's *On Racine* (1964) from 1963 is considered as an investigative achievement and as a milestone in structuralist method in literary criticism. Conversely, Barthes's 1967 text *The Fashion System* (1983a) is usually deemed a disappointment. His analysis of "The Vestimentary Code" (1983a: 59–187), which does not contain a single reference to luxury fashion, is seen as contrived and unpersuasive. It does not understand or explain the two chief features of fashion, specifically, the charm of independence and the pressure for continuous transformation. On the other hand, in "The Contest between Chanel and Courrèges," which appeared in the women's magazine *Marie Claire*, also in 1967 (and subtitled by the magazine "Refereed by a Philosopher"), Barthes concerns himself with a "contest" taking place in the French luxury fashion industry (2006: 99–103).

Though not a systematic thinker, Barthes successfully shows himself a consummate philosopher of luxury clothing and its codes as he convincingly interprets the meanings behind Chanel's different luxury fashion ranges, how little these have changed, how the worn and the durable in Chanel stand in opposition to the new offerings of André Courrèges (1923–2016), the French luxury fashion designer known for his streamlined 1960s creations influenced by modernism and futurism that exploited modern technology and new fabrics in the construction of the low-heeled women's white "go-go boot" and the popularization of the miniskirt in France. There was thus a "contest" taking place in the French luxury fashion industry of the 1960s, Barthes suggested, between the classicism of Chanel and the modernism of Courrèges. The article also differentiates the conception of the individual body in the respective luxury fashion houses. Finally, Barthes indicates the importance of this "contest": on the same level as literature, film, and music, luxury fashion, as a form of lavish "taste," reflects and inflects people's way of thinking about luxury and many other topics and thus represents a form of historical and sociological mentality.

But what is structuralism and Barthes's connection to the structuralist method? Structuralism postulates a methodical questioning of language, culture, politics, and society. It originated from Saussure's (1983) proposal that articulation is informed and ruled by the structural system upon which it is founded. Saussure presented this system in linguistic terms, differentiating three dichotomies: *langue* (language) and *parole* (speech), *synchrony* and *diachrony,* and *signifier* and *signified. Langue* is the fundamental system upon which communication is established, and *parole* is articulation itself. *Synchrony* denotes the system of language in the moment, and *diachrony* to shifts in the growth of the system. The *signifier* designates the acoustic or visual component of articulation, and the *signified* is the mental concept linked with it.

Structuralism presented a challenge to analytic philosophy. It rejected essentialist ideas of truth and reality, with Saussure suggesting that individual units of language are random because they stem from tradition. Meanings are comprehended as effects of the host sign system wherein articulation happens.

Structuralism was unconcerned with the questions of individuality and style that characterize Barthes's work. For example, in applying the structuralist method in the social sciences, the French anthropologist Claude Lévi-Strauss (1966) exposed the generative grammar of mythical thought. Lévi-Strauss thought that a fundamental structure connects the myths and rituals, oral traditions, kinship systems, and modes of symbolic representation between seemingly diverse cultures, political systems, and societies. His method consequently reveals the superficiality of form and the complexity and unity of structure.

Yet, from *Writing Degree Zero* onward, Barthes *supported* individuality as the hallmark of the author. He argued that this arose from the biological body of the author, the sole corpus of viewpoints. As noted above, Barthes differentiated between language, style, and writing. Language, he suggested, is the natural order of meanings united by custom. It is the border or the horizon that literature and criticism must exceed if it is to be noted. Style is the images and language that spring from the body. They are the pictures, statements, and accounts of the writer's personal experience and the medium of the events that have formed him or her. Vital to the contention is the suggestion that writers have no choice in the style of their body of knowledge and standpoints. These appear from the medium and substance of culture, politics, and society wherein the writer is associated by virtue of birth. Barthes thus hypothesizes a pessimistic structure in writing as no writer can select or decide the roots or conditions of their birth. Nevertheless, Barthes declines what structuralism offers, which is that writers are lacking in choice because they reveal the beliefs of the structural atmosphere and ground wherein they are entrenched. His idea of writing highlights the individuality and commitment of the writer.

Nonetheless Barthes is also concerned with repudiating the implication that writers are individualists, arguing that they have no control over the effects of their writing on culture, politics, and society, which acquire priority, outwardness, and restraint over individual intentionality and conduct. Barthes's examination of writing argues that the writer inhabits a valiant position in disputing the customs of language and style. But, his resolve on the ascendancy of the cultural, political, and social structures rejects the implication, and generates a conflict that persists throughout his writing.

Barthes's literary and cultural writings divulge him not as a would-be novelist but as a critic with a somewhat artificial voice that he dispensed with after his lyrical turn to poststructuralism in the 1970s. This most self-assured of critics was then uncomfortable with exposing himself through a work of fiction. Still, *Camera Lucida* (1981) shows Barthes's transition from the systematic and aspirant scientific procedures of structuralism to the fictional, poetic, and playful methods of poststructuralism while remaining attached to the tradition of criticism. Although Barthes considered writing a work of fiction (2011), he died before the aspiration could be fulfilled.

With *S/Z* (1974), Barthes acknowledged that his concern with structuralism was over. Henceforth, the subjects of Barthes's publications change trajectory without restrictions. *S/Z* is an interpretation of the French novelist and playwright Honoré de Balzac's (1799–1850) short story "Sarrasine." Barthes divides the story into 561 components or "lexia," extricating five codes to enable comprehending it: *hermeneutic* denotes issues of interpretation; *seme* alludes to the system of allusions, metaphors, and connotation; *symbolic* implies the system of symbolic oppositions, for instance light and shade; *action* conveys the narrative content; and *reference* expresses the web of cultural codes regarding places, events, personalities, and stereotypes. Yet *S/Z* is no conventional structuralist investigation, despite Barthes's identification of the multiplicity of codes and his modification of structuralist literary criticism.

Indeed, Barthes undermines the hopes of the reader and disarms structuralist rhetoric by stating that the semic code is irregular and unreliable (Allen 2003: 83–8). He explains the lexias, which are the main critical systematizing principle in the study, as devices to interrupt the text, thus refuting unity. He proposes that the structuralist principle of uniformity should be substituted by a new principle of *différence*, which signifies the fertility and play of language (1974: 3). Narrative is criticized as a seductive code that silences the reader into obedience while Barthes implores readers to become inventive agents in clarifying the text.

Barthes's method of analysis concerning "Sarrasine" thus not only reads the story gradually and systematically but also parts company with the conventional "bourgeois" style of reading that assumes the preeminence of the author, a linear narrative, and symmetry between character and story line. For Barthes, the text is a labyrinth of meaning: stunning, seductive, volatile, disentangling in unexpected viewpoints. Primarily, Barthes praises the "free play" of meaning and the delight of reading as an inventive agent (Kritzman 1984).

After *S/Z*, Barthes embarked, for example, upon an analysis of the sign world of Japan in *Empire of Signs* (1982), showing how a culture outside of the system of the Western world interrupts and disassembles presumptions about how signs function and what meaning is. Yet, Barthes's visit to and analysis of Japan are not meant as an exact consideration of Japanese culture but as a rather contentious if productive reaction to the material signs of an alien (Other) culture that offers freedom from the Western fixation with meaning. There is mention in Barthes's text of the phenomenon of luxury in

Japan: the luxury, for instance, of the Japanese love of packages "wrapped with as much sumptuousness as a jewel" and the luxurious rooms Barthes inhabits in places that have no other limits than their "carpet of living sensations, of brilliant signs (flowers, windows, foliage, pictures, books)" (Barthes 1982: 46, 107). Here, luxury in Japan and Japan itself are interpreted by Barthes as texts without definitive, transparent, unchanging, or unique meanings. Yet luxury in Japan and Japan as text remain, finally, impenetrable, thus causing Barthes the reader of luxury and the country to become a writer once more and to further investigate the poststructuralist philosophies which were now influencing and altering his work as a writer. In *Empire of Signs* and elsewhere, Barthes writes of the luxurious delights of language and explanation, love, and other writers, with his work pursuing a single idea that he studies for enjoyment through a sort of textual decadence.

Certainly, luxury as pleasure, as the state or feeling of being pleased or gratified, as a source of enjoyment or delight, amusement, diversion, sensual gratification or indulgence becomes a central motif of Barthes's later work. Writing about words and their function in signifying and diverting meaning, Barthes's concern with the corporeal body of the writer fades, along with interest in conducting empirical or comparative examination to evaluate his ideas. Similarly, while for Barthes the purpose of myth may well be to render what is a historically specific interpretation into something "natural," he never offers a historical viewpoint to explain the geneses and development of the process. Instead, Barthes rejects what he called "The Reality Effect" (1986: 141–8) and, in his essay "The Discourse of History" (1986: 127–40), the "imperious warrant" of historical science as an "imaginary narration" which is no more of a "rational" exposition than the novel (1986: 127). Disclosing the enervation he experienced with conventional structuralism and his liberation through poststructuralist methodology, Barthes critiqued the idea of interpretation, of notions of a unitary structure, of a deep meaning, and of explanation, arguing instead for "a new discourse" whose objective is "the establishment of an interplay of multiple structures" (1986: 154). Such an establishment itself must be "*written*, i.e. uncoupled from the truth of speech; … it is the relations which organize these concomitant structures, subject to still unknown rules, which must constitute the object of a new theory"

(Barthes 1986: 154; original emphasis). From this point onward, Barthes's early work is left in the past, the structuralist stage of his writing discarded, along with systematic thought.

S/Z is the beginning of Barthes's new and adventurous poststructuralist phase. Deserting the search for a self-styled scientific interpretation of literature and culture, politics, and society under the inspiration of, among others, Jacques Lacan (1901–81) (Lacan 1977), the French psychoanalyst and psychiatrist, Barthes investigated the concept of "intertextuality" (1977a: 146), a term implying that individual texts are inevitably related to other texts and that their meanings are correspondingly temporary and plural consistent with how these relations are perceived and emphasized. Contra Saussure, Barthes reconceptualized language as an open system where meanings are organized and defined but do not submit to rules of closure: "We know," wrote Barthes, "that a text is not a line of words releasing a single 'theological' meaning … but a multi-dimensional space in which a variety of writings, none of them original, blend and clash. The text is a tissue of quotations drawn from the innumerable centers of culture" (1977a: 146). The very commitment to such rules can be understood as playful, for they are an illogicality. Structure without closure preserves the authority of structuralist thinking while concurrently refusing the prerequisite of structuralist philosophy.

Concurrent with this refusal was Barthes's newfound fervor for the play of meaning and the plurality of the text. His *Image-Music-Text*, for example, demonstrates Barthes's rejection of the idea that the authorial voice or the sign system has ascendancy over articulation and upholds that the reader plays an inventive part in re-aestheticizing and redefining texts to such an extent that he writes of "The Death of the Author" (1977a: 142–8).

A Lover's Discourse: Fragments from 1977, by contrast, is the most novelistic of all Barthes's works, especially in his use of the term "image-repertoire" (Barthes 2002: 4). Structured around eighty figures arranged in alphabetical order, so as to surmount the insinuation of a dominant authorial voice, Barthes's text describes these figures rising in the mind of the amorous subject like "the printout of a code" (2002: 4); they are the intertextual components of the lover's discourse. The figure of "Exuberance," for instance, Barthes (2002: 84–6)—perhaps unconsciously echoing Georges Bataille (see Chapter 6)—describes the amorous subject pursuing and wavering "to place love in an economy of pure expenditure, of 'total loss.'" For Barthes, love is not just an obsession but a transgressive force wherein the lover lavishes their time, their abilities, and their wealth without counting the cost. Expending their love every day in an aberrant economy of dispersal, excess, and tumult, the lover lavishes for nothing, for no objective. Amorous expenditure is asserted without limit or repetition to produce "that brilliant and rare thing which is called exuberance, and which is equal to beauty" (Barthes 2002: 85). Amorous exuberance is the exuberance of vain manifold pleasures that nothing can restrain. However, when interwoven with sadness, such exuberance contaminates the lover's discourse with a volatility, with a "black economy" that marks the lover "with its aberration and, so to speak, with its intolerable luxury" (Barthes 2002: 86). The result of such figures is to decenter the association between the author and text as the focus of literary, cultural, political, and social critique. For Barthes, "the amorous subject draws on the reservoir (the thesaurus?) of figures, depending on the needs, the injunctions, or the pleasures of his image-repertoire" (2002: 6). The paradox of the amorous subject is that love, that allegedly most individual of feelings, is experienced by the subject as the appearance of snippets of code originating from a socialized thesaurus. The reason the subject does not comprehend this paradox involves Barthes's Lacanian psychoanalytically influenced idea of the image-repertoire. The image-repertoire is Barthes's term for the imaginary. In "incident" after unrelated "incident," Barthes (2002: 6) offers the image-repertoire of the amorous subject. The lover's discourse, which is aimed at the "you," the beloved object, is an intertwining of intertextual signs from literature and psychology, philosophy, religion, music, and personal experience. Driven by a wish to defend the lover's discourse as part of the imaginary, Barthes notes that it "is spoken, perhaps, by thousands of subjects … but warranted by no one: it is completely forsaken by the surrounding languages: ignored, disparaged, or derided by them" (2002: 7). Contending that it is owing to this social separation that the lover's discourse becomes a place for "affirmation," Barthes declares that that affirmation is the topic of the book. Barthes's text therefore affirms the lover's discourse through the lover, the figure who says "I" in his text. However, the lover does not experience love as an affirmation but as a loss, as irritation, nervousness, postponement, expectation, and as a fearful quest after an indefinable positive meaning associated with unimportant signs. Barthes's lover is a reader and productive agent of signs who hunts for meaningful signs in other subjects and objects that the Other (the beloved) participates in the imaginary fiction of the lover's self-authored drama. Yet, since the loved one is Other to the lover's imaginary, such a quest after positive meanings in self-selected signs can only cause dissatisfaction. The quest for signs of requited love, of a mutual image-repertoire, is complemented by the lover's need to offer signs of love, to persuade the loved one, or the image of the loved one, that the lover's imaginary is real. The amorous subject, the "I" of Barthes's text, is a meaningful character in a novel of unrequited love, of the vexation of the imaginary clashing with reality who wants to be a character in another novel wherein the imaginary becomes reality. Barthes has thus written the "feigned," "fabricated," "discourse of *a* lover" that is "pieced-together" like a mosaic (1985: 284–5; original emphasis). The consequences of such a textual mosaic are multifaceted. First, Barthes's writing of the lover's discourse uncovers the deceptive nature of the discourse of love. Second, Barthes's text discusses its character (the discourse of love, the "I" that says "I love you") with love, affirms it, saves it from intellectual refusal. The result is a text that reveals the fictional and gullible nature of amorous discourse while sidestepping its critique. *A Lover's Discourse: Fragments* is Barthes's writing poised between the demystifying of the lover's discourse and its romanticization; it is a text that presents readers with an imaginative critique of a cultural myth that, concurrently, most people identify with. The consequence is that the act of reading becomes an act of conception: it is challenged in its own relation to the discourse of love without being offered the comfort of a conclusive, objective, let alone structuralist or scientific, philosophy of that discourse.

Faithful to hedonistic poststructuralist investigation, the topics of Barthes's writing following *A Lover's Discourse: Fragments* were rarely chosen for reasons of topicality or strategy, focusing instead on a kind of textual or immaterial rather than material cultural politics with an antibourgeois attitude of critique yet written in a tranquil voice replete with politeness and suitable decorum.

Style is the leading theme of Barthes's structuralist and poststructuralist luxury philosophy. He differentiated between two kinds of writing: the *écrivain*, which is the thickly conditioned style of conventional academic writing; and the *écrivant*, which is the personal style associated with the creative writer that, from *A Lover's Discourse: Fragments* onward, became Barthes's hallmark (Calvet 1994: 127–34). Yet, despite his aversion to academic writing, no novel or even short-form fiction appeared in Barthes's lifetime, leaving him to speculate near the end of his life that his critical work on structuralism and poststructuralism had perhaps run its course (Calvet 1994: 237–42).

Luxury Mythology

Barthes's prestige as a founder of cultural and media studies and an idiosyncratic luxury philosophy resides in his use of the signifier/signified contrast in the investigation of popular culture (see, e.g., Fiske 2010). Elaborating on Saussure, Barthes explored sign systems in advertising and television, travel guides, science fiction, and race, along with other components of popular culture practices, beliefs, artistic output, and objects. For Barthes, nothing in popular culture is what it appears to be and can be decoded. Barthes's arguments, reflexivity, and method of writing luxury philosophy disclose that people "naturalize" codes of communication, with his cultural, political, and social studies ousting earlier assumptions.

Barthes's commitment to the study of structures and structuralism throughout the 1960s led to his belief in the necessity of limits, enforced by the priority, externality, and constrictions of the cultural, political, and social orders. The implication that meaning is a connection in the sequence of decoding indicated bourgeois class rule as a final limit in popular culture. For Barthes, attempting to combine Marxian and Saussurean structuralism, it was the dominant bourgeois power structure that "naturalized" and perpetuated misrepresentation in culture, politics, and everyday life in society.

Barthes's use of Saussure was certainly distinctive given that Saussure postulated that meaning is random, with the meaning of a word springing from its location in the language sequence of which it is a part. In contrast, Barthes ascribed symbolic or, rather, ideological, meaning to components in sign systems. A classic example of Barthes's luxury philosophy is the somewhat neglected examination in *Mythologies* of "Soap-powders and Detergents"

(Barthes 1993: 36–8). Barthes writes of "Omo euphoria" in the advertising campaigns for detergent in the France of the 1950s: "in the Omo imagery," he declares, "dirt is a diminutive enemy, stunted and black, which takes to its heels from the fine immaculate linen at the sole threat of the judgement of Omo" (1993: 36). Advertisements for Omo signify the result of the merchandise and "reveal its mode of action," which entails "the consumer in a kind of direct experience of the substance, make him [*sic*] the accomplice of a liberation rather than the mere beneficiary of a result; matter here is endowed with value-bearing states" (1993: 37). Observing that Omo uses two of these value-bearing states, which Barthes argues are new in the category of detergents, he develops a luxury philosophy or, rather, a luxury mythology, of "the deep and the foamy" (1993: 37). Omo, for example, "cleans in depth" on the newfound assumption that "linen is deep," thus gratifying "those obscure tendencies to enfold and caress which are found in every human body" (1993: 37). Yet, for Barthes, it is foam that "signifies luxury" for foam "appears to lack any usefulness"; it is also abundant, proliferates, and "issues a vigorous germ, a healthy and powerful essence, a great wealth of active elements in a small original volume" (1993: 37). Satisfying in "the consumer a tendency to imagine matter as something airy, with which contact is effected in a mode both light and vertical," foam is "sought after like that of happiness" (Barthes 1993: 37). "Foam," Barthes proposes, "can even be the sign of a certain spirituality," given that "spirit has the reputation of being able to make something out of nothing, a large surface of effects out of a small volume of causes" (1993: 37). Omo advertising campaigns for detergent thus entail the art of concealing "the abrasive function of the detergent under the delicious image of a substance at once deep and airy which can govern the molecular order of the material without damaging it" (1993: 37–8).

A characteristic of this exemplar is the imprecision that buttresses its seeming exactness. Barthes implies that matter is endowed with value-bearing states. It is a crucial move in his contention, as it supports his argument that the subliminal influence of the deep and the foamy is not merely to caress the human body but also to highlight foam as a signifier of luxury and, as with Bataille (see Chapter 6), the virtues of the useless, the abundant, and all those active elements that proliferate, whether beginning in small volumes or not. There are two ways of considering this example, one positive, the other negative: positively, Barthes offers a thought-provoking if quirky and freewheeling essay on the possibilities of understanding matter becoming airy, light, and vertical, and the basis for a kind of human happiness; negatively, Barthes's essay can be read as further evidence of his intellectual nomadism wherein foam becoming "a sign" of spirituality is simply declared rather than established through structuralist methodology.

Citing the example of "Soap-powders and Detergents" also demonstrates Barthes's distinction between denotation and connotation which is central to his scrutiny of luxury mythology. Following Danish linguist Louis Hjelmslev (1961), Barthes alludes to denotation as the truthful or objective expression of a concept or image whereas connotation denotes the sequence of representations that the concept or image means. For Barthes, however, connotation is not merely an innocent succession of representations but a series of ideological ideas and images whose implied meaning is signified for the semiologist of luxury in, for instance, foam.

Barthes's interpretation of the influence of the ideology of Omo centers upon form before content. What fascinates Barthes is foam creating "something out of nothing" or its ability to produce "a large surface of effects out of a small volume of causes." Omo advertising campaigns are therefore not simply representations of detergent but perform an important ideological task, which is the art of concealing "the abrasive function of the detergent" within images of substances that are "deep and airy." As to the positions of Omo's scientists attempting to govern the molecular order, its advertising executives, copywriters, and photographers, Barthes simply supposes that they are ideological functionaries, paid by the bourgeoisie, committed to representing the language of advertising as "naturalized" truth. There is, though, a critical, not to say quasi-Marxian historical materialist, political economy implied in his interpretation, which is Barthes's insistence that readers do not forget that most soap-powders and detergents, from Omo to Persil, are owned and controlled by one giant Anglo-Dutch conglomerate: Unilever (1993: 38). Barthes does not philosophize on this aspect of his reading, leaving it to readers to imply the essential links between bourgeois class rule and the "naturalized" misrepresentations of popular culture.

Barthes's luxury mythology is complex, self-reflexive, critical, and intended to disentangle, if not wholly decipher, the taken-for-granted suppositions of bourgeois luxury philosophy, even if it evades an engagement with, for example, Marxian historical materialism and fails to offer an alternative reality to bourgeois fictions. Yet, in the 1950s and 1960s, readers encountering Barthes slaying luxurious myths about soap-powders, detergents, and numerous other topics found in his method and self-styled socialism a liberating alternative to the simple clichés of the emerging consumer monoculture forged after the Second World War.

However, when Barthes repeated the form of *Mythologies* in *Le Nouvel Observateur* in the 1970s, it lasted a matter of months (Calvet 1994: 232). Not only the position of the left-leaning critic of the values of petit-bourgeois consumer culture and politics but also the standing of intellectuals within society was less straightforward than in the 1950s and 1960s. Cultural politics in the 1970s was increasingly concerned with models constructed under multiple sexual identities rather than the "natural" form of heterosexuality; similarly, people no longer felt compelled by nationalist collective ideologies in the era of globalization and the consequent realignment of classes, ethnicities, and identities (see, e.g., Bauman 1998, 2004). Multivalent and unstable, cultural identities could only be read by an array of codes of association or practice that mix and conflict in interaction. No longer governed by unchanging codes of conduct, the governance of everyday life was also questioned by new philosophical formations arising from postmodern, postcolonial, and postfeminist cultural critics who achieved preeminence in the years after Barthes's death in 1980.

Appraisal of Key Advances in Luxury Philosophy and Controversies

Barthes's use of Saussure's signifier/signified contrast was influential, with residues of it obvious in, for instance, the postmodernism of Jean Baudrillard (1929–2007) (Baudrillard 2020; also see Chapter 6). Founding the rule that culture is structured like a language, Barthes supplied significant foundational components of modern semiology, cultural studies, subsequent analytical work on codes of signification, and, of course, luxury philosophy.

But his work is susceptible to two objections. First, Barthes failed to offset his support of the plurality of the text with a plausible epistemology. Following *S/Z*, his poststructuralist thought dissociated itself from conceptualizing classifications in terms of transpersonal experience. In his Collège de France inaugural lecture, Barthes (1983b: 461) argued that language is inherently ideological and thus subliminally induced subjective surrender, with the inference that communication cannot be entrusted to make sense of the world: "In speech," Barthes asserts in his inaugural lecture, "servility and power are inescapably intermingled," with freedom from power and freedom to subjugate no one occurring "only outside language" (1983b: 461). "Unfortunately," declared Barthes, "human language has no exterior: there is no exit" (1983b: 461).

Expounding a writerly refusal to accept limits, Barthes sought to pass through the curtain of received language alone, disregarding trust in and collaboration with other human beings in the provision of cultural, political, and social agency. Ever the individualist seeker of historical, cultural, and other knowledge, Barthes avoided causative accounts in favor of textual readings abstracted from historical and cultural events. Yet historical and cultural events, such as the emergence of the luxury fashion designer André Courrèges in the 1960s, Barthes's own trip to Japan in the 1970s, or his experience of exuberance, soap powder, and detergent advertising are not just "referential illusions" and signifiers, denotations, connotations, categories, referents, and effects as Barthes claims (1986: 148) but also real experiences that profoundly alter the course of people's lives, inclusive of the eventful life of Roland Barthes (1977b). Barthes, therefore, had no epistemological research frame to draw on that would allow him to distinguish between textual, historical, and cultural interpretations.

Second, while Barthes's work increasingly emphasized the aestheticization of everyday life (see, e.g., Featherstone 2007: 64–80) through luxury fashion and so forth, it also swung from the critique of literary codes to the critique of visual codes in, for example, *Camera Lucida: Reflections on Photography* (1981) and *Empire of Signs* (1982). Barthes's interest in visual codes is an understandable response to the upsurge of media and consumer culture from the 1950s onward that included the growth of advertising-driven magazines, the spread of television, and the habitual consumption of ubiquitous visual data and stimulus. People in industrial societies looked to popular magazines for role models and "personalities" whose "achievement" was that they were now idols of consumer culture in, for instance, cinema. Barthes's interest in luxury and other mediated mythologies, such as his essay in *Mythologies* on "Romans in Films" (1993: 26–8) featuring discussion of Marlon Brando's fringe in Joseph L. Mankiewicz's Shakespearean epic, *Julius Caesar* (1953), is thus the expression of the increase in visual codes in popular culture which occurred in the 1950s.

It might be argued that Barthes never produced an adequate philosophy of visual culture, with his semiology remaining illustrative and tentative concerning the implied meanings connoted by signifieds. However, as I demonstrated in *Luxury and Visual Culture* with regard to the role of luxury fashion in contemporary visual culture, while Barthes's conceptions of visual consumption and semiotics, representation, signs, language, meaning, and communication in everyday life may not amount to a complete philosophy of visual culture, they can be utilized as methodological bases and inspiration for the analysis of visual subjects and representational themes (Armitage 2020: 37–66). Incorporating the nature of visual codes, the work of reading, and the configuration and fragmentation of texts, Barthes's writings on visual culture challenge readers to think through the myths of, for example, luxury fashion and the ideology of luxurious contemporary visual culture, of spectacular luxury fashion as a sociocultural order, set of representations, and discourses of pleasure, and, finally, as luxury-branded visual representations that frequently appropriate the written word. Similarly, when Barthes's deliberations shift toward problems concerning the politics of philosophy, the examination of visual culture, it could be suggested, becomes vague and passé. Yet, while he criticizes the bourgeois, Barthes's political examinations are not so much lacking in philosophical awareness as predicated on the distinction he makes "between 'the political' and 'politics'" (1985: 218). "To me," Barthes argues, "the political is a fundamental order of history, of thought, of everything that is done, and said. It's the very dimension of the real" (1985: 218). Politics, however, is "the moment when the political changes into the ... discourse of repetition" (Barthes 1985: 218). Barthes's profound interest in ideology, in the process of class rule, is therefore attached to the political and to history rather than explicated through the empirical investigation typical of politics and its discourse of repetition.

Barthes's considerations of class rule are not meant to convince anyone of his own political position which, by his own admission, was divided and guilt-ridden (1985: 218–19). Understanding that the use of the signifier/ signified contrast problematized authority as such, Barthes's semiology and critical analyses gradually eschewed the objective of substituting one class with another and sought, instead, for a mode of presence within the discourse of the political that would not be based on repeating the same old values and power formations. Nonetheless, seeking an alternative methodology that would deflate the inflation of contemporary political discourse within the context of myriad ideological activities and discourses was no easy task, especially when the connotations of all those old, denoted values were raised to the heart of Barthes's study of meaningful interpretations founded on individual rather than collective meaning. Furthermore, as semiology teaches that signs are volatile, the possibility of transcendence necessarily becomes singular and provisional.

Barthes examined the implications of individual rather than collective meaning and the possibility of transcendence in his poststructuralist work. Yet, his insights into questions of interpretation and literary and cultural analysis can lead readers to the conclusion that writers face a never-ending task of interpretation in the face of a human language that is fundamentally ideological and, from Barthes's perspective, often difficult to share with other human beings when trying to understand the world. For Barthes, the gap between individual and collective meaning is a chasm, which leaves the question of transcendence unanswered, lost somewhere not so much in issues of interpretation as in language as a structure possessing importance, externality, and restraint over articulation. However, as Barthes's pre-poststructuralist writing in *Writing Degree Zero* (2001: 14) makes apparent, language and certainly authorial style are states of human embodiment that come involuntarily from the author's body, personal history, and the nature of the author's personality: they are not things that authors can choose. Moreover, given that Barthes's own interpretations in *Mythologies* (1993) indicate that people are equipped with semiotic awareness and have the literary and cultural analytical ability to rewrite, reread, and reinterpret ideology, there is no reason in principle why people cannot resist its distorting effects on human consciousness and the language of political discourse in society. But it must be remembered that Barthes never sought to contend with themes that are directly political, inclusive of ideological codes of communication (1985: 268). For Barthes, what was important was for everyone to become sensitive to the many meanings of the ubiquity and endurance of the spectacle of power (1985: 269).

Additionally, Barthes acknowledges resistance and describes it in aesthetic terms, linking it in his *The Pleasure of the Text* (1975: 23) to the individualized luxury or "scandalous pleasure" of an "atopic" reading, which denotes the interpretation of cultural codes. By "atopic," Barthes signifies aesthetic interventions that engage with the question of luxury and produce a surplus of meaning over the bourgeois codes which dominate contemporary culture. "Does luxury of language belong with excessive wealth, wasteful expenditure, total loss?," asks Barthes: "Does a great work of pleasure … participate in the same economy as the pyramids of Egypt?" (1975: 23). Certainly, for the late Barthes of *The Preparation of the Novel*, "what has to be *wrenched from life*" is "the remainder, the surplus, the *luxury*," a surplus that for writers is essential because it leaves them in a morally ambiguous position wherein they are "monstrously idle and yet a participant in the organization of social movement" (2011: 219; original emphases). Through creating luxurious language and surplus meaning, individual writers problematize petit-bourgeois codes of cultural, political, and social control for they scandalize, offend, and thus unmask the limits of a cultural regime built on class rule.

In the structuralist stage of Barthes's work he contended that structure, not the individual self, is the center of meaning, thus offending the petit-bourgeois belief in the freedom of the individual and the power of rational communication. In the poststructuralist stage of Barthes's work, he denied that meaning is possible, except in brief occurrences at a site of aestheticized luxury characterized as pleasure or "bliss"; a site that offers "the possibility of a dialectics of desire, of an *unpredictability* of bliss" (Barthes 1975: 4; original emphasis). The language that petit-bourgeois culture employs to understand itself is denounced as ideological "*prattle*" (Barthes 1975: 4; original emphasis). Barthes's poststructuralist work, it might be argued, is unacceptable because it fails to disclose the relations between aesthetics and politics. But Barthes's focus on bliss is meant to be "unacceptable" in the sense that what it offers is an unsettling challenge to aesthetics and a more "open" politics founded on his self-proclaimed (Barthes 1985: 268) anarchist perspective on modernist and avant-garde texts such as those of Phillipe Sollers (Barthes 1987b).

Barthes's later work is fueled by a resistance to the orthodoxies of mass culture and left-wing "politics" rather than the contrast between the individual and society. It presents what Barthes styles as a "transgression of transgression" (1977b: 65), a theme that buttressed all of his late writings on luxury mythology and many other subjects. In the final phase of his writing career, Barthes's conception of resistance was to allow into his philosophical discourse "*a touch of sentimentality*" (1977b: 66; original emphases). His suspicion of left-wing "politics" propelled him beyond aesthetics and the discourse of repetition and into the realm of transgression. Nevertheless, Barthes's belief was not that transgression is adequate to elucidate luxury in culture and society (1977b: 66). Rather, it was that, together with the mythology of love, transgression can challenge the common beliefs of left-wing discourse and protect writing (*écriture*) from hardening into such common beliefs, into that which represses and covers over plurality and difference regarding people as individuals and as luxury and pleasure-seeking subjects.

References

Allen, G. (2003), *Roland Barthes*, Abingdon: Routledge.
Armitage, J. (2020), *Luxury and Visual Culture*, London: Bloomsbury.
Barthes, R. (1964), *On Racine*, trans. R. Howard, New York: Hill and Wang.
Barthes, R. (1974), *S/Z*, trans. R. Miller, New York: Hill and Wang.
Barthes, R. (1975), *The Pleasure of the Text*, trans. R. Miller, New York: Hill and Wang.
Barthes, R. (1977a), *Image—Music—Text*, trans. S. Heath, London: Fontana.
Barthes, R. (1977b), *Roland Barthes by Roland Barthes*, trans. R. Howard, London: Macmillan.

Barthes, R. (1981), *Camera Lucida: Reflections on Photography*, trans. R. Howard, New York: Hill and Wang.

Barthes, R. (1982), *Empire of Signs*, trans. R. Howard, New York: Hill and Wang.

Barthes, R. (1983a), *The Fashion System*, trans. M. Ward and R. Howard, New York: Hill and Wang.

Barthes, R. (1983b), *Barthes: Selected Writings*, ed. S. Sontag, London: Fontana.

Barthes, R. (1984), *Elements of Semiology*, trans. A. Lavers and C. Smith, London: Jonathan Cape.

Barthes, R. (1985), *The Grain of the Voice: Interviews 1962–1980*, trans. L. Coverdale, New York: Hill and Wang.

Barthes, R. (1986), *The Rustle of Language*, trans. R. Howard, New York: Hill and Wang.

Barthes, R. (1987a), *Michelet*, trans. R. Howard, New York: Hill and Wang.

Barthes, R. (1987b), *Sollers Writer*, trans. P. Thody, London: Athlone Press.

Barthes, R. (1993), *Mythologies*, trans. A. Lavers, London: Vintage.

Barthes, R. (2001), *Writing Degree Zero*, trans. A. Lavers and C. Smith, New York: Hill and Wang.

Barthes, R. (2002), *A Lover's Discourse: Fragments*, trans. R. Howard, New York: Hill and Wang.

Barthes, R. (2006), *The Language of Fashion*, trans. A. Stafford, ed. A. Stafford and M. Carter, London: Bloomsbury.

Barthes, R. (2011), *The Preparation of the Novel: Lecture Courses and Seminars at the Collège de France (1978–1979 and 1979–1980)*, trans. K. Briggs, New York: Columbia University Press.

Baudrillard, J. (2020), *The System of Objects*, trans. J. Benedict, London: Verso.

Bauman, Z. (1998), *Globalization: The Human Consequences*, Cambridge: Polity.

Bauman, Z. (2004), *Identity: Conversations with Benedetto Vecchi*, Cambridge: Polity.

Calvet, L.-J. (1994), *Roland Barthes: A Biography*, trans. S. Wykes, Cambridge: Polity.

Featherstone, M. (2007), *Consumer Culture and Postmodernism*, 2nd edn, London: Sage.

Fiske, J. (2010), *Understanding Popular Culture*, 2nd edn, Abingdon: Routledge.

Hjelmslev, L. (1961), *Prolegomena to a Theory of Language*, trans. F. J. Whitfield, Madison: University of Wisconsin Press.

Kritzman, L. D. (1984), "Barthesian Free Play," *Yale French Studies*, 66 (The Anxiety of Anticipation): 189–210.

Lacan, J. (1977), *Écrits: A Selection*, trans. A. Sheridan, London: Tavistock.

Lévi-Strauss, C. (1966), *The Savage Mind*, London: Weidenfeld & Nicolson.

Picard, R. (1969), *New Criticism or New Fraud?*, trans. F. Towne, Pullman: Washington State University Press.

Sartre, J.-P. (2002), *What Is Literature?*, trans. B. Frechtman, London: Routledge.

Saussure, F. de (1983), *Course in General Linguistics*, trans. R. Harris, La Salle, IL: Open Court.

9

Luxury Philosophy Today: A Conclusion

When people write about the influence of philosophers, they are inclined to commit the error of producing quantitative assessments, as if influence were a unique thing of which a philosopher can have a great deal or a small amount. One of the influences of luxury philosophy ought to be that it makes people reassess luxury philosophers, for example the seven figures of influence detailed in *Luxury Philosophy*. There are numerous types of influence. One method of disclosing this fact is to reflect on what I mean by an expression such as "luxury philosophy today." The word "today" has many philosophical reverberations. We may think of the "present day." The present day is a "time," often connected to "the age." We may also think of the present day, time, or "this day," as distinct from yesterday or tomorrow. We need also to contemplate the word today in its literal sense. If we turn to a dictionary, we discover that the word has different meanings: that which is "the present age," for instance, something that takes place during or on this day; but also, that which takes place "nowadays," or, in other words, something that is present this day or something that is present in the current "era." Thus, the word "today" can mean "these days" or it can mean "up-to-date."

The first sense of the word "today," the present day, guides us to the meanings of the words "present-day influence," especially to the question of whether the work of luxury philosophers, from Rousseau and Saint-Lambert to Marx, Levinas, Bataille, Adorno, and Barthes, has made available material for later luxury philosophers and critics to model themselves on. The second sense of the word "today," "up-to-date," entails us in the more compound patterns of the influences of the work of luxury philosophers, including what components of their work have been supplanted and surpassed, but also what components still remain or even have yet to be fulfilled in luxury philosophy today, such as the work of Rousseau and Saint-Lambert. This last is important because the work of luxury philosophers has had, and continues to have, a multilayered and enduring influence that it is as imperative to comprehend today as it was in the eighteenth, nineteenth, and twentieth centuries.

The Present-Day Influence of Luxury Philosophy

The influence of the ideas of those luxury philosophers specified in Chapters 2–8 of *Luxury Philosophy* has had an enormous impact on numerous diverse subjects within the arts and the humanities. No one writing luxury philosophy today, for example, can examine questions of visual culture, still a disputed concept, without alluding to the work of luxury philosophers such as Roland Barthes, discussed in the previous chapter, on haute couture fashion. The luxury goods and services industry is of course developing at an unparalleled rate globally. Yet, important questions remain. For instance, in contemporary digital culture does luxury still dwell in material objects, or instead in the look of objects? Indeed, a Barthesian argument can be made that luxury is experiencing a change from material culture to the immaterial culture of the visual, presenting new types of luxury engagement and unmatched levels of enjoyment never before presented to the senses. Consequently, new Barthesian interpretations of luxury in the shifting visual panorama of contemporary society are needed that encompass a variety of cultural forms, including fashion and photography, social media, television, and art, in addition to investigating the important questions of globalization, digitization, consumer identity, and mass luxury. Concepts such as media and communication continue to have an important impact on cultural studies and are permanently marked by the pivotal work of luxury philosophers such as Barthes's on these subjects. Paula von Wachenfeldt and Magdalena Petersson McIntyre (2024), for example, employ image and film advertisements, interviews, social media, and public and private archives in their co-edited collection *Luxury Fashion and Media Communication: Between the Material and Immaterial,* which presents a Barthesian-influenced methodology for the examination of the often-ambiguous value of luxury objects. Von Wachenfeldt and Petersson McIntyre's volume thus investigates the material and immaterial meaning of luxury and how it is shared and communicated between the luxury industry and consumers in France and Italy, Spain, China, and the United States. Above all, the book emphasizes the contradictory narratives concerning luxury objects and services as simultaneously exclusive yet widely available through mass-marketed luxury brands. The modern disciplines and practices of visual, media, and cultural studies are filled with the influence of Barthes and, in their contemporary forms, can be said to elicit much of their justification from texts such as Barthes's *Mythologies* (1993), and many essays extending throughout his career as a luxury philosopher. Verena Andermatt Conley's (2020) "Inhabiting Luxury Spaces," for instance, is focused on contemporary urban kinds of living and being luxurious. Ever more, in the urban landscape, Conley argues, established communities are being displaced to clear the way for redevelopment and gentrification. Concentrating on New York and Boston in the United States, Conley demonstrates how traditional models of luxury continue to be superseded by an explosion of mass-marketed luxury products, just as Barthes (1993) observed in his *Mythologies* in the 1950s. Revamped and suitably marketed with minimal fittings and fisheye photography, small apartments magically become luxurious dwellings. For Conley, the fantasy of space and luxury is produced by architects and designers eliminating walls, utilizing special lighting, and expertly positioning mirrors. She contends that it is through an imaginary, not to say mythological, consumption of "luxury" that an ideology of identity and community is imposed. Accordingly, the real and the imaginary jointly create an illusion of occupying luxury residences. No academic or student engaged in a research procject on luxury or a course on luxury and the visual, on luxury and the media, or luxurious forms of representation, or the cultural politics of luxury can afford to continue without an awareness of Barthes's work on luxury philosophy.

Philosophical discussions of luxury still depend on the groundbreaking work of luxury philosopher Georges Bataille in this area; subdivisions of the modern disciplines of fashion and lifestyle studies are still influenced by his work. For Calefato (2014), for example, luxury has been praised and censured throughout history up to the present day because of its association with expenditure and extravagance, longing, social standing, consumption, and economic value. Surveying why luxury remains conspicuous and utilizing a Bataillian-influenced viewpoint on cultural studies, semiotic research, and aesthetics, Calefato offers a variety of case studies on urban space and recent technologies, travel, interior design, cars, fashion advertising, and jewelry to examine what luxury signifies, and why, in the contemporary world.

New topics of philosophical and critical work on luxury, chiefly those involved with the historical and contemporary meanings of luxury in political terms, draw from the writings of luxury philosophers such as Karl Marx. An innovator in the domain of communal luxury philosophy and practice, Kristin Ross's (2015) *Communal Luxury: The Political Imaginary of the Paris Commune* gives a prime place to Marx in her work. Ross's tour de force on luxury within the Communard uprising of 1871 resounds with the stimuli and events of contemporary protest, inclusive of occasional protests against luxury brands, which has discovered its articulation in the cultural, political, and social recovery of public space. Today's anxieties, such as the standing of art, structure and inform Ross's restaging of particular Communards concerning luxury. Her innovative exploration of an event and its influences on the question of luxury animate the workers in Paris who became revolutionaries, the importance they ascribed to their fight, and the amplification and continuance of their thought about luxury in the encounters that took place between the insurrection's survivors and defenders like Marx. Other leading luxury philosophers, such as Ulrich Lehman (2016), study how "luxury-as-dominance" and the duality of capital and labor allow people to reconsider and develop their and our comprehension of the structure of luxury. Here, Marx's work on political economy and systems of production and consumption continues to be one of the most advantageous models upon which to ground such research.

Marx's work is, therefore, indissolubly connected to the idea and practice of luxury philosophy. When people engage in philosophical work of whatever type, they practice a style or styles of discourse that luxury philosophers like Marx helped to found. References to and quotes of the work of luxury philosophers such as Marx still flourish in numerous areas of philosophy. Yet it remains correct to state that no one practices luxury philosophy today. For luxury philosophy is specifically not an expert discourse that can be followed systematically. To be sure, there are luxury philosophers in the world, but they do not find their communal identity in a store of shared ideas. Luxury philosophers, it can be argued, invent roles for themselves that consist in undermining the knowledge intrinsic in the discourse of luxury, and in undertaking that role they make themselves unique. However, there can be no "disciples" of this or that luxury philosophy, only practitioners pursuing their own discourses and new conceptual knowledge concerning luxury. Reintroducing the somewhat neglected critical theory of the Marxian philosopher and, along with Theodor Adorno, member of the Frankfurt School, Herbert Marcuse (1964), for instance, it is possible to identify the ongoing cultural form of what can be conceptualized as "luxury new media" (Armitage and Roberts 2014). Contending that luxury new media is a new kind of luxury that is generating groundbreaking types of luxury new media goods and services that lead to "euphoria in unhappiness" (Armitage and Roberts 2014) and the contemporary development of what Marcuse called "false needs" (1964: 7), it thus becomes possible to interrogate the growth in significance of luxury new media as a type of managed consumer choice that is problematic because it generates not only boundless and continuous forms of elation but also discontent through the endless pursuit of manufactured false needs. Similarly, within the concept and practice of haute couture's contemporary engagement with the discourse on and virtual worlds of the "metaverse," a new shared virtual environment that features online gaming and augmented reality, it is reasonable to interpret the important fashion ideas of, for example, the French haute couturier Julien Fournié from the perspective of a continental philosopher not usually associated with luxury philosophy such as the phenomenologist Martin Heidegger (Armitage 2023).

Readers of *Luxury Philosophy* are in a position to understand why luxury philosophers are not luxury philosophers others can emulate. Those who desire to follow the work of luxury philosophers such as Emmanuel Levinas on *Totality and Infinity* (1969) must be conscious of how he came to undo such themes through the elaboration of a distinctive approach to philosophical examination. Those who would follow Levinas's philosophical practice in books such as *Totality and Infinity* must be mindful that, in this work, Levinas described and analyzed luxury as voluptuosity within the discourse of continental philosophy but through a continuously recurring writing style. Those who would emulate Levinas's mature, rhythmic style of criticism cannot evade the fact that such a standpoint is by definition almost beyond the realms of a cultural and political, social, and intellectual commentary, beyond, namely, anything that is shareable and therefore susceptible to emulation. As Jacques Derrida wrote in his *Writing and Difference*, in *Totality and Infinity*, Levinas's

> thematic development is neither purely descriptive nor purely deductive. It proceeds with the infinite insistence of waves on a beach: return and repetition, always, of the same wave against the same shore, in which, however, as each return recapitulates itself, it also infinitely renews and enriches itself. Because of all these challenges to the commentator and the critic, *Totality and Infinity* is a work of art and not a treatise.
>
> (Derrida 1978: 312)

People cannot write today as a rhythmic stylist in imitation of Levinas.

The luxury philosophers described in *Luxury Philosophy*, I have suggested, were dedicated throughout their writings to discourses that were new or at any rate withstood simple classification. During their lives, luxury philosophers such as Bataille gave voice to discourses that had not, as yet, been acculturated by the dominant ideology of necessity: recall Bataille's observation that the essential cultural, political, and social problem facing humankind *"is not necessity but its contrary, luxury"* (1989: 12; original emphases). What this means for the heritage of luxury philosophers such as Bataille and others is that many concepts, promising beginnings or articles, a multitude of unique descriptive methods and analytical approaches, await those who come after them today. None of these components, though, add up to an unchanging and enduring explanatory method or analytical outlook for understanding luxury because, as has been shown all the way through this book, the seven key luxury philosophers did not trust in the possibility of a descriptive method or analytical approach for understanding luxury that could wholly circumvent absorption by the dominant ideology and culture of necessity. The work of these luxury philosophers, therefore, forces people to interrogate what they mean by the words "luxury" and "philosophy." Is luxury philosophy an instructive methodology by which people can methodically examine luxurious philosophical and cultural, political, and social texts and practices? Or is luxury philosophy an unruly force that challenges all accessible descriptive methods and analytical views on luxury but never offers a definite illustrative method or analytical approach in their place? Is luxury philosophy a positive force within the subjects that make up the arts and the humanities (the visual arts and architecture, filmmaking, painting, photography, literary studies, fiction, drama, poetry, prose, performing arts, dance, music, theater, cultural studies, history, sociology, linguistics, and, of course, philosophy)? Or is luxury philosophy a negative force that interrupts and dislocates the descriptive methods and analytical points of view by which the numerous subjects within the arts and humanities would describe themselves? The influence of luxury philosophy is so dispersed and so hard to classify specifically because it lies resolutely on the negative side of these two choices for philosophy.

The work of the luxury philosophers explained in *Luxury Philosophy* asks people to follow after it today by discovering new critical objects of luxury philosophy and new critical methods of luxury philosophy before attempting the unfeasible project of emulating its explicatory methods and its analytical styles of luxury philosophy in the arts, design, the media, and elsewhere (see, e.g., Armitage and Roberts 2016). The numerous approaches of luxury philosophers, it is also accurate to register, remain accessible for people to use in a restricted, focused, or planned way, picking them up for a specific task but always with a sense of the provisional nature of such an assignment. People cannot depend on luxury philosophers for an informative or analytical method, as some analytic philosophers still depend on the scientific method (West 2010: 114–15). It is, in truth, impractical to emulate luxury philosophers, as the question of which luxury philosopher people are emulating among the various luxury philosophers that are available, from Rousseau to Barthes, disturbs the idea of the emulation of a luxury philosopher. To be a luxury philosopher today is, inconsistent as it may appear, to avoid emulating luxury philosophers. Luxury philosophers such as Rousseau and Marx should not and cannot be relegated, by those who come after them today, to "the luxury philosopher of the enervation of virtue" or "the luxury philosopher of necessity." Many luxury philosophers, such as Levinas and Bataille, thoughtfully sidestepped becoming "a luxury philosopher" with a command of the subject in this sense: for them, luxury philosophy did not bring about the formation of a movement, although Adorno's membership of the Frankfurt School of thought might be considered an exception to the rule (West 2010: 60–72); the meaning of luxury philosophy for Barthes, instead, lies within the pursuit of luxury philosophy itself sooner than in what people are expected to produce by that pursuit such as a full-blown luxury philosophy. "In my case," Barthes commented, "I have taken on the responsibility of a certain hedonism, the return of a philosophy discredited and repressed for centuries: first of all by Christian morality, then again by positivistic, rationalistic morality, and unfortunately once again by a certain Marxist ethic" (1985: 206).

For Barthes, luxury philosophy has a meaning tied to hedonism or, perhaps, to a disruption of the Christian and positivistic, rational, and Marxist meanings of hedonism rather than to a production of the meaning of hedonism.

The Influence of Contemporary Luxury Philosophers

The thirty years between Levinas's death and the appearance of this book have been typified by concerns, philosophical debates over luxury, and widespread cultural, political, and social changes that were only coming into existence when Levinas, the last living luxury philosopher with a chapter dedicated to his work in *Luxury Philosophy*, died in 1995. Today, African feminist luxury philosophers, while certainly not the dominant luxury philosophers contributing to the luxury debate in this era, are taking significant concepts and philosophical examples from luxury philosophy. But they are doing so through innovative rereadings of the work of luxury philosophers that guide that work toward subjects which were not its initial or main emphasis. Mehita Iqani and Simidele Dosekun's *African Luxury: Aesthetics and Politics* (2019), for example, critically questions the visual and material cultures of luxurious consumption present on the African continent through the work of Adorno, Barthes, and Marx, among many others. Organizationally, philosophically, and systematically, the edited collection disassembles accepted beliefs that the West is the basis and center of lavish and attractive material cultures. The book surveys what the culture of consumption denotes in Africa in historical and contemporary circumstances, examining varied luxury phenomena embracing fashion advertising, reality television, retail, gendered consumption, and gardening to refocus the debate on extant contemporary luxury cultures throughout the continent.

Jessica Clark and Nigel Lezama's *Canadian Critical Luxury Studies: Decentring Luxury* (2022) performs an analogous function for luxury philosophy in that it contests Euro- and US-centric views that attach luxury to either a colonial history or to a consumerist present. The edited volume focuses on Indigenous and Canadian examples of luxurious manufacture, experiences, and locations to suggest a novel characterization of luxury that comprises regional practices underlining that Canadian luxury focuses on community and association. Examining luxury from diverse philosophical perspectives to appreciate why it has prospered or failed in the Canadian environment, the book considers, among other topics, the history of the fur trade and Indigenous fashion, the Made-in-Canada campaign, Toronto Fashion Week, public art commissions, and Montréal's future-forward fashiontech sector. Still, people may ask, what have the seven important luxury philosophers debated in *Luxury Philosophy* got to tell them about the critical questions concerning luxury in the present moment of history? If the contemporary history of luxury is dominated by questions concerning the globalization of luxury, rhetorical and yet simultaneously real sustainable luxury-driven campaigns against "waste," the resurgence noted above of national luxury, such as Canada's, connected to existing nation-states, matters rotating around the relation between physical and digital luxury increasingly reliant not on humans but on AI, the luxurious human body and the luxurious technological body found in videogame avatars dressed in haute couture, the relation between bricks-and-mortar luxury flagship stores and the world of luxury retailing on the internet, then does the work of these seven luxury philosophers still have significance besides the sparks of enlightenment and luminous suggestiveness they obviously continue to offer?

The work of the luxury philosophers deliberated in *Luxury Philosophy* spans more than three centuries, primarily in French and German contexts, and circles around the debates between the moral and liberal, revolutionary, phenomenological, avant-garde, and critical theoretical in luxury philosophy and a bourgeois philosophy fixated on necessity that luxury philosophers saw as the prevailing force in their cultures, political systems, and societies. Is it unwise to evaluate the significance of the luxury philosophers examined in this book when they have all passed away? After all, the luxury philosophers considered in *Luxury Philosophy* cannot partake in the luxury debates and the increasingly luxurious conditions of the twenty-first century. Will they remain forever part of the epoch from the eighteenth to the twentieth centuries? Are their books and articles unreflective of the present period and marooned in yesteryear's quarrels and priorities concerning luxury? Does their often-sophisticated and stylish luxury philosophy appear out-of-date? On the other hand, while terms such as enervation and the luxury of appearances that luxury philosophers like Rousseau and Saint-Lambert developed in the eighteenth century do not regularly feature in contemporary contexts, they could, in fact, be the subject of explicit discussion, despite their obvious lack of visibility in luxury debates today. It would be fair to say, then, that these two important areas—the role of luxury as a debilitating and enfeebling social force and as the driver of cultural appearances founded on social class, perceptions of goodness (e.g., the phenomenon of "virtue signaling" by luxury fashion brands such as Louis Vuitton concerning their sustainability credentials), and wealth—are where Rousseau's and Saint-Lambert's work might be further explored and expanded upon at the present time. The world people live in today, of course, is different from the world Rousseau and Saint-Lambert, Marx, Levinas, Bataille, Adorno, and Barthes were born into and in which they lived. Levinas died only three decades ago, yet the world map of luxury and the related questions that concern people have changed radically in that interval.

Yet, clearly, people must be cautious if they wish to propose that the significance of luxury philosophers and thus their possible influence has expired. Actually, such a declaration would only seem sensible if it were aimed at luxury philosophers who expounded elucidatory methods and analytical viewpoints that were meant to be pertinent in all conceivable settings. For such luxury philosophers and for such descriptive methods and analytical approaches, changed circumstances in culture and politics, society, and culture can be ruinous. The main luxury philosophers reviewed in *Luxury Philosophy*, however, thoughtfully circumvented all such claims to universal meaning and importance. Indeed, they wrote about the many aspects of luxury and presented revealing questions about them that explain luxury which may otherwise have remained unconsidered. Unquestionably, their books and articles offer readers helpful methods, analyses, and standpoints on concepts and practices concerning luxury that are relevant today. Moreover, luxury philosophers managed to disassociate their names and writings from all those processes that entail support for constant and unchanging forms of philosophy. A significant danger is how luxury philosophers, as happened to Barthes, can be turned into an image, for instance as a Hermès silk scarf (Armitage 2020: 63–6). The image on the Hermès silk scarf at issue here is a luxury-branded visual representation of Barthes's book, *A Lover's Discourse: Fragments* (2002), a literally fabricated scarf, a stereotype that stifles his luxury philosophy in a semirigid appearance of meaning. As a luxury philosopher, Barthes was a practitioner, not a cultural, political, or social value, a messenger whose task was, if not to obliterate the message, to complicate it, to resist its processes of absorption into the name, into the image, and into the meaning of "Roland Barthes"; one of his important contributions to luxury philosophy was to highlight how people could oppose their transformation into simple, unchanging, and communicable entities based on a fixed meaning. For Barthes, what was important was to produce a philosophical method and analytical approach that rejected any possibility of "disciples" attempting to practice luxury philosophy in his image today.

In conclusion, Barthes and the other important luxury philosophers in this book present their readers less with an influence than with exemplars. The example of critiquing the process of Barthes becoming a Hermès silk scarf entails a practice instead of a rigid collection of concepts or methodological techniques: the practice of a style of luxury philosophy that is dedicated to the communication of that which is not as yet absorbed, of that which is not yet part of an intellectual or a broad cultural, political, and social unanimity. To be influenced by Barthes, and by any of the other luxury philosophers in *Luxury Philosophy*, is to be touched, to be moved, and, yes, to be disturbed by their examples of practicing luxury philosophy which are unique and yet which, in all their countless forms, show the continued possibility of a style of dedication. What such dedication implies has been an important theme of *Luxury Philosophy* and can only be encapsulated through recourse to the field of luxury philosophy. The influence of luxury philosophers, of Rousseau and Saint-Lambert, Marx, Levinas, Bataille, Adorno, and Barthes, can be sensed by their readers when a luxury philosopher or anyone in the arts and the humanities contributes a new concept to the existing language of luxury or contributes a philosophical idea that was previously unimaginable. The exemplars of luxury philosophers are not only notions that speak to people from their books and articles, and therefore from the past, but also notions that people can use in their daily lives today to become something different in the future.

References

Armitage, J. (2020), *Luxury and Visual Culture*, London: Bloomsbury.

Armitage, J. (2023), "Rethinking Haute Couture: Julien Fournié in the Virtual Worlds of the Metaverse," *French Cultural Studies*, 34 (2): 129–46.

Armitage, J. and J. Roberts (2014), "Luxury New Media: Euphoria in Unhappiness," *Luxury: History, Culture, Consumption*, 1 (1): 113–32.

Armitage, J. and J. Roberts, eds. (2016), *Critical Luxury Studies: Art, Design, Media*, Edinburgh: Edinburgh University Press.

Barthes, R. (1985), *The Grain of the Voice: Interviews 1962–1980*, trans. L. Coverdale, New York: Hill and Wang.

Barthes, R. (1993), *Mythologies*, trans. A. Lavers, London: Vintage.

Barthes, R. (2002), *A Lover's Discourse: Fragments*, trans. R. Howard, New York: Hill and Wang.

Bataille, G. (1989), *The Accursed Share: An Essay On General Economy, Volume I—Consumption*, trans. R. Hurley, New York: Zone Books.

Calefato, P. (2014), *Luxury: Fashion, Lifestyle and Excess*, trans. L. Adams, London: Bloomsbury.

Clark, J. and N. Lezama, eds. (2022), *Canadian Critical Luxury Studies: Decentring Luxury*, Bristol: Intellect.

Conley, V. A. (2020), "Inhabiting Luxury Spaces," in J. Roberts and J. Armitage (eds.), *The Third Realm of Luxury: Connecting Real Places and Imaginary Spaces*, 67–84, London: Bloomsbury.

Derrida, J. (1978), *Writing and Difference*, trans. A. Bass, Chicago: Chicago University Press.

Iqani, M. and S. Dosekun, eds. (2019), *African Luxury: Aesthetics and Politics*, Bristol: Intellect.

Lehman, U. (2016), "The Luxury Duality: From Economic Fact to Cultural Capital," in J. Armitage and J. Roberts (eds.), *Critical Luxury Studies: Art, Design, Media*, 67–87, Edinburgh: Edinburgh University Press.

Levinas, E. (1969), *Totality and Infinity: An Essay on Exteriority*, trans. A. Lingis, Pittsburgh, PA: Duquesne University Press.

Marcuse, H. (1964), *One Dimensional Man: Studies in the Ideology of Advanced Industrial Society*, London: Routledge & Kegan Paul.

Ross, K. (2015), *Communal Luxury: The Political Imaginary of the Paris Commune*, London: Verso.

von Wachenfeldt, P. and M. Petersson McIntyre, eds. (2024), *Luxury Fashion and Media Communication: Between the Material and Immaterial*, London: Bloomsbury.

West, D. (2010), *Continental Philosophy: An Introduction*, 2nd edn, Cambridge: Polity.

Index